Scott Reeves

Developing and Delivering Practice-based Interprofessional Education

Scott Reeves

Developing and Delivering Practice-based Interprofessional Education

VDM Verlag Dr. Müller

Imprint

Bibliographic information by the German National Library: The German National Library lists this publication at the German National Bibliography; detailed bibliographic information is available on the Internet at http://dnb.d-nb.de.

Any brand names and product names mentioned in this book are subject to trademark, brand or patent protection and are trademarks or registered trademarks of their respective holders. The use of brand names, product names, common names, trade names, product descriptions etc. even without a particular marking in this works is in no way to be construed to mean that such names may be regarded as unrestricted in respect of trademark and brand protection legislation and could thus be used by anyone.

Cover image: www.purestockx.com

Publisher:
VDM Verlag Dr. Müller Aktiengesellschaft & Co. KG , Dudweiler Landstr. 125 a, 66123 Saarbrücken, Germany,
Phone +49 681 9100-698, Fax +49 681 9100-988,
Email: info@vdm-verlag.de

Zugl.: London, City University, TU, Thesis, 2005

Produced in USA and UK by:
Lightning Source Inc., La Vergne, Tennessee, USA
Lightning Source UK Ltd., Milton Keynes, UK
BookSurge LLC, 5341 Dorchester Road, Suite 16, North Charleston, SC 29418, USA

ISBN: 978-3-8364-8110-6

Contents

Tables and figures

Tables

Figures

Acknowledgements

I would like to thank the three people who supervised this study. Firstly, I would like to thank Julienne Meyer for her invaluable guidance, encouragement and support throughout the course of this study. I would also like to thank Della Freeth for her direction and support during the write-up stage of this work. My thanks also go to Richard Barron for providing initial advice on the study before his retirement.

I would also like to acknowledge the help of the medical, nursing, occupational therapy and physiotherapy staff and students who made this study possible by generously giving up their time to work with me.

I am indebted to a number of friends and colleagues who have supported this work over the years, notably, Emma-Jane Berridge, Mike Cook, Bob Heyman, Simon Lewin, Lynn Summerfield Mann, Anthony Pryce, Elaine Stewart and Merrick Zwarenstein. A particular note of thanks goes to Hugh Barr for his advice and ideas on interprofessional education.

I would also like to thank family members, in particular, Sheila and Ray for their support during the writing of this thesis and William, Ewan and Joshua for their patience while I was completing this study.

Finally, I would like to acknowledge the special role of my wife Ruth for her continued encouragement and support throughout the duration of this work.

Abstract

This thesis presents a study of interprofessional education within a health care setting. It explores the processes linked to the development and delivery of a practice-based interprofessional education initiative: the Training Ward. It focuses on the activities of a steering group in developing this initiative and the experiences of students and facilitators who participated in a pilot version of the ward delivered by the group.

The study emerged from two concerns (one empirical, one theoretical) related to the literature. Firstly, an over-reliance on reporting outcomes in the research literature meant that the processes related to the development and delivery of interprofessional education were overlooked. As a result, two 'black box' problems could be identified in the literature: one associated with development activities, the other associated with delivery activities. Secondly, a limited use of theoretical perspectives in the literature has resulted in a largely under-theorised understanding of the development and delivery of interprofessional education.

Employing an interactionist ethnographic approach, the study focused on exploring the successes and challenges connected with developing and delivering the Training Ward. Qualitative data derived from interviews, observations and documents were gathered over a two-year period to obtain a comprehensive understanding of this initiative.

The study indicated that while a number of successes were achieved in both the development and delivery of the Training Ward, a range of internal and external challenges were also encountered. Four interlinked factors (enthusiasm, backstage work, negotiation and group development) emerged from the study as key in understanding the development and delivery of this interprofessional initiative. To help illuminate these four factors, Janis' (1982) theory of groupthink, Goffman's (1963) concept of backstage performance, Strauss' (1978) negotiated order perspective and Tuckman & Jensen's (1977) model of group development are employed. The thesis goes on to argue that groups involved in the development of interprofessional education need to manage the effects of the four factors identified by the study. A failure to do so when developing an initiative is likely to result in the emergence of problems when delivering it, as development and delivery activities are closely entwined.

This study contributes to the interprofessional education literature in two ways. Firstly, it opens the 'black boxes' associated with development and delivery activities to provide a unique empirical insight into the nature of these factors. Secondly, the study's use of theoretical perspectives provides new ways of thinking about the development and delivery of interprofessional education.

Abbreviations

ACLS	Advanced cardiac life support
ASSIA	Applied Social Science Index and Abstracts
BEI	British Education Index
BSA	British Sociological Association
CAIPE	UK Centre for the Advancement of Interprofessional Education
CINAHL	Cumulative Index to Nursing and Allied Health Literature
CQI	Continuous quality improvement
CV	Curriculum vitae
ERIC	Education Resources Information Centre
GP	General practitioner
IEPS	Interdisciplinary Education Perception Scale
IPE	Interprofessional education
NHS	National Health Service
OSCE	Objective structured clinical examination
OT	Occupational therapist
PBL	Problem-based learning
PC	Personal computer
PHCT	Primary health care team
TQM	Total quality management
UK	United Kingdom
WHO	World Health Organisation

Codes

For the purpose of clarity, the following codes have been used:

1. All extracts are indented

2. *Italics* are used for data extracts

3. [...] indicates words, phrases or sentences that have been omitted from an extract

4. A word or phrase within square brackets [ ] indicates information added to make the context or meaning of an extract clearer

5. Rounded brackets ( ) at the end of a data extract gives the source of the extract and the month/year the data were gathered

Definitions

For clarity, this thesis employs the following definitions:

1. 'Black box' is a research term that describes a situation whereby one has an awareness of the 'inputs' and 'outputs' connected to an intervention, such as interprofessional education, but little or no idea of the processes that connect these two points (Pope & Mays 1996).

2. 'Collaboration' is defined as an interactive, synchronous or asynchronous, activity undertaken between two or more health and social care professions to enhance the delivery of care (Henneman et al. 1995).

3. 'Group' and 'team' are used interchangeably. This use of terminology follows the work of authors, such as Douglas (1983) and Adair (1986), who regard the interactions that occur within both groups and teams as similar.

4. 'Interprofessional education' is defined as: "occasions when two or more [health and social care] professions learn from and about each other to improve collaboration and the quality of care" (CAIPE 1997:1).

Chapter 1: Development of the study

Introduction

This chapter presents a description of the process related to the development of the study to help 'set the scene' for the thesis. The chapter is divided into four sections. Section 1.1 provides an insight into how the study evolved from empirical and theoretical limitations in the interprofessional education literature and how a funded evaluation provided an opportunity to undertake this study. Section 1.2 goes on to present the research aims and objectives for the study. Section 1.3 outlines how the study makes an original contribution to the interprofessional education literature. Finally, Section 1.4 offers an overview of the thesis.

1.1. Origins of the study

The actual seeds for this study can be traced back to 1995. At this time, I was working as a research assistant on an evaluation of an interprofessional education module delivered to medical, nursing and dental students (Pryce & Reeves 1997). Whilst reviewing the literature for this project, I found that it only provided limited accounts of the nature of interprofessional education. For example, it often mentioned 'barriers', 'hostilities' and 'rivalries' that existed between learners (e.g. Leiba 1993, Zungolo 1994), but did not go on to offer a sufficient explanation of the nature of these issues. The interprofessional education literature therefore provided a partial account of what appeared to be a more complex activity. Indeed, my undergraduate and postgraduate degree studies had introduced me to a wealth of literature that offered a range of insightful accounts into the complexity of interprofessional relationships between health and social care practitioners (e.g. Becker et al. 1961, Dingwall 1980a, Hughes 1988).

These early concerns about the literature increased while undertaking work on two further projects. The first examined the effectiveness of interprofessional education delivered in a variety of different settings and professional groups in six sites across Wales (Freeth et al. 1998). The second was a systematic review of the effects of interprofessional education (Zwarenstein et al. 1997).

My involvement in this work helped me to identify a central limitation with the literature: an over-reliance on reporting outcomes without examining processes. For example, interprofessional education evaluations often collected questionnaire data and reported a range of outcomes in relation to improvements in learner attitudes and/or knowledge of collaboration (e.g. Brown & Adkins 1989, Anderson et al. 1994, Gould et al. 1998).[1] As a result of this focus on outcomes, the literature only provided a poor insight into the processes associated with interprofessional education. I therefore decided to undertake a study that could begin to explore and uncover this shortfall.

1.1.1. Identifying two 'black box' problems in the literature

The lack of attention to examining processes connected to interprofessional education has resulted in the production of a 'black box' problem (Pope & Mays 1996). A 'black box' is a term employed when research accounts present data on both the 'inputs' and 'outputs' of a specific intervention, but have little or no data regarding the processes that connect these two points.

In relation to the limitations in the interprofessional education literature, two black box problems could be identified:

- *A black box related to the development of interprofessional education*
  Although the literature provided brief descriptions of planning group activities linked to the development of an initiative (inputs), and offered an understanding of the impact of the initiative on participants (outputs), there was little indication of the processes linked to the activities that lay between these two points.

- *A black box related to the delivery of interprofessional education*
  While one could find good descriptions of inputs (e.g. details of participants, range of learning activities) and outputs (e.g. changes in attitudes, acquisition of knowledge) linked to the delivery of an initiative, there was an unclear understanding of what actually occurred between these two positions.

1.1.2. A lack of theory

In addition to the empirical concerns discussed above, I identified another shortfall in the literature: a limited use of theory. In general, I found that most published accounts of interprofessional education had not explicitly employed theoretical perspectives in their

---

[1] The focus on the outcomes of interprofessional education, in many ways, should be expected due to the need to demonstrate the effects of 'interventions' within health services (e.g. Davies et al. 2000).

work. (Nevertheless, as discussed in Section 2.4.1.1, it is possible to discern an implicit use of theory in some interprofessional education studies). Of the small number of accounts that did draw upon a theoretical perspective, these were largely restricted to the theories of adult learning, organisational learning and groupwork (see Section 2.4). While this use of theoretical work has helped develop our understanding of interprofessional education, it inevitably means we only have a partial insight into the development and delivery activities associated with this form of education.

1.1.3. The Training Ward project: an opportunity to open the 'black boxes'

In early 1997 senior managers in two universities initiated an interprofessional steering group, consisting of educational and clinical staff, to develop and deliver a practice-based interprofessional education initiative. Based on a model developed in Sweden (Sandén & Walhström 1996, Walhström et al. 1996), the Training Ward aimed to provide interprofessional teams of senior pre-qualification students with a clinical practice placement where, under supervision, they took the lead in planning and delivering care to patients. (See Section 4.3 for a full description of the Training Ward initiative).

Following a series of steering group meetings during 1997, it was decided that the initiative needed to be evaluated to understand the impact on its participants (students, facilitators and patients). Funding for an evaluation project was therefore obtained and a research post was advertised. In late 1997, I applied for and was appointed to this post. Working with Della Freeth (principal investigator) we decided to examine the impact of the Training Ward by collecting:

- Questionnaires, interviews and observations with students about their views and experiences of participating in the Training Ward;
- Interviews and observations with facilitators about their ideas and experiences of facilitating the students;
- Patient questionnaires about their perceptions of care they received from the students;
- Training Ward documents to provide an additional understanding of the nature of this initiative.

Findings from the funded evaluation of the Training Ward can be found in the final project report (Freeth & Reeves 1999) and in three peer-reviewed papers (Freeth et al. 2001, Reeves et al. 2002a, Reeves & Freeth 2002).

My involvement in the Training Ward presented me with a useful opportunity to undertake a PhD study that could 'open' the two black boxes of interprofessional education and begin to understand the processes associated with its development and delivery. I therefore decided to collect observations and interviews with the steering group developing the project as well as draw upon the data from funded evaluation – observations and interviews of the students and facilitators who participated in the initiative delivered by the steering group. (Chapter 5 contains a detailed description of the data gathered for this study). To ensure that I had ethical approval for the study, the application I submitted to the local research ethics committee covered work on both the funded evaluation and the PhD study. (See Section 5.4.3 for further information on the ethical considerations connected to the study).

While this PhD study drew upon the student and facilitator data gathered for the funded evaluation, there are three crucial differences between these two pieces of empirical work:

- The PhD study collected observation and interview data from Training Ward steering group members over a two-year period to explore the processes attached to the development of this interprofessional initiative.
- The student and facilitator data (gathered for the funded evaluation) have undergone a far more in-depth analysis for the PhD study than was undertaken for the time-limited evaluation.
- Although the funded evaluation examined the general *impact* of the Training Ward on its participants (students, facilitators and patients), the study focuses on understanding the *processes* involved in developing and delivering this initiative.

(A more detailed explanation of the links between the funded evaluation and this PhD study is presented in Appendix 1).

1.2. Aims and objectives

In attempting to 'open' the black boxes associated with the development and delivery of interprofessional education and begin to understand their contents, the study is based upon the following research aim:

To explore the successes and challenges of introducing a new interprofessional education initiative (the Training Ward) in clinical practice.

Linked to this aim are the following three objectives:

1. To explore the factors (roles, relations, interactions, processes) that influenced the *development* of this interprofessional education initiative.

2. To explore the factors that influenced the *delivery* of this interprofessional education initiative.

3. To examine the relationship between the development and delivery of this interprofessional education initiative.

1.3. The need for the study

The study makes an original contribution to the interprofessional education literature in two ways. Firstly, it provides a rare exploration of the processes linked to the development and delivery of a practice-based interprofessional education initiative (see Chapters 6 and 7). Secondly, the use of theoretical and conceptual work drawn from sociology and social psychology provides new ways of thinking about the development and delivery of interprofessional education and the relationship that exists between these two activities (see Chapter 9).

1.4. Thesis overview

The thesis is presented ten chapters. This chapter has provided relevant 'scene setting' information for the study. The next chapter explores the emergence of interprofessional education and considers the background concepts that have helped to shape it. The chapter also critically reviews the theoretical literature related to the development and delivery of interprofessional education. Chapter 3 offers a critical review of the research literature related to the development and delivery of interprofessional education. Information relating to research context, participants and locations is offered in Chapter 4. Chapter 5 offers a description and discussion of the methodology and methods employed in this study. The next two chapters present and discuss the study's findings in relation to the successes and challenges of developing (Chapter 6) and delivering (Chapter 7) the Training Ward. Chapter 8 describes the use of a structured case comparison, a technique that can help enhance the validity of findings from a single case study. Chapter 9 goes on to offer a discussion of the successes and the challenges of the Training Ward and draws together the study's findings and considers them in relation to social psychology and sociological theory. This chapter also discusses how the thesis makes an original contribution to the interprofessional education literature. Finally, Chapter 10 offers conclusions and implications for the development and delivery of interprofessional education.

Presenting any thesis in such a fashion imposes a rather 'artificial' structure on the research process. While this structure does mask the messiness of undertaking research in the 'real world' (Robson 1993), it has been important to take this approach to provide an accessible and readable account of the study.

Chapter 2: Interprofessional education – background and theory

Introduction

This chapter is the first of two chapters that critically review the interprofessional education literature. In this chapter, Section 2.1 describes the process undertaken to search and obtain literature for the thesis. Section 2.2 outlines why interprofessional education emerged as a key approach to enhancing the collaborative work of health and social care professionals. Section 2.3 provides an overview of the background concepts that have helped shape interprofessional education. Finally, Section 2.4 reviews the use of theory in the development and delivery of interprofessional education. The overall aim of this chapter is to outline the context in which interprofessional education has emerged, to understand the concepts that have moulded this form of education and offer an insight into how theory helps support the development and delivery of interprofessional education.

2.1. Search processes

A range of electronic databases from health and social care, education and sociology (e.g. Medline, CINAHL, BEI, ASSIA, ERIC) were searched to obtain the literature for the study. My involvement in systematic review work on the effectiveness of interprofessional education (Zwarenstein et al. 1997, 1999, Barr et al. 1999a&b) was particularly helpful in providing the basis of a robust strategy for the database searches. (The search strategies employed in this thesis are presented in Appendix 2). Policy, research, theoretical, discussion and opinion papers/documents were included in the searches to obtain a comprehensive understanding of the literature. In addition, all databases were searched from their year of inception to the present day. The first literature search was undertaken in 1998 and repeated once a year during the study.

Hand searches of health and social care journals that published interprofessional initiatives were also undertaken (e.g. *Journal of Interprofessional Care*, *Nurse Education Today*, *Medical Education*, *International Journal of Rehabilitation and Therapy*, *Social Work Education*, *Learning in Health and Social Care* and *Sociology of Health and Illness*).

These searches were helpful in ensuring that any relevant papers missed by the database searches were obtained.

Relevant books were also obtained by searching the different library catalogues at three separate universities: City, Queen Mary and London South Bank. In addition, a search of the Internet was undertaken using key terms from my search strategy to discover books, policy documents and the grey (unpublished) literature.

As result of these searches, I collected over 600 papers, documents and books on interprofessional education and practice for the study.

2.2. The emergence of interprofessional education: a socio-political response

Effective collaboration between the various health and social care professions has long been regarded as an essential ingredient for delivering high quality patient care (e.g. Barker 1964, Shaw 1970, Kindig 1975, Evers 1981, Gregson et al. 1991, Firth-Cozens 1998, Rafferty et al. 2001, Penthybridge 2004). Writing in 1974, Eichhorn offers an early example of why this approach is needed:

> "Because health problems have become defined in complex and multi-faceted terms, health organisations have discovered it is necessary to have the information and skills of many disciplines in order to develop valid solutions and deliver comprehensive care to individuals and families" (Eichhorn 1974 cited in Larson & LaFasto 1989:17).

Such sentiments have been regularly re-emphasised in the health and social care policy literature (e.g. World Health Organisation 1976, 1988, Department of Health and Social Security 1974, Department of Health 1988, 1996, 1998, 2000, 2001, 2002). For example, the Department of Health's (1997) policy document on modernising the NHS states that the complexity of patients' health and social care needs means:

> "It will be increasingly important for the staff [...] to work efficiently and effectively in teams within and across organisational boundaries" (Department of Health 1997, Section 6.10).

Despite a growing body of research indicating that effective collaboration can reduce staff absenteeism (Lies & Sunderland 2001), create a more satisfying work environment (McGrath 1991) and improve the quality of care delivered to patients (Feiger & Schmitt 1979, Schmitt 2001, Litaker et al. 2003), interprofessional relationships continue to be problematic. Often they are undermined by boundary infringements, a lack of understanding of one another's roles, limited communication and poorly co-ordinated teamwork (e.g. Hughes 1988, Walby et al. 1994, Allen 1997, Skjørshammer 2001, Pethybridge 2004). Indeed, failures of collaboration were found to be at the centre of a number of well-publicised health and social care inquiries, such as the:

- Cleveland child abuse inquiry (Butler-Sloss 1988);
- Christopher Clunis murder inquiry (Department of Health 1994);
- Bristol heart surgery inquiry (Kennedy 2001);
- Victoria Climbié inquiry (Laming 2003).

In an effort to improve interprofessional practice, policy documents have repeatedly advocated the use of interprofessional education (e.g. Department of Health 1989, 1997, 2000, 2001, 2002, Committee of Vice Chancellors and Principals 1997, O'Neil & Pew Health Professions Commission 1993, College of Occupational Therapists 2000, General Medical Council 2001, Nursing and Midwifery Council 2002, World Health Organisation 1976, 1988).[2]

The collective view of the above policies and the wider literature (e.g. Szasz 1969, MacDougall & Elahi 1974, Jones 1986, Barr 1994a&b, Larson 1999) is that because professionals are trained separately from one another they are not equipped with the attitudes, skills or knowledge to work effectively together to deliver patient care. It has therefore been argued that interprofessional education offers a way to resolve this problem, as the World Health Organisation (1988:16-17) state:

"[Interprofessional education] develops the ability of students to share knowledge and skills collaboratively and thereby provide individuals and the community with more efficient health care ".

As a result of this interest there has been a steady growth of interprofessional education within the health and social care systems in the United Kingdom and abroad, most notably the United States, continental Europe and Australia (Goble 1994, Tope 1996, Graham & Wealthall 1999, Ross & Southgate 2000, Barr 2002).

Interprofessional education is now a widespread and diverse activity. Initiatives have been reported in both pre-qualification (e.g. Parsell et al. 1998, Scott et al. 2005) and post qualification (e.g. O'Boyle et al. 1995, Jones & Salmon 2001, McKeown et al. 2005) professional education.

---

[2] More detailed discussion of these policies and their implications for interprofessional education can be found in both Pittilo & Ross (1998) and Forman & Nyatanga (1999).

It can be university-based (e.g. Gill & Ling 1995, Hind et al. 2003) or undertaken within clinical practice (e.g. Falconer et al. 1993, Elliot et al. 2002). It can also be employed as a part of a continuous quality improvement (CQI) or total quality management (TQM) initiative (e.g. Hunter & Love 1996, Cleghorn & Baker 2000). Interprofessional education can also be found both in primary health care settings (Long 1996, Gentry et al. 2001) and acute settings (e.g. Harmon et al. 1998, Elliot et al. 2002) and can involve a range of different health and social care professions such as nurses, speech therapists and nutritionists (Arlton 1986); doctors, nurses, occupational therapists and physiotherapists (Van der Horst et al. 1995); social workers, nurses and psychologists (DePoy *et al.* 1997). (Papers illustrating this diversity are discussed later in this chapter).

2.3. Background issues and concepts

Having outlined the emergence of interprofessional education, this section provides an insight into the background concepts related to the development and delivery of this type of education. Specifically, it discusses terminology, goals, learning activities, typologies and debates related to interprofessional education.[3]

2.3.1. Terminological issues

While, as noted in the section above, there has been a growth in interprofessional education, terms describing this type of education are varied with authors employing a variety of phrases such as 'shared learning', 'multiprofessional education' and 'interdisciplinary education' (Leathard 1994, 2003). Consequently, Pirrie (1999:122) has noted that interprofessional education has been described as a "fuzzy concept." To help clarify this confusion, CAIPE (1997:1) developed the following definition:

> "Occasions when two or more professions learn from and about each other to improve collaboration and the quality of care".

Employing this definition, interprofessional education has a clear focus on *interaction* between participants. For its advocates, the interaction that occurs within this type of education ensures a key goal: the development of attitudes, knowledge, skills and behaviour required for effective collaboration (e.g. Barr 1996, 2002, Hammick 1998).

---

[3] For those interested in understanding the historical development of interprofessional education, Tope (1996) and Barr (2000, 2002) provide excellent overviews. In addition, the literature offers a number of helpful discussion papers (e.g. Headrick et al. 1998, Graham & Wealthall 1999, Cable 2002, Humphris & Hean 2004, Gosling 2005, Ross & Harris 2005).

This contrasts with 'multiprofessional education', where there is no interaction between participants.[4]

As noted in the Definitions Section (page xi), to avoid possible confusion with terminology, the thesis employs CAIPE's definition of interprofessional education.

2.3.2. Goals and learning activities

As noted above, interprofessional education is an interactive learning activity that involves participants from two or more professions. As such, it aims to develop the attributes (attitudes, knowledge, skills and behaviour) required for effective collaborative practice (e.g. Funnell 1995, Gill & Ling 1995, Barr 1996, 2002, Horder 1996, Hammick 1998). As Parsell & Bligh (1998:89) state, a central goal of interprofessional education is to:

"Enable learners to acquire knowledge, skills and professional attitudes [about collaboration] that they would not acquire effectively any other way".

Once equipped with these attributes, it is argued that practitioners will be able to collaborate together in a more effective manner, which in turn will enhance the quality of patient care they deliver (e.g. Casto 1994a&b, Funnell 1995, Barr 2002). Indeed, findings from systematic reviews into the effectiveness of interprofessional education have indicated that it can produce a positive impact on both professional practice and patient care (Koppel et al. 2001, Freeth et al. 2002, Barr 2005).

In offering a more comprehensive insight into the interactive nature of interprofessional education, Barr (1996) outlines five different types of interactive learning methods used in interprofessional education:

- Exchange-based learning (e.g. seminar-based discussions);
- Observation-based learning (e.g. joint visits to patients/clients);
- Action-based learning (e.g. problem-based learning);
- Simulation-based learning (e.g. simulating clinical practice);
- Practice-based learning (e.g. interprofessional clinical placements).

In relation to the literature, one discovers that these five learning activities are regularly employed within interprofessional education initiatives. For example, Freeth et al. (1999)

---

[4] CAIPE (1997:1) defines multiprofessional education as "occasions when two or more professions learn side-by-side for whatever reason."

report the use of exchange-based learning in an interprofessional seminar focused on discussing how general practitioners (GPs), practice nurses, district nurses and pharmacists can enhance their joint work in the care of patients with Alzheimer's disease. Another example is offered by Ker et al. (2003) who describe the use of simulation-based learning in a ward environment for small teams of nursing and medical students to collaborate in the care 'patients' with a range of simulated medical conditions.

To maximise opportunities for interaction, several learning activities are typically employed within interprofessional education initiatives. For example, Mires et al. (1999) have detailed the use of exchange-based, action-based and simulation-based learning in a series of interprofessional sessions for medical and midwifery students. Similarly, Wahlström & Sandén (1998) have described the use of action-based and practice-based learning in their evaluation of an interprofessional placement for medical, nursing, occupational therapy and physiotherapy students. (See Sections 3.2.1.2 and 4.2.3, respectively, for a more detailed discussion of these two initiatives). In addition, electronic learning (e-learning) methods, such as electronic bulletin boards and video conferencing, are increasing being used within interprofessional education (e.g. Cornish et al. 2003, Farrell 2005). The use of e-learning allows students based in separate geographical locations to interact electronically (in either a synchronous or asynchronous fashion) while they learn together. Often, interprofessional education initiatives that employ e-learning methods also use traditional learning methods, such as seminar discussions, to create a 'blended learning' approach (Richardson & Cooper 2003)

2.3.3. Typologies

The literature offers a number of typologies to help understand how interprofessional education might be developed (e.g. Forbes & Fitzsimons 1993, Hilton et al. 1995, Bond 1997, Newton et al. 1998). For example, Harden (1998) offers an eleven-stage typology in which course developers can map their progress in creating opportunities for collaborative learning (see Table 1, page 13). While Harden provides a useful idea of how an interprofessional education initiative may be developed, no published account could be located that has employed this typology. Therefore, it is difficult to establish the usefulness of this particular model.

Miller et al. (2001) offer another typology designed to map the development of collaborative knowledge and skills for pre-qualification students (see Table 2, page 13).

The authors identify three stages (pre-clinical, clinical novice and probationer), each requiring a different form of interprofessional education input.

Stage	Description
1. Isolation	Each profession organises its own teaching and is unaware of what might be taught or learned in other professions
2. Awareness	Teachers are aware of what is covered by other professionals but there is no formal contact
3. Consultation	Consultation about learning programmes between teachers from differing professions begins
4. Nesting	Aspects relating to the work of other professions are included in otherwise uniprofessional courses
5. Temporal co-ordination	Timetable arranged so that two or more professions can be scheduled for one part in a course, e.g. a joint lecture with little interaction between learners
6. Sharing	Two professions plan and implement joint teaching, with interaction between learners in one part of a course
7. Correlation	Sessions are scheduled in the programme for multiprofessional consideration of topics in an otherwise uniprofessional course
8. Complementary programme	Multiprofessional teaching alongside uniprofessional teaching
9. Multiprofessional	Each profession looks at themes from the perspective from its own profession
10. Interprofessional	Each profession looks at themes from the perspective of its own and other professions
11. Transprofessional	The education is based on the experience of the real world which provides a filter for student learning

Table 1: Eleven-stage typology of collaborative learning (Harden 1998:405)

Stage of learning	Activity
Stage 1: Pre-clinical	Students begin developing an understanding of interprofessional communication from shared seminar discussions
Stage 2: Clinical novice	Students are based in a clinical setting to begin developing their knowledge about different professional roles and how collaboration operates within teams.
Stage 3: Probationer	Students spend more time within a clinical setting and develop a more comprehensive insight into collaborative practice, such as understanding the varying strategies required for effective teamwork.

Table 2: Developing knowledge and skills of collaboration
(adapted from Miller et al. 2001)

Again, while the typology offered by Miller and her colleagues offers a helpful insight into the types of interprofessional learning activities that could be employed, there is no published account of this typology being used by a course developer. Therefore, one cannot tell how useful this work might be for interprofessional education.

2.3.4. Debates

In addition to understanding the goals, learning activities and typologies connected to interprofessional education, there are two key debates that need to be considered in relation to its development and delivery activities. The first debate centres on identifying the most 'effective' time to deliver interprofessional education. For some authors, pre-qualifying interprofessional education is more effective as it can help diminish the negative effects of professional socialisation, such as hostile stereotyping (e.g. Tope 1996, Horder 1996, Graham & Wealthall 1999). As Parsell & Bligh (1998:527) note:

"Beginning shared [interprofessional] learning as early as possible in undergraduate courses may help to change negative attitudes or prevent the formation of stereotypical views."

In contrast, other authors (e.g. Dombeck 1997, Pirrie et al. 1998) maintain that post-qualifying interprofessional education is more effective, as participants have a firmer understanding of their own professional identity and role. For Dombeck (1997:15) learning to collaborate with other professional groups can be difficult when "one is unsure of one's professional identity".

A further viewpoint in this debate advocates that interprofessional education should form a part of all practitioners on-going professional development, starting in their pre-qualification programmes and continuing throughout their careers. This will ensure that early learning is built upon:

"Interprofessional experience and learning could and should be consciously and deliberately built into education opportunities available to practitioners as they move along [...] further and higher education and to professional training, practice and continuing professional development" (Mathias & Thompson 1997:103).

In relation to this debate, I agree with Mathias & Thompson's argument that interprofessional education should be an on-going part of an individual practitioner's continuing professional development, as it will ensure that early gains from interprofessional education (e.g. knowledge and skills of collaboration) can be developed and built upon in a logical fashion. Nevertheless, as evidence for the most effective time to deliver interprofessional education remains elusive (e.g. Hall & Weaver 2001) this debate continues.[5]

The second debate is linked to an uncertainty of the potential role interprofessional education could play in the development of a 'generic' health and social care worker (e.g. Loxley 1997, Barr et al. 1999a, Sims 2002). The UK government has recently outlined its vision for a more flexible workforce (Department of Health 2000). The aim of this policy is focused on modernising the NHS workforce by attempting to loosen the rigid differentiation that has traditionally existed between professional groups. It is envisaged that common or generic skills will be developed, using common learning (Department of Health 2001), to allow professionals to work closer together in practice. For its advocates, interprofessional education is employed to improve collaboration without losing the diversity that exists between health and social care professionals. It is therefore not employed to produce a 'generic worker' (e.g. CAIPE 1996, Barr 1994a&b, 2000). For Finch (2000) the use of interprofessional education to produce a generic worker will create tension and territorial competition as the different professions protect their separate roles, boundaries and identities. On this point, Mathias & Thompson (1997:103) argue:

> "Professionals will rightly continue to strive for differentiation, specialisation and the development of profession-specific [...] knowledge and skills. There are arguments for general, generic approaches to education and training which fail to recognise the plurality, diversity and specialisation of the professions active in health and social care".

In relation to this debate, I agree with Finch's (2000) argument that attempting to use interprofessional education for generic purposes will be particularly problematic, as the health and social professions will inevitably protect their traditional areas of expertise. Indeed, as noted above, research into the introduction of generic working has suggested that this type of approach can cause tension in teams, as members become unclear of their own professional contribution and professional roles overlap (e.g. Brown et al. 2000, Ross et al. 2000, Parker 2001).

2.4. Using theory in interprofessional education

Having discussed salient background issues and concepts related to interprofessional education, this section reviews the literature in relation to how theory has been employed

---

[5] Despite the lack of evidence, in the UK, the Department of Health has decided to focus its attention on advancing pre-qualification interprofessional education (Department of Health 2001).

in the development and delivery of interprofessional education.

2.4.1. Theories employed when developing interprofessional education

As noted in Section 1.2.2, there is a limited amount of theory in the interprofessional education literature. Of the small number of studies that incorporate theoretical perspectives into the development of an interprofessional initiative, these tend to employ adult learning, organisational learning or groupwork theories.

2.4.1.1. Adult learning theories

Despite a large theoretical literature on adult learning (e.g. Rogers 1969, Knowles 1975, Vygotsky 1978, Schön 1983, Eraut 1994, Barnett 1994), it is possible to summarise key principles that these theories rest upon. In general, adults are considered to be: problem-centred; reflective; collaborative; life-long learners who tend to draw upon their previous experiences as a resource when learning. While agreement exists around the principles of adult learning, there is debate over whether these theories do form a distinct subset of general theories of learning (e.g. Jarvis 1995). Furthermore, some authors argue that given the lack of supporting evidence for these theories (Norman 1999, Prideaux 2000), there is doubt around whether they can, indeed, be considered theories or rather "axioms of adult learning" (Fry et al. 1999:25). Nevertheless, critics do generally acknowledge that these perspectives have been influential in supporting adult learning.[6]

In general, there is little explicit use of adult learning theory within the interprofessional education literature. Of the small number of studies that do incorporate these theories, they tend to draw upon the work of Knowles (1975), Schön (1983), Barrows & Tamblyn (1980), Kolb (1984) and Lave & Wenger (1991). To help understand how these theories are employed in the interprofessional education literature three examples are described and critiqued. The first is Lia-Hoagberg et al. (1997) who provide an insight into how Knowles' theory was used to develop an interprofessional course that aimed to develop an understanding of teamwork for 48 nurses, social workers, nutritionists and medical assistants. For Knowles (1975), adult learners are intrinsically motivated by 'problems' they identify and solve themselves. Adult learning is therefore more permanent when knowledge has direct application to an adult's work and incorporates a task-centred learning approach. Lia-Hoagberg et al. report that participants were offered opportunities

---

[6] While acknowledging this debate, for clarity, I employ the term 'theory' when referring to the work of authors such Knowles (1975) and Kolb (1984).

to discuss a range of issues linked to interprofessional collaboration (e.g. teamwork skills, conflict resolution). A needs assessment exercise was undertaken before delivering the course to allow participants to identify relevant clinical topics for their discussions. Questionnaires collected before and after the course indicated that participants enjoyed their interprofessional experience and felt they had obtained a better understanding of teamwork issues. However, while the authors' description of the use of Knowles' theory suggests that it helped structure the interprofessional learning in such a way that it was enjoyable for the participants, insufficient information on the development of the course means it is difficult to establish a comprehensive insight into how Knowles' work was used in supporting learning in this interprofessional initiative.

Mann et al. (1996) provide an insight into how Barrows & Tamblyn's (1980) theory of problem-based learning (PBL) was employed to develop an interprofessional course to improve understanding of health promotion issues for 35 doctors, nurses, dieticians, pharmacists and social workers. For Barrows & Tamblyn, adult learners are collaborative in nature. They acquire knowledge and skills in the context of problems they encounter in their work. Learning is effective if undertaken in small groups, where learners overcome 'problems' by identifying gaps in their knowledge or skills and agree what information is needed to address these problems. Working in small interprofessional groups, Mann et al. state that participants were encouraged to discuss four problem-based cases linked to various aspects of health promotion and agree 'solutions' to the problems contained in each case. A mixed method evaluation of the course indicated that participants "enjoyed the case approach to learning" (Mann et al. 1996:55) and acquired a better understanding of each other's roles in relation to health promotion. The authors conclude by stating that the use of PBL helped participants gain knowledge about how they might work together in future. Like the paper presented above, while the use of PBL helped structure the interprofessional learning in a positive way, insufficient information on the development of the course means it is difficult to establish a detailed understanding of the exact contribution PBL made to the learning in this course.

Freeth & Nicol (1998) offer an example of how Kolb's (1984) theory on experiential learning was employed to develop an interprofessional initiative that aimed to improve the clinical and communication skills of seven final year medical students and seven newly qualified nurses. For Kolb, learning occurs through an integrated four-stage cycle: initial experience (stage 1), observation and reflection (stage 2), formation of abstract concepts (stage 3) and testing concepts in new situations (stage 4). Through this cycle, the learner uses observation and reflection to develop their experiences into ideas. In outlining their interprofessional initiative, Freeth & Nicol state that participants were offered four half-day sessions in which they discussed patient scenarios linked to the management of diabetes, wound care, pain management and cardiac care. The initiative was developed to ensure it offered experiential learning to participants by encouraging them to discuss patient scenarios drawn from their clinical practice:

> "The scenario, which provided the focus for the course, could be a patient relevant to their current clinical experience and so likely to result in more effective learning [...] it was expected that this contextualisation would aid meaningful learning and allow participants to draw upon their practice experiences" (Freeth & Nicol 1998:457).

An evaluation of the initiative, using questionnaires, observations and interviews, indicated that both medical students and nurses enjoyed their interprofessional experiences and felt that their knowledge of one another's professional roles was improved. Once again, while the use of Kolb's theory appeared to structure the learning activities in such a way that they were enjoyable and they also helped enhance knowledge, limited information on the development of the initiative means there is an unclear idea of how Kolb's work supported the learning that occurred in this initiative.

Unlike the studies discussed above, more typically the empirical literature tends to draw implicitly upon the principles of adult learning theory (e.g. Dienst & Byl 1981, Rutter & Hagard 1990, Barber et al. 1997, Alderson et al. 2002). An illustration of this approach is provided by Stark et al. (1984) who describe an interprofessional course delivered to 34 students from medicine, nursing and physiotherapy who visited nursing homes to talk to residents and their families to understand their health and social needs. Information gathered from these conversations was later used to inform a series of interprofessional discussions. Questionnaires were completed by students before and after their interprofessional course. It was found that the students valued their interprofessional learning and felt they gained knowledge into how they might work together as a team. While the authors offer no explicit idea of which theory they employed, it is likely that they implicitly drew upon the principles of adult learning devised by theorists such as Knowles (1975) which, as noted above, emphasises the need to apply learning directly to the working context of learners.[7] However, given that one cannot be entirely certain which adult learning theory was employed, it is difficult to establish a detailed understanding of

---

[7] In implicitly drawing upon the principles of adult learning theory, it is possible that course developers have also been influenced by the work of other theorists, such as Rogers (1969), Vygotsky (1978), Eraut (1994) and Barnett (1994).

how a particular theory (or theories) may have supported the learning activities that take place during an interprofessional education initiative.

Another, more recent, example of this approach to using adult learning theory is offered by Edward & Preece (1999) who describe an evaluation of an interprofessional course for 40 senior nursing and 40 medical students, which was focused on understanding ethical issues involved in the delivery of patient care.   Students were offered four one-hour seminars focused on truth telling, informed consent, confidentiality and death and dying. Working together in small interprofessional groups, students were asked to reflect upon the "ethical dilemmas" (Edward & Preece 1999:302) linked to these four issues that they may have encountered during their practice placements. Questionnaires distributed to both students and facilitators directly after the final seminar indicated that both groups enjoyed their interprofessional experiences. Again, while the authors do not explicitly cite the use of an adult learning theory in the development of their course, the focus on reflection upon the participants' experience within the course suggests that they drew implicitly upon Schön's (1983) work. However, as discussed above, given that one cannot be completely certain which adult learning theory was employed, it is difficult to obtain an informative insight into the role of adult learning theory in this initiative.

As indicated in this section, while the explicit use of adult learning theories appear to structure interprofessional learning in ways that support positive learning experiences, limited information on the use of these theories means it is difficult to establish, with certainty, their contribution to learning within an interprofessional initiative. This problem is exacerbated by the implicit use of adult learning theory, which further restricts the understanding of how theory has contributed to interprofessional education.

2.4.1.2. Organisational learning theory

Another key approach employed in the interprofessional education literature is organisational learning theory (Argyris & Schön 1978). For these authors, organisational learning is a process whereby individuals work and learn together to collectively improve the quality of their work environment and the products or services they provide. Through on-going learning, often linked to a continuous quality improvement (CQI) or total quality management (TQM) initiative,[8] an organisation can improve its performance in terms of developing high staff morale, improved interprofessional collaboration, effective use of

---

[8] Despite the difference in terminology, CQI and TQM are identical in their use of organisation learning theory (Almaraz 1994).

resources and enhanced user/consumer satisfaction. Almaraz (1994:9) states that a central aim of organisational learning theory is to establish:

> "Organised continuous improvement activities in an organisation in a totally integrated effort toward improving performance at every level".

While, as noted above, the use of this approach offers a number of advantages for organisational life, the notion of a learning organisation is problematic, as it is not the organisations that learn, it is the individuals, often working collaboratively in groups where the learning occurs.

A growing number of interprofessional education studies are beginning to draw explicitly upon organisational learning theory as a way to enhance collaboration and improve the quality of care delivered to patients (e.g. Falconer et al. 1993, Hickey et al. 1996, Heckman et al. 1998, Wilcock et al. 2002). A useful example of this approach is provided by Townes et al. (1995) who describe a TQM initiative that involved teams of doctors and nurses from a surgical department who attended a two-day interprofessional workshop to learn about TQM and how to implement this approach in their workplace. Following these sessions, staff concern at the inefficient use of operating theatres led them to develop an initiative focused on improving collaboration to reduce the efficiency of the theatres. An evaluation of this initiative, drawing upon clinical audit data collected over a two-year period, indicated that a TQM approach achieved success in improving interprofessional co-ordination which helped reduce theatre inefficiency and patient delay for surgery. The authors go on to conclude that the use of interprofessional education linked to a TQM initiative can be effective in enhancing the co-ordination and delivery of patient care. Despite providing a convincing account of the positive effects that were achieved in employing a TQM approach, a lack of information on the development of this initiative means that it is difficult to establish, with certainty, the role TQM played in underpinning this initiative.

Cox et al. (1999) offer another example of using organisational learning theory to develop an interprofessional initiative for GPs and receptionists. Difficulties related to an increasingly high workload for the receptionists at one practice led a senior GP to examine the problem. It was found that the receptionists regularly encountered difficulties obtaining repeat prescriptions, which in turn, resulted in patient complaints. Working with an external facilitator, a GP, the practice manager and three receptionists began to resolve this problem through the use of a CQI initiative. Following a series of planning meetings, the group established a more systematic approach to their repeat prescription system (where information was stored electronically and where GPs could be contacted at specific times for authorising repeat prescriptions). Audit data were gathered to provide an indication of the effects of this new system. These data suggested that the prescription system became more efficient with 99% of prescriptions being ready within 48 hours, which in turn reduced patient complaints. The authors conclude that a CQI initiative can be particularly effective in allowing staff:

"To share understanding of their current ways of doing things and to use this knowledge to generate ideas for change [and] improvements in practice" (Cox et al. 1999:124).

Like the study undertaken by Townes and his colleagues, this study offers a persuasive account of the positive impact of a CQI approach. Nevertheless, this work is, again, restricted by a lack of information on the role of CQI in the development of the initiative.

Gilbert et al. (2000) provide an interesting insight into the effectiveness of using an organisational learning approach on student teamwork. The authors describe a simulation exercise for 21 students from 12 professional groups including nursing, occupational therapy, speech language and social work. Students were divided into four teams, with each student being ascribed a separate team role (e.g. project manager, engineer, assembler) and asked to recreate a complicated Lego model. Each team was encouraged to apply the principles of a separate organisational theory (traditional, values-based, process-focused and learning-based). These different types of teams represented separate points on a continuum: from a bureaucratic team (based on the use of a 'top-down' leadership approach), to a learning-based team model (founded on a more democratic approach). Questionnaire data collected during, after and six months following the initiative consistently indicated that the students in the learning-based team out-performed all the other types of team. The authors conclude that the use of an organisational learning approach can be regarded as:

"Best suited to the needs of a complex, ambiguous task, similar to many treatment situations" (Gilbert et al. 2000:230).

Again, while providing a well-written account of the benefits of employing an organisation learning approach, limited information on the development of this initiative means that it is difficult to obtain a detailed understanding of how an organisational learning approach underpinned this initiative.

In general, although the use of organisational learning theory appears to ensure that interprofessional initiatives are based on sound foundations, limited descriptions of the development processes of many initiatives has resulted in a somewhat restricted understanding of how this theory contributes to interprofessional education.

2.4.1.3. Groupwork theories

A handful of groupwork theories are also used in the development of interprofessional education. While the use of contact theory (Allport 1954) is now well established in the interprofessional education literature, Hind et al (2003) have also introduced realistic conflict theory (Brown et al. 1986), social identity theory (Ellemers et al. 1999) and self-categorisation theory (Turner, 1999). Although these theories are widely employed to help understand the nature of how groups function, they have nevertheless been criticised for focusing too heavily on interpersonal group relationships at the expense of neglecting wider societal influences, such as gender and social class (e.g. Giddens 1993).

Contact theory

Contact theory was developed by Allport (1954) from his work examining the origins of prejudice between different social groups. For Allport, the most effective way to reduce tension between groups was to bring them together. He maintained, however, that simply placing people together would be insufficient to effect positive change. Allport outlined three conditions that needed to be met if prejudice between groups could be reduced. These were the need for:

- Equality of status between groups;
- Groups to work on common goals;
- Groups to co-operate during their contact.

Building upon Allport's work, Hewstone & Brown (1986) provide a more detailed range of requirements needed for positive contact. For positive contact, Hewstone & Brown argued that additional conditions needed to be met, including, positive expectations, that groups were successful in their joint work and that they focus on understanding differences and similarities between themselves.

Three key papers provide an insight into how contact theory has been employed in the development of interprofessional education. Firstly, Carpenter's (1995a&b) papers describing an interprofessional course for 39 medical and nursing students. Secondly, Carpenter & Hewstone's (1996) paper detailing an interprofessional course for a similar number of medical and social work students. In an attempt to ensure positive attitude change, each course incorporated the conditions required by contact theory, outlined above. Thus, the courses provided students with an opportunity to work together in a co-operative fashion discussing patient cases and focusing on how they could enhance their interprofessional communication. The courses ranged in length from one to two days. Pre and post course questionnaires were used to measure changes in students' attitudes towards and knowledge of each other's profession. Both studies reported improvements in student attitudes towards each other and improvement in knowledge of one another's professions. While this work provides a useful insight into the positive use that contact theory can have in shaping interprofessional learning, the lack of a longitudinal perspective means that we have no idea whether these initial gains were maintained over time.

More recently, Carpenter and his colleagues (Barnes et al. 2000a&b, Carpenter et al. 2003a) evaluated a postgraduate interprofessional programme in community mental health for nurses, occupational therapists, social workers, psychologists and other mental health staff. Again, the programme drew upon contact theory. The authors examined the impact of this programme on participants' attitudes towards different professional groups. Findings from this work indicated that participants' attitudes changed little during the course. In conclusion, the authors note that limited opportunities for interactive learning was the likely reason for the lack of positive change. In relation to contact theory, as noted above, while both Allport (1954) and Hewstone & Brown (1986) outlined a number of factors required for positive contact, they did not identify time as a factor.

Multiple theories

Hind et al. (2003) have employed four group work theories to inform the development of their interprofessional initiative for pre-qualification students from five different professional groups. The first, contact theory, has been described above. The second, realistic conflict theory (Brown et al. 1986) assumes that groups holding divergent objectives will have hostile and discriminatory inter-group relations whereas groups with common objectives will display conciliatory behaviour. The third, social identity theory (Ellemers et al. 1999), proposes that a person will identify more closely with members from their own social group than with members from other groups. The fourth, self-categorisation theory (Turner, 1999) retains the focus on self and group identity, but does not regard them as being bipolar in nature, but based more upon a continuum. In their evaluation, Hind et al. collected 933 questionnaires from medical, nursing, dietetics, pharmacy and physiotherapy students about to commence interprofessional education. The authors found that the students, in general, felt ready for this type of learning experience. In addition, it was reported that students held positive views of their own professional group also "viewed other groups favourably" (Hind et al. 2003:33). While this

23

work provides a useful insight into students' early attitudes, as the authors note, such positive initial attitudes may alter over time as the students progress through their respective professional courses.

Although the use of these groupwork theories appear to provide interprofessional education with some useful foundations, the small number of studies combined with a single data collection method (usually questionnaires), mean we only have a partial understanding of how such theories contribute to the development of interprofessional education.

2.4.1.4. Exploring the contribution of potential theories

In addition to studies that have drawn upon theory to inform their work, in the last few years, a small number of discussion papers have been published that explore the *potential* contribution theory may have on the development of interprofessional education. Two such papers were located: one exploring the use of complexity theory (Cooper et al 2004); the other discussing the potential use of Biggs' presage-process-product model (Freeth & Reeves 2004).

Cooper et al. (2004) present a discussion paper that draws on complexity theory. Describing its initial emergence, the authors note that this theory was generated in response to the generally accepted notion of the social world being a stable and predictable place. In contrast, complexity theory assumes a world where complexity and disorder are more central. Drawing on the work of authors such as Harvey & Reed (1997) and Cilliers (1998), who developed this approach in the context of understanding the complicated nature of how organisations function, Cooper et al. present the five general principles of complexity theory:
- Complex systems consist of multiple components;
- There are general boundaries to phenomena within such systems, but within these boundaries exact outcomes are uncertain;
- Phenomena can exhibit orderly and chaotic behaviours;
- Complex systems are sensitive to change;
- Such systems are open, when observed the observer becomes part of the system.

In beginning to apply this theory to the development of interprofessional education, the authors argue that this form of education constitutes a complex system with a multitude of (orderly and chaotic) factors such as financial constraints, temporal-spatial issues, curricular issues, professional socialisation issues and multiple stakeholder needs.

Consequently, Cooper et al. argue that in understanding the complex nature of developing interprofessional education, an evaluator must employ multi-methods designs to investigate cognitive, emotional and social-environmental issues attached to this form of education. In conclusion, Cooper et al. (2004:197) state:

> "Essentially, a complexity framework can provide the scaffolding on which to build IPE and provide clear guidance for its future development".

Despite offering a potentially useful approach to help understand the development of interprofessional education, complexity theory has yet to be empirically tested within this context. Therefore, uncertainty exists in relation to how effective such a theory may be for interprofessional education.

Freeth & Reeves (2004) offer a discussion paper that draws upon the 3P (presage-process-product) model of learning and teaching devised by Biggs (1993). In his original paper describing the model Biggs regarded 'presage factors' as the socio-political context for education and the characteristics of the individuals (planners, teachers and learners) who participate in learning and teaching. 'Process factors' were regarded as the approaches to learning and teaching that were employed in an educational experience and 'product factors' were seen as the outcomes of the learning.

Freeth & Reeves describe how the 3P model could be applied to the development of an interprofessional education initiative. Specifically, they discuss how interprofessional education has been shaped by a number of presage factors such as government policies and negative professional stereotypes held by both teachers and learners. They also discuss the various facilitation approaches that can be employed, the different types of assessment that can be used (process factors) as well as the various learning outcomes that can be achieved to promote collaboration (product factors). The authors conclude by stating that the 3P model offers a "potentially useful tool" (Freeth & Reeves 2004:54) to help the development of interprofessional education. While this paper, again, describes a potentially useful approach to help understand the nature of developing interprofessional education, it has not been empirically tested. Therefore, it is not possible to detect how effective such an approach is for interprofessional education.

2.4.2. Theories used in the delivery of interprofessional education

In addition to the limited amount of theory that has been drawn upon to underpin the development of interprofessional education, on rare occasions theoretical perspectives are employed to help illuminate the nature of empirical findings related to the delivery of an initiative. This section describes and discusses the handful of studies that employ theory in their work.

2.4.2.1. Professionalisation

One of the theories used in the evaluation of interprofessional education is Freidson's (1970) sociological theory of professionalisation. For Freidson, professionalisation is a process undertaken by occupational groups to secure exclusive ownership of specific areas of knowledge and expertise. In obtaining exclusivity, Freidson argues that occupational groups secure autonomy of practice, which in turn leads to economic reward and status enhancement. To protect the gains obtained from professionalisation, Freidson claims that all groups guard the areas of knowledge and expertise they have acquired primarily through the regulation of entry and the maintenance of professional standards.[9] Tension is likely to arise if it is perceived that a member from another profession is infringing their area of expertise.

Like the implicit use of adult learning theory described in Section 2.4.1.1, when issues related to Freidson's theory (e.g. friction around professional boundaries) are discussed, they tend to be done so in an implicit manner. An example of this approach is provided by Skovholt et al. (1994) who describe an evaluation of a series of interprofessional workshops for community-based prenatal health and social care professionals. The aim of the workshops was to improve the co-ordination of the service offered by these professionals. Findings from a mixed method evaluation indicated that while participants reported an improvement in their understanding of one another's roles, some noted the emergence of tension due to interprofessional "turf issues" (Skovholt et al. 1994:779). The authors, however, do not provide details on the nature of these tensions or explicitly draw upon Freidson's (1970) theory.

Connolly (1995) offers another illustration in her evaluation of an interprofessional mental health placement for 87 senior nursing, social work, occupational therapy, nutrition and recreational therapy students. The aim of the placement was to prepare students for the demands of collaborative practice. As well as working together on the placement, the students attended seminars where they discussed their clinical experiences. Using questionnaires distributed to the students directly after their placement, Connolly reported

---

[9] However, more recently, it is argued that the effectiveness of professionalisation has been undermined due to the increasing influence of management on the health and social care professions (e.g. Elston 1991, Hunter 1994). For some, a result of this process has been a de-professionalisation of these professions, in particular medicine (Haug 1993).

that a number of students felt, on occasions, that their professional boundaries were encroached upon while learning together. These perceived professional boundary infringements were reported to cause friction between the students, as they attempted to protect their own boundaries. Connolly fails, however, to offer detailed information in relation to the nature of this problem and also neglects to draw upon a sociological theory, specifically Friedson's work, that could have offered an insightful explanation of her findings.

2.4.2.2. Loss and change

Another approach used in the evaluation of interprofessional education is Marris' (1986) psychodynamic theory of loss and change. For Marris, when change occurs individuals often experience a number of losses. For example, when an individual retires they can incur a number of economic losses (e.g. the loss of a full-time income) and social losses (e.g. a loss of status associated with being employed). Fearful of these changes, Marris maintains that unconscious feelings of anxiety arise, which can create resistance to change.

Holman & Jackson (2001) draw upon Marris' theory in their evaluation of seven interprofessional workshops for staff caring for older adults. The sessions aimed to enhance collaborative practice and improve the delivery of patient care. In total, 27 nurses, a psychologist, a bereavement officer and a chaplain attended the workshops and participated in the evaluation. To examine the impact of these workshops, interviews with the participants and the workshop facilitator were undertaken. Findings indicate that, although participants enjoyed their interprofessional experience, they reported that it had not altered their approach to collaboration. In using Marris' theory, Holman & Jackson argue that the failure of staff to change their practice after participating in the workshops was due to resistance generated from unconscious feelings of anxiety. While this study provides an illuminating account of the use of a psychodynamic theory, the authors' analysis is unconvincing. If one is to believe that unconscious processes are behind the limited changes reported in this paper, a leap of imagination is required. Indeed, other plausible explanations for this failure of change (i.e. a lack of time to implement change) are overlooked.

2.4.2.3. Social power

Two of Foucault's theories of social power – discourse theory (Foucault 1972) and surveillance (Foucault 1979) have been employed in the evaluation of interprofessional education. For Foucault (1972) a discourse helps to define a particular culture, its language and the behaviour of individuals who belong to that culture. Discourses therefore contain the power to provide the overall shape to a culture and define what becomes accepted as 'truth' and 'fact'. While discourses shape culture and language, Foucault (1979) believed that surveillance was required to help maintain the existence of a particular discourse. Therefore, Foucault saw surveillance as another dimension of social power. Indeed, the use of self-surveillance and surveillance by others was crucial in ensuring that individuals remained compliant to a particular discourse.[10]

In his PhD thesis, Koppel (2003) explored how the growing influence of health service management had affected the education of health care professionals. Drawing on interviews with doctors, nurses and health service managers, Koppel reported that these professionals were particularly concerned about the increased control managers had in shaping their continuing professional development. Consequently, these professionals felt that management was attempting to control their behaviour and thus erode their autonomy. Employing both of Foucault's theories, Koppel argues that, supported by government policy, health service management had employed a 'discourse of efficiency' to advocate the use of interprofessional education to ensure that professionals would learn and then work together in a more 'efficient' manner. In addition, for Koppel, surveillance within interprofessional education was a central element in controlling professional behaviour. By learning together, individuals are open to scrutiny by colleagues from other professions. Thus, a profession's uniqueness of knowledge and expertise can be questioned, as each is open to a critique of their actions, thoughts and attitudes. Consequently, their autonomy can be undermined and moulded to fit into the management-led discourse. Koppel's use of Foucault's work on power provides a thought-provoking account of a possible 'darker' dimension to interprofessional education. Nevertheless, it could be argued that given the problems that occur when health and social care professions fail to collaborate effectively (see Section 2.2), a management influence on encouraging involvement in interprofessional education may not be as problematic as this work suggests.

Regan de Bere (2003) also draws upon Foucault's (1972) theory of discourse in her paper that evaluated an interprofessional course for doctors, nurses, social workers and service users based in mental health settings. Individual interviews were undertaken with participants before, after and six months following the delivery of the course to elicit their

---

[10] See Porter's (1996) paper critiquing Foucault's theories of power for an illuminating account of how difficult these theoretical approaches are to operationalise.

perceptions and experiences of interprofessional education. Employing discourse theory to help illuminate the nature of her findings, Regan de Bere reports that before the initiative was delivered participants held a range different discourses:

"Generally, people were able to draw simultaneously on both personal and professional discourses, as they tended to complement each other. They also appeared to be compatible with, and amenable to, IPE discourses" (Regan de Bere 2003:118).

(Unfortunately, the author does not offer any description of the nature of these different discourses). Data gathered directly after the course indicated that the discourses held by the various practitioners had begun to merge to form a more "generic collaborative discourse" (Regan de Bere 2003:119) that stressed an appreciation of different professional roles, respect of other professional groups and a support of teamwork. However, the author also found that while the practitioners' discourses emphasised this generic discourse, service users reported the emergence of a 'them and us' (professional versus non-professional) discourse. Similar findings were reported in the follow-up data, collected six months after the delivery of the course. In conclusion, the author states that despite the development of a collaborative discourse, this interprofessional course also has "negative implications for the service user" (Regan de Bere 2003:119). Although the author presents an interesting discussion of her findings, the paper is limited in two key respects. Firstly, she does not include any interview extracts, which mean that it is difficult to judge any claims made about the data. Secondly, the author's use of discourse theory focuses mainly on the use of different *narratives* employed by participants, rather than using this theory to explore the underlying social power relations linked to a discourse, thus overlooking a crucial element of this approach.

2.4.2.4. Inter-group relations

Recently, social identity theory has been employed to help illuminate the findings of a study that evaluated the impact of a short interprofessional course delivered to physiotherapy and podiatry students (Mandy et al. 2004). As outlined in Section 2.4.1.3, social identity theory proposes that a person will identify more closely with members from their own group (or profession) than with members from other groups (Ellemers et al. 1999). Mandy et al. drew upon this theory to help explain the findings from their before-and-after questionnaire study with 130 students. The study indicated that students' initial negative stereotypes of one another's professions were reinforced following the delivery of an interprofessional course whose aim was to provide students with an opportunity to understand and value the roles of different health and social care professions. Given their findings, the authors argue that the limited effect of this course can usefully be understood in relation to social identity theory, which stresses inter-group discrimination:

> "The different professions each have their own distinct occupational culture, which will lead to distinct tribal groups. Each professional group will develop its own characteristic style of communication and language, which in turn lead to stereotypical judgements" (Mandy et al. 2004:165)

Consequently, the authors argue that any negative professional stereotypes are complex and very difficult to change. Although Mandy et al. offer an interesting discussion of the use of social identity theory, they fail to acknowledge the presence of any other explanations for the limited impact of their students' interprofessional experiences. For example, the failure of this interprofessional course to alter stereotypes may be linked to the students receiving poor quality facilitation during their interprofessional experience.

2.4.3. Theoretical perspectives offering 'new' insights into interprofessional education

As discussed in this chapter, only a small number of studies have employed theoretical work to underpin the development of an interprofessional education initiative. These are largely restricted to the use of adult learning, organisational learning and groupwork theories. In addition, the use of theory in the delivery of interprofessional education is limited to the following theories: professionalisation; loss and change, surveillance and discourse and social identity theory. Due to the limited use of theoretical work in the literature, this thesis draws upon perspectives from the sociological and social psychological literature to offer new insights into the development and delivery of interprofessional education. Specifically, it employs:

- Janis' (1982) theory of groupthink;
- Goffman's (1963) concept of backstage performance;
- Strauss' (1978) negotiated order perspective;
- Tuckman & Jensen's (1977) model of group development.

Chapter 9 provides a description of these approaches, a rationale for their inclusion in the thesis and a discussion of how these different approaches illuminate the study's findings.

Summary

This chapter has offered an insight into the issues related to the emergence of interprofessional education. Importantly, it has described how interprofessional education emerged from political and social concerns about poor collaboration between health and social care professions. The chapter also reviewed how theory was employed in the development and delivery of interprofessional education and found only a limited use of such work. Consequently, the chapter argued that there is a partial understanding of development and delivery activities. To help overcome these shortfalls the chapter presented four perspectives that are employed in the thesis to help illuminate development and delivery activities related to an interprofessional education initiative.

Having critically reviewed the theoretical literature, the next chapter presents a critical review of empirical literature related to the development and delivery of interprofessional education.

Chapter 3: Research into the development and delivery of interprofessional education

Introduction

In presenting a critical review of the interprofessional education research literature this chapter is divided into two main sections. Initially, Section 3.1 describes and discusses the limited number of studies that have evaluated the development of interprofessional education. Section 3.2 describes and discusses the more much substantial literature that evaluates the delivery of interprofessional education. The aim of this chapter is to provide an insight into the research literature related to both the development and delivery of interprofessional education. It also aims to identify the shortfalls in this literature and outlines how this study can address them by in order to meet its research objectives (see Section 1.2).

3.1. Studies on the development of interprofessional education

In general, there are few empirical accounts of the development of interprofessional education. Given the limited number of research studies, this section begins by presenting the larger descriptive literature in this area, before presenting the small amount of empirical literature.

3.1.1. Author descriptions

The vast majority of the interprofessional education literature fails to provide an empirical insight into the development processes of an interprofessional education initiative. Instead, the literature focuses on reporting the outcomes related to the delivery of an initiative. Nevertheless, most studies tend to offer a brief description (based on the authors' recollections) of how they developed an initiative (e.g. Barber et al. 1997, Brandon & Knapp 1999, Sengupta et al. 2003, Stone et al. 2004, Donovan et al. 2005).

McCarey & Mires (2002) offer a helpful example of this approach in their evaluation of an interprofessional programme for 145 medical and midwifery students. In their paper, the authors provide a limited description of the planning processes involved in their initiative:

> "The organisers of the programme met regularly to establish mutually desirable outcomes derived from existing outcomes used by the two schools. Concessions were made on both sides to achieve this goal and this was central to the running of the initiative. These common objectives therefore provided focus and direction to the programme [...] the common curriculum was arrived at through negotiation, co-operation and a desire to make the programme succeed" (McCarey & Mires 2002:64).

Later in their paper, when reflecting upon their involvement in this initiative, the authors also note that all members of the planning group "worked in a co-operative atmosphere" (McCarey & Mires 2002:75). Apart from these comments the authors offer no other idea of the issues related to the development of this interprofessional initiative. Instead, as noted above, these authors focus their paper on reporting the outcomes associated to their evaluation of student learning in this initiative.

Yarborough et al. (2000) provide another illustration of this approach in their evaluation of an interprofessional ethics course for over 100 first-year medical, nursing, physician assistant, physical therapy and pharmacy students. Drawing upon their recollections of planning group meetings, the authors (as group members) describe some of their experiences:

> "The cohesiveness and shared vision achieved and enjoyed by the original steering committee gave way when the committee changed [...] new people brought new philosophies of teaching and leadership that had to be processed by all" (Yarborough et al. 2000:797).

The authors also point out that the development of the initiative was impeded by the group having to navigate their way around the course timetables of the different institutions involved in the initiative. Despite these difficulties, the authors report a favourable set of findings in relation to students' reactions to the course, with most agreeing that the course enhanced their understanding of the ethical issues related to interprofessional practice.

While these accounts provide some idea of the planning group's activities, they tend to focus on reporting the impact of an initiative on the learners. Consequently, they offer little indication of the processes that lay between these two points. Therefore, as argued in Section 1.1.1, there is a 'black box' problem (Pope & Mays 1996) in relation to the development of interprofessional education.

While, as noted above, the literature typically offers a number of brief descriptions of the planning activities related to the development of an interprofessional initiative, two papers were found that offered more in-depth discussions. The first, by Satin (1987), outlines the development of four (two pre-qualification, two post-qualification) interprofessional education initiatives. Drawing on his experience of these initiatives, Satin offers five key issues related to success in initially developing and then sustaining interprofessional education, the need for:

- The interprofessional nature of an initiative to remain a central focus of the planning group;
- Senior management support for the initiative;
- A careful assessment of the local context before attempting to embed an initiative;
- Honesty, trust and respect within the planning group responsible for developing the initiative;
- Sufficient resources (time and money) to ensure an initiative can be properly developed and embedded.

Satin also stresses that planning groups share a commitment for interprofessional education, as well as being creative and flexible in their developmental work. He goes on to offer the following conclusions:

> "[Developing interprofessional education] is a hard road to travel, with few guides and only sketchy maps. It requires flexibly, creativity, persistence, and, above all, commitment to find ways of continuing to exist" (Satin 1987:67).

Clark (2004) presents a discussion of his experiences of developing an interprofessional course for nursing, pharmacy and nutrition students from which he proposes two 'laws' for the development of interprofessional education.[11] The first is termed 'the law of academic inertia' and relates to how staff will usually resist the introduction of an interprofessional programme unless there is an "external force such as grant funding or accreditation requirements" (Clark 2004:254). The second is called 'the law of permanency of academic change' and relates to how both positive factors (e.g. senior management support, creativity and commitment of development group members) and negative factors (e.g. lack of resources, sustaining momentum) affect the longevity of an interprofessional programme. Based in these two laws, Clark argues that groups involved in the development of interprofessional education need a range of attributes:

> "[They] must be constantly vigilant in identifying and marshalling resources, creative in building structural coalitions and partnerships, and persistent in keeping alive the vision of what interprofessional [education] should and can be" (Clark 2004:260).

---

[11] The use of the term 'law' is a rhetorical device designed "to provoke continued debate and dialogue" (Clark 2004:260).

Although these papers provide some illuminating descriptions of the issues attached to the development of interprofessional education, their anecdotal nature (based on the author's description) means the validity of such accounts, in comparison to well conducted empirical work, is in question.

3.1.2. Empirical accounts

In contrast to the large amount of authors' descriptions of development issues, only three interview-based studies (all examining the views of course planning groups on their developmental work) were found. The first study, undertaken by Stanford & Yelloly et al. (1994), provides an insight into the planning processes related to the development of two interprofessional courses in child protection. The first course was a ten-week introductory course on issues around inter-agency child protection; the second was a two-year course that led to a Master's degree in the subject. Both courses were jointly validated by the then professional bodies for nursing, the English National Board for Nursing, Midwifery and Health Visiting (ENB) and social work, the Central Council for Education and Training in Social Work (CCETSW)

While the main focus of the paper by Stanford & Yelloly et al. is upon reporting the impact of these courses on the participants (see Section 3.2.4.1), the authors also undertook interviews with five members of the group who developed both courses. Findings from this part of their evaluation indicated that a number of factors were critical in supporting the development of the courses. Importantly, the interviews suggested that enthusiasm for interprofessional education was a central requirement for success. The need to share "common objectives and values in relation to child protection" (Stanford & Yelloly et al. 1994:114) to help ensure that group members could work together in an effective manner was another key factor. The findings also indicated that group members' initial efforts in clarifying different terms was helpful in ensuring that they all held a common understanding of their work. A further key element of success was the equal representation in the planning group of the participating professions (medicine, nursing, social work, police, education), which resulted in no single profession dominating group discussions and decisions. In addition, a flexible approach to working together and mutual support between members emerged as necessary aspect to their work, as did senior management support to ensure that "sufficient resources of time and staff for collaborative planning" (Stanford & Yelloly et al. 1994:44) were available for the group.

Although the data gathered by Stanford & Yelloly et al. offer a rare account of planning group members' perspectives of developing an interprofessional education initiative, collecting data at one point in time means that this study cannot provide any information on how such perspectives may alter over time. Furthermore, the authors' sole use of interviews means that the study is dependent upon the accuracy of a participant's memory to recall events that occurred some time in the past. Consequently, such data does not always provide an accurate picture of what actually happened, due to problems of recall.

The second paper, by Richards & Horder (1999), presents an interview study of 13 professionals involved in establishing an interprofessional course for practitioners working in mental health. Four key themes emerged from their analysis. The first theme, 'a local champion', described the need for an enthusiast to initiate the development of the initiative:

> "The project team relied on one person, P, to provide enthusiasm, commitment and focus for the work [...] loyalty developed towards him and several participants credited their interest and involvement to P, whom they saw as having a pivotal role" (Richards & Horder 1999:455).

The second, a 'critical mass', described the need for a subgroup of enthusiasts who worked together to operationalise their shared vision of developing this interprofessional course:

> "Seven members of the group had a high level of energy and commitment to the project. It would have been very difficult for one person to get this off the ground and the members involved helped create a sense of momentum" (Richards & Horder 1999:456).

The third, 'time', outlined the need for the planning group to spend sufficient amounts of time together to be able to work as an effective team. The last theme, 'liking', described the importance that all group members liked one another, as this element helped to create mutual trust and an incentive to work together.

The authors also highlighted the need for the individual commitment of group members to help ensure that are motivated to work together in the development of an interprofessional course. They also note that on-going external pressures for change within public sector organisations restrict the opportunities for individual commitment to be nurtured between the different professionals engaged in developing interprofessional education. Although Richards & Horder offer an illuminating insight into the views of a group who had developed an interprofessional initiative, like Stanford & Yelloly et al., the sole use of interviews (collected at one time point) limits the overall ability of the study to provide a comprehensive account of this process.

The final paper is a study by Roberts et al. (2000) who interviewed the two course organisers involved in developing a five-week community-based interprofessional placement for fourth year medical and third year nursing students. While the main focus of their paper is upon reporting the impact of this placement on the students (see Section 3.2.2), the authors offer a helpful insight into the issues related to the development of this initiative. Findings from their evaluation indicated that both course organisers needed to cope with an additional workload to overcome the logistical and curricula constraints (e.g. timetable clashes between courses, agreeing shared budgets, finding suitable space for a 'new' interprofessional placement). Due to the extra amount of work needed, Roberts et al. pointed out that course organisers need a good deal of enthusiasm for interprofessional education. Indeed, the authors note that such enthusiasts can often become the "champions" (Roberts et al. 2000:391) for this type of education. They go on to point out, however, that given the range of educational hurdles, course organisers should balance their enthusiasm with what they can realistically achieve:

> "Enthusiasm for shared learning must be tempered with realism about current nursing and medical education" (Roberts et al. 2000:391).

The study also indicated that both course developers felt their collaborative work on the placement resulted in the strengthening of links between their respective educational institutions. Indeed, the study indicated that the development of this interprofessional project provided the foundations for further work:

> "The groundwork was set for learning lessons from the project and applying them for future shared learning initiatives" (Roberts et al. 2000:388).

Again, however, as these authors only gathered interview data (at one point in time), this work contains similar the same limitations as the other two studies reported in this section.

Collectively, the papers presented in this section offer some helpful (although restricted) insights into the development of interprofessional education. Indeed, they identify a number of similar issues related to this activity. In relation to the descriptive accounts offered in Section 3.1.1, both Satin and Clark note that the support of senior managers, creativity and commitment within the planning group and sufficient resources are all needed for success in the development of an initiative. In addition, the three empirical papers discussed in Section 3.1.2 offer a number of similar findings:

- All the studies indicated that the enthusiasm of planning group members was central to the successful development of their initiatives;

- Richards & Horder and Roberts et al. reported a need for the planning group to have champions (key enthusiasts) for interprofessional education to help support its development;
- Stanford & Yelloly et al. and Roberts et al. reported a need for planning groups to be given sufficient time for their collaborative work.

However, as discussed above, this literature provides only a partial insight into the development of interprofessional education. Indeed, the anecdotal nature of the papers presented above means that the validity of such accounts is questionable. In addition, the sole use of interview data means that these studies only provide a partial insight into this area, which this study, through its research aim and objectives (see Section 1.2), attempts to address.

3.2. Studies on the delivery of interprofessional education

In contrast to the limited number of studies that examine the development of interprofessional education, there is a more substantial amount of empirical literature describing the outcomes associated with the delivery of interprofessional education. To help understand the nature of these studies, this section presents and discusses them in relation to the range of research designs and methods they employ.

3.2.1. Questionnaire studies

Predominately, studies of interprofessional education employ questionnaires to evaluate the outcomes produced from an initiative. In general, these studies use self-developed questionnaires and incorporate either a post-course or a before-and-after research design.

3.2.1.1. Post-course studies

A popular approach for questionnaire studies is the post-course design (e.g. Chesney & Chesney 1981, Hemman et al. 1995, Savage & MacDowell 2000, Doyle et al. 2003). Typically, this type of study collects questionnaire data from learners directly after they complete their interprofessional course. Collier (1981) provides an early insight into this type of study, in which he describes a one-week community-based interprofessional placement for five medical, four nursing and two pharmacy students. Students worked together in small interprofessional teams while on the placement. In addition, they attended seminar-based discussions where they explored their interprofessional experiences. A formative evaluation[12] of the placement was undertaken to understand its impact on the students. Questionnaires distributed directly after their programme indicated that the students enjoyed their collaborative experiences and felt they had a better understanding of one another's professional roles. Despite providing an interesting insight into this initiative, Collier's study is limited by a failure to provide a clear research aim and a lack of clear information relating to data collection and data analysis. The neglect of such details reduces the overall quality of the study and restricts its ability to provide generalisable information. In addition, the study's focus on reporting outcomes means it contributes to the 'black box' problem related to the delivery of interprofessional education.

Another illustration of this approach is provided by Banks & Janke (1998) who describe the delivery of an interprofessional session to nursing, occupational therapy, physiotherapy and social work students. The aim of the session was to develop students' understanding of one another's professional roles. A questionnaire that assessed students' views of their interprofessional experiences was given to them directly after the session. Findings indicated that the students felt they had gained a better understanding into each other's professional roles and an insight into how they could collaborate with one another. While Banks & Janke provide clear information relating to their research aims, this study is limited by a lack of information concerning its methods of data collection and data analysis. This work is also limited by a poor description of the participants and the learning activities they undertook on this course.

3.2.1.2. Before-and-after studies

Another popular approach taken with questionnaire studies is the before-and-after design, in which data are collected directly before and after the delivery of an interprofessional course (e.g. Hasler & Klinger 1976, Nash & Hoy 1993, Green et al. 1996, Gould et al. 1998, Tunstall-Pedoe et al. 2003, Ponzer et al. 2004). In general, this type of study is more reliable than a post-course design, as the collection of baseline data means that a better understanding of change can be obtained. Stark et al. (1984) provide a useful illustration of this approach in a before-and-after study that evaluated four interprofessional sessions offered to 44 medical, nursing and physiotherapy students. Working together in small interprofessional groups, students visited nursing homes to

---

[12] As most reported interprofessional education initiatives are in pilot form, their evaluations tend to be formative in nature.

understand the health and social needs of the residents. The experiences gained from these visits were later used in seminar discussions where students explored the issues and implications related to collaboration in this context. Findings from students' questionnaires indicated that 70% of them rated the sessions as 'excellent'. In addition, when pre-course data were compared with post-course data, gains in both attitudes and knowledge were reported. Despite offering a helpful description of this initiative, this study is limited by a lack of methodological information concerning the aims and methods of data collection and analysis. Like the studies discussed in the section above, the failure to include such details means that the overall quality of the study is limited and its ability to offer generalisable findings is restricted.

Another illustration of this type of study is provided by Mires et al. (1999) who describe an evaluation of a short interprofessional course for 141 medical and 35 midwifery students. The course aimed to improve students' attitudes towards each other's professional group and their knowledge of working together within an obstetrics setting. Based explicitly upon Barrows & Tamblyn's (1980) PBL theory, the course consisted of one lecture, three PBL sessions, a two-hour clinical skills session and a two-hour seminar. Questionnaires that aimed to capture attitudinal and knowledge change were distributed to students directly before and after their interprofessional learning. Findings indicated that students reported improvements in their attitudes towards each other's profession and increases in their knowledge of working together. Mires et al. (1999) go on to argue that interprofessional courses can be successfully delivered in medical and midwifery curricula:

> "[Interprofessional learning] can be an effective educational strategy as judged by its ability to meet its objectives in terms of knowledge and attitude change" (Mires et al. 1999:284).

Although this paper provides detailed information relating to both data collection and analysis, the authors provide no discussion of the limitations of their study. For example, like many studies, the use of a self-developed questionnaire means there is uncertainty around the validity of findings. In addition, while the use of a before-and-after design is helpful in detecting changes immediately after an educational experience, they offer no idea whether such changes are sustained over time.

3.2.1.3. Follow-up studies
A small number of studies incorporate follow-up questionnaires (in the weeks or months after an interprofessional course has been delivered) to provide a better understanding of the longer-term impact of interprofessional education (e.g. Hunter & Love 1996, McKeown

et al. 2005). The use of this approach means that the problems related to post-course and before-and-after studies, in relation to providing no insight into the longer-term effect of interprofessional education, can begin to be addressed. An example of this approach is provided by Strasser (1995) who collected five-month follow-up questionnaires from 37 community-based doctors, nurses and unspecified 'allied health professionals' working in rural settings in Australia. These participants undertook a one-day workshop designed to enhance their understanding of teamwork issues in mental health. The workshop was delivered to professionals based in two separate rural locations and offered educational credits. It involved a combination of presentations, large and small group discussions based on patient cases nominated by the participants. Following the delivery of the workshop a questionnaire was distributed to participants to assess their views of this interprofessional experience.

Findings from this evaluation indicated that nearly all participants valued the structure, content and organisation of the workshop. In addition, participants felt they had gained insights into the problems faced by other health professionals and that they had developed an appreciation of need for mutual support in their work. Follow-up questionnaires posted to the participants five-to-six months after the workshops indicated that early gains in relation to knowledge of teamwork issues had been maintained. However, Strasser (1995) reported receiving mixed response rates: in one area he received an 80% response rate; in the other he only received a 45% rate. (Unfortunately, the author does not discuss the contrasting response rates). Based on his evaluation, Strasser (1995:61) states:

"These workshops were very successful [...] there is potentially great value in multidisciplinary continuing education for rural heath professionals".

While this study provides a useful insight into the longer-term impact of participant views of interprofessional education, it fails to provide an idea on whether this workshop actually had an impact on their professional practice. However, given the short time scale of this initiative (one day), it is unlikely that it did have any significant effect.

Parsell et al. (1998) provide a similar account in their use of six week follow-up questionnaires gathered from 28 final year medical, nursing, dental, occupational therapy, physiotherapy and radiography students who participated in a two-day interprofessional course. Explicitly underpinned by the work of Knowles (1975), Kolb (1984) and Schön (1983), the course aimed to enhance the students' understanding of their different professional roles and develop a better knowledge of teamwork. Students participated in three learning activities: presentations on interprofessional issues in the NHS; group discussions and a group problem-solving session based on four different patient cases. To evaluate the initial impact of this interprofessional experience, self-developed questionnaires were distributed to students at the beginning and again at the end of the programme.

Findings from the evaluation indicated that all the students reported gains in their knowledge of each other's professional roles. In addition, 25 reported that the course had improved their understanding of the roles undertaken by other professional groups and provided them with useful insights into teamwork. Follow-up questionnaires distributed to the students six weeks after the course indicated that the initial gains were maintained. However, the authors are cautious about the significance of their findings as they note that it is uncertain if such gains will be "carried over into working practice" (Parsell et al. 1998:310). They therefore recommend that a further longitudinal investigation is needed. (To date, no longer-term research has been published from this interprofessional initiative). While this study provides a better understanding of the longer-term impact of interprofessional education, the paper is limited as it only provides sketchy information on the actual processes of data collection and analysis that were undertaken, restricting its overall validity.

3.2.1.4. Control groups

To produce a more rigorous understanding of the effects of interprofessional education, a few questionnaire studies incorporate the use of control groups (e.g. Finset et al. 1995, LaSala et al. 1997, Crutcher et al 2004). The use of control groups is particularly useful in helping to detect whether a change has occurred as a result of an intervention (i.e. interprofessional education) or is due to some other confounding influence. Edinberg et al. (1978) provide a helpful example of how this type of questionnaire study is employed, in their evaluation of a 12-week interprofessional course for students from seven professions including medicine, nursing and nutrition. Fourteen students were recruited to work together in small interprofessional teams in community-based practice placements. These formed the intervention group. In addition, 19 students were recruited to act as a control group who undertook a course on bio-ethics in which there was no focus on teamwork.

Findings from the pre-course questionnaires indicated that students' knowledge of teamwork and understanding of the different professional roles were similar in both intervention and control groups. In contrast, post-course questionnaires suggested greater improvements for the intervention group in their knowledge of teamwork and understanding of other professional roles when compared to control group. The authors offer the following conclusions:

"A team experience, with its emphasis on interdisciplinary communication, collaboration and planning, is qualitatively different from most classroom or clinical training experiences students receive [...] despite the uniqueness of the team experience, compared with the rest of the students' education activities, participants felt there were immediate benefits" (Edinberg et al. 978:671).

This type of research provides a more insightful understanding of the outcomes connected to interprofessional education. Indeed, the collection of both pre and post course data, and the use of a control group means that change can be more accurately detected. However, the studies presented in this section contain a number of limitations. In general, their small-scale nature, their reliance on a single method of data and their implicit use of theory restricts the quality of this work.

3.2.1.5. Pre-validated tools

As noted in the preceding sections, most studies of interprofessional education employ self-developed questionnaires. While such tools are relatively easy to construct, their validity and reliability is open to question. In beginning to address this shortfall, a small number of authors have developed and pre-validated interprofessional education evaluation tools to overcome this problem (e.g. Parsell & Bligh 1999, Hyer et al. 2000, Mackay 2004). A useful example is offered by Hayward et al. (1996) who used the Interdisciplinary Education Perception Scale (IEPS) designed by Luecht et al. (1990). Developed as a pre-test and post-test tool, the IEPS aims to measure changes in learners' attitudes resulting from an interprofessional course:

"The scale is a perceptual attitudinal inventory consisting of 18 response items designed to measure the professional perceptions of students exposed to interdisciplinary practice applications related to their own professions" (Hayward et al. 1996:321).

To help detect changes in attitude, the IEPS was constructed around four factors: professional competence; perceived need for interprofessional collaboration; perceptions of actual interprofessional co-operation and attitudes towards the value of working with other professions. Hayward et al. used the IEPS to understand the impact of a community-based interprofessional practice placement for students from nursing, medicine, social work, physiotherapy and pharmacy. The placement aimed to develop students' understanding of interprofessional collaboration and support the development of positive perceptions of one another's professional groups. These authors' use of this tool helped identify positive changes in health care students' perceptions towards one another following their involvement in a practice-based interprofessional course.

Although studies that employ pre-validated questionnaires can, potentially, provide more valid and reliable findings, they nevertheless contain many of the limitations described in the studies presented in the preceding sections. For example, their focus on reporting outcomes mean they contribute to the 'black box' problem (Pope & Mays 1996) related to the delivery of interprofessional education.

3.2.2. Interview studies

In contrast to the large-scale use of questionnaires, there are a small number studies that employ interviews (e.g. Swanson et al. 1998, James & Anderson 1999, Alderson et al. 2002, Carlisle et al. 2004). These studies generally collect interview data from participants after their course and, like many of the questionnaire studies discussed above, focus on capturing participant perceptions of interprofessional education.

Perkins & Tryssenyer (1994) provide an example of this approach. These authors describe an evaluation of the impact of a series of interprofessional tutorials on senior physiotherapy and occupational therapy students. Collectively, the tutorials had two aims: to enhance student understanding of each profession's role and contribution to care; and to prepare students to work more effectively together when they qualified. Group interviews with the 14 students after these tutorials indicated that most valued their interprofessional experiences. In addition, the students felt that these sessions had helped to increase their awareness of each other's professional role and how they could collaborate together in practice. As the authors state:

> "Students felt the clinical tutorials were a useful place to interact with the other discipline, as discussion could be linked to real world situation [...] this allowed them to become accustomed to the interaction" (Perkins & Tryssenyer 1994:139).

While the study provides a useful picture of the impact of this initiative, the lack of explicit theory and the collection of data at a single point in time (directly following the course) means that it contains many of the limitations as the other studies cited above.

A more interesting interview study is offered by Long (1996) who describes an evaluation of a two-day residential teambuilding workshop delivered to primary health care teams (PHCTs). Two PHCTs, each consisting of a GP, a practice nurse, a receptionist, a health visitor, a district nurse and a midwife participated in this workshop. Due to the residential nature of this experience not all team members could attend, as a small number of staff were required to provide cover for their colleagues. Nevertheless, it was noted that these members would receive a similar workshop at a later date. The workshop aimed to improve each team's understanding of the different professional roles each member held and how they could enhance their collaborative work. An experienced facilitator worked with each team to provide guidance in establishing objectives, identifying problems and planning team solutions.

Semi-structured individual interviews collected before and after the workshops indicated that the participants reported a number of improvements. For example, most felt there was more agreement over team goals following the workshop. However, while the workshops made some useful gains, participants felt that interpersonal friction between certain team members was unaltered. Indeed, it was felt that the "traditional hierarchical relations" (Long 1996:940) created by financial and status inequalities between the GPs and other team members meant that the essential character of team relations were largely untouched. Although Long's study provides a more detailed picture of the outcomes produced from an interprofessional education initiative, like most studies it is let down by a poor description of methodological details related to data analysis and a lack of discussion of the study's limitations.

Roberts et al. (2000) present another interesting interview study in which they describe an evaluation of a five-week interprofessional placement for medical and nursing students based in a general practice and a community nursing unit. The placement aimed to develop students' understanding of their respective professional roles and responsibilities. To understand the impact the placement, individual interviews were undertaken with the students. Findings from this work suggested that while students enjoyed their interprofessional experience, many were "resistant to interdisciplinary group work" (Roberts et al. 2000:390) as they wanted the placement to have a more profession-specific focus. The authors also reported that the students continued to hold negative stereotypes of one another following their interprofessional learning. In addition, the students were unhappy that the placement did not contribute to the formal assessment of their respective courses. The authors conclude that despite providing students with a rewarding interprofessional experience, problems of stereotyping and resistance to interprofessional education undermined the placement. They go on to state that such issues need "proactive management and skilled facilitation" (Roberts et al. 2000:391) to ensure success in the delivery of interprofessional education. Although this evaluation provides a detailed insight into the issues related to participating in an interprofessional education initiative, like most studies reported above, its small scale nature and the lack of follow-up (to understand the longer term impact of interprofessional education) limits the quality of this study.

Unlike the bulk of studies of interprofessional education, Fallsberg & Hammar (2000) provide a rare insight into the processes that occur during the delivery of an interprofessional initiative. These authors evaluated an interprofessional placement for community care supervision, medical, medical laboratory technology, nursing, occupational therapy and physiotherapy students. The placement provided students with opportunities to work together in order to develop an insight into the nature of interprofessional collaboration. Individual interviews undertaken with seven students provided a number of insights into the nature of their interprofessional interactions. It was found that students employed a range of different approaches to their interactions while working together on the placement. For example, Fallsberg & Hammar (2000:342) reported that while medical students used a "one-way" approach to passing information, nursing students employed a more open discussion-based approach. The authors also reported that students employed different approaches to their interprofessional learning. For some, their learning was based upon undertaking "dialogue and discourse" (Fallsberg & Hammar 2000:345). For other students, reflection upon their interprofessional experiences was an important part of the learning process. While Fallsberg & Hammar's study provides an insight into the interactions that occur during an interprofessional education initiative, its sole use of interview data to report processes is problematic. The use of interviews relies upon the accuracy of a participant's recall of events. Unfortunately, such recall does not always provide an accurate picture of what actually happened.

3.2.3. Observing interaction

In helping overcome the limitations of solely using interviews to understand the processes that occur within an interprofessional education initiative, a small number of studies have gathered observations of student interactions. These data are useful as the researcher can witness social interactions as they occur, rather than relying upon an individual's ability to recall events after they have happened. In two related papers, Pryce & Reeves (1997) and Reeves (2000) provide a rare insight into the nature of interaction during an interprofessional community module.[13] The module offered first and second year medical,

---

[13] Both papers were based on a Department of Health funded evaluation in which I undertook data collection, analysis and writing activities with a colleague from City University.

nursing and dental students opportunities to work together to understand the health and social needs of service users. Observational and interview data were collected with students, facilitators and service users. While pre-module interviews indicated that students held a variety of negative stereotypes of each other's professions, observations of their interprofessional sessions found that none of the facilitators spent time exploring or unpacking these stereotypes. Consequently, post-module interviews suggested that student stereotypes remained largely unaltered. Nevertheless, it was found that an important aspect to the students' enjoyment of the module was the informal learning activities they undertook after the formal learning:

> "In addition to their work during the placement, students continued to interact after their 'formal' education by going to nearby cafés and pubs. Here, students shared the more informal, relaxed side to interprofessional teamwork, where they discussed their differing courses and reflected upon their work. Students valued these informal meetings and saw them as a central feature to building and maintaining constructive interprofessional relationships" (Reeves 2000:272).

Indeed, this informal time allowed the students to explore their different roles and how they worked together on the module. However, a lack of time to amend the nursing students' curriculum before the module commenced meant that they did not receive any educational credit for completing this module, unlike the medical and dental students. This educational inequality between the student groups was considered problematic, as it undermined the nursing students' overall enjoyment of the module. While this study provides an understanding into the nature of the interactions that occur within interprofessional education, these insights are limited to only a few hours of observations on the module.

Another study that examined the nature of interaction within interprofessional education is provided by Freeth et al. (1998, 1999).[14] Drawing upon observations and interviews collected from an evaluation of the effectiveness of interprofessional education across seven sites in Wales, the authors found that interprofessional interaction between participants was generally good, with all professionals participating in learning activities. The following extract describes an observation of an interprofessional session for a number of health professionals, including GPs, practice nurses, distinct nurses and pharmacists, which explored how they worked together to care for patients with Alzheimer's disease:

---

[14] Both papers were based on an evaluation funded by the Clinical Effectiveness Unit (Wales) in which I undertook data collection, analysis and writing activities along with colleagues from City University.

"The meeting was highly interactive, with questions during the presentations and substantial debate after each. Most of those who did not present offered their knowledge and experiences. The debate included: a request from district nurses for their earlier involvement by GPs; GPs clarifying with the pharmacist and representatives from the local day hospital the effects of the available drugs; GPs clarifying with the day hospital representatives various referral options and the services offered by the day hospital [and] a discussion of liaison with informal carers and carers' groups" (Freeth et al. 1999:131-132).

While participants were generally positive about their interprofessional education experiences, course organisers did identify a number of mainly logistical problems (e.g. funding, timetabling) that undermined the sustainability of many of these initiatives. Again, although this study offers a helpful insight into the processes that occur within interprofessional education, these data were collected from short (three-to-four hour) site visits. Therefore, they continue to provide only a partial view of these interprofessional interactions.

3.2.4. Mixed method studies

The interprofessional education literature offers a larger amount of mixed method evaluations, which employ a range of data collection methods, including:

- Questionnaires and interviews (Bailey 2002, Wakefield et al. 2003, Lempp et al. 2003);
- Questionnaires and documentary data (Itano et al. 1991, DePoy et al. 1997);
- Questionnaires, interviews, observations (Rutter & Hagart 1990, Lough et al. 1996, Lacey 1998, Harris et al. 2003);
- Questionnaires, interviews and documentary data (Tepper 1997);
- Questionnaires, interviews, observations, documentary data (Spratley 1990, Birnbaum et al. 1994, Mann et al. 1996, Tope 1996, Cable 2000);
- Questionnaires, interviews, observations and clinical audit data (Glanz et al. 1992, Skovholt et al. 1994, McCormack & Wright 1999).

As mixed method studies employ two or more methods of data collection, they tend to provide more comprehensive findings than studies which employ a single method. For instance, Jones & Salmon (2001) describe a mixed method evaluation in which questionnaire and focus group interview data were gathered to evaluate the impact of a university-based interprofessional course for 64 qualified nurses, social workers, community/youth workers and midwives. The course aimed to improve participants' understanding of issues and policies related to interprofessional practice. Findings from the questionnaires indicated that participants enjoyed and valued their interprofessional experiences. Interview data provided a more in-depth insight into the participants' views, suggesting that the course improved their understanding the nature of teamwork, which helped "sharpen their practice and outlook" (Jones & Salmon 2001:71) concerning issues and policies linked to teamwork. The study also indicated that the course encouraged participants to share and understand the different "discourses" attached to each of their professions (Jones & Salmon 2001:72). The authors provide one of the better mixed method evaluations as they offer detailed information relating to their methodology, present their findings in a clear fashion and provide a helpful discussion of the study's limitations.

However, a common problem with the way this type of evaluation is employed in the interprofessional education literature is that, while they provide detailed descriptions of the outcomes of an initiative, they tend to under-report the processes which underpin these outcomes. Itano et al. (1991) provide a typical example of this problem in their evaluation of an eight-week interprofessional course for medical, nursing and social work students working in an oncology setting. Despite providing detailed descriptions of their outcome-based data relating to knowledge and attitudinal change, process-based data from the students' diaries (logs) are given scant attention. The following sentence offers the only insight into the nature of these data:

> "[Student] logs also documented some role overlapping, and therefore conflict, between nursing and social work students" (Itano et al. 1991:224).

This cursory treatment of the student log data means that the paper does not provide a sufficient explanation of why problems occurred around role overlap, an oversight that limits the quality of the study. A similar problem can be found in the study undertaken by DePoy et al. (1997) with students from nursing, social work, speech therapy and psychology. Despite offering detailed information on the outcomes from questionnaire data in relation to an improved understanding of teamwork issues, process-based data from student diaries are given very little attention. Again, this oversight limits the quality of the research.

3.2.4.1. Processes and outcomes

In contrast to the bulk of evaluations of interprofessional education, a small number of mixed method studies offer more helpful insights into both the processes and outcomes of interprofessional education (e.g. Glanz et al. 1992, Birnbaum et al. 1994, Skovholt et al. 1994, Freeth & Nicol 1998, McCormack & Wright 1999). Stanford & Yelloly et al. (1994) provide a useful example of this approach in their evaluation of two interprofessional university-based courses in child protection. In total, 26 participants from nursing, health visiting, midwifery, the police and youth work took part in these courses. The collection of observations, documents, interviews and questionnaires before, during and after both courses indicated that participants were highly satisfied with their interprofessional experiences and felt their knowledge, professional roles and contributions in the field of child protection had improved. In relation to the observational data, it was reported that the participants encountered a number of professional issues during their learning. For example, many participants used stereotypical banter, especially in the first introductory course. In addition, during one of their role-play sessions, participants resorted to "blaming [...] other professionals" (Stanford & Yelloly et al. 1994:42) for a number of the problems they encountered in their work. Furthermore, it was reported that there was a general reluctance in "challenging one another on practice issues" (Stanford & Yelloly et al. 1994:74) during most of the group discussions. While this evaluation provides some helpful insights into the nature of interactions that occur during these two interprofessional courses, the overwhelming focus of this work is upon reporting the impact of these courses in terms of knowledge gained by the participants.

Another more recent example of an evaluation that offers an insight into processes and outcomes is provided by Ker et al. (2003), who evaluated the impact of a simulated ward environment where teams of nursing and medical students worked together to provide care for 'patients'. Questionnaire and observation data were collected from all participants. Findings from the questionnaire data indicated that all students enjoyed their interprofessional experiences, and considered that this simulated environment provided a realistic insight into the demands of working together. Findings from the observations provide some illuminating insights into the nature of student interactions. For example, these data suggested that there were a few minor difficulties in some student groups:

> "Limited collaboration was observed in some teams [as] medical student expected nurses to assist them in some of the tasks but were not observed to reciprocate" (Ker et al. 2003:253).

The observation data also indicated that a lack of leadership in several of the student groups resulted in problems prioritising their workloads. Despite these difficulties, it was reported that, in general, students worked well together in this environment. Although this study offers a rare insight into the processes that occur between different professional groups, like many studies of interprofessional education it offered no information on how the observational data were either collected or analysed.

3.2.4.2. Multiple perspectives

While the majority of studies focus on understanding the impact upon the learner, a few studies examine learner and tutor perspectives (e.g Tope 1996, Willis et al. 1997) or learner and patient perspectives (e.g. Glanz et al. 1992, Crawford et al. 1998). In general, these studies provide a more detailed understanding of the impact of interprofessional education. An example of this approach is provided by Lough et al. (1996) who describe a mixed method study of an interprofessional placement for medical, nursing and social work students. The placement offered students a four-week experience working together in the community. It aimed to enhance students' understanding of different professional roles and provide them with an insight into community-based teamwork. Interviews, observations and questionnaires were collected from students, tutors and patients following the delivery of the placement. Findings indicated that students felt they had a better understanding of different professional roles and had also had a useful teamwork experience. The tutors reported that they thought the students worked well together in their teams during the placement, while the patients indicated that they enjoyed the high levels of attention they were given by the student teams who cared for them.

Another illustration of this approach is offered by Birnbaum et al. (1994), who describe a mixed method evaluation of an advanced cardiac life support training (ACLS) for doctors and nurses based in an acute cardiac unit. The course aimed to provide participants with a better understanding of how to work as a team during a cardiac resuscitation. Twelve weekly three-hour sessions were offered to participants. The sessions provided them with presentations of resuscitation techniques, simulation exercises in which they worked as a cardiac resuscitation team and discussions of their collective performance after the simulation exercises. Interviews and questionnaires were gathered from the participants directly after the course. In addition, to understand the impact of the course on patients, patient case notes and outcomes data were also gathered three months after the course was delivered. Findings indicated that participants both enjoyed the course and felt better prepared to work together as a cardiac resuscitation team. In addition, it was found that the mortality rates of patients who underwent cardiac resuscitation following the course decreased from 17.4% to 13.4%. In conclusion, the authors state:

> "Training directed to the entire team likely to participate in the provision of ACLS [...] favourably affects the practice of ACLS and the survival rate of patients" (Birnbaum et al. 1994:741).

While both studies provide useful range of perspectives into the impact of interprofessional education, this work is let down by a common problem in the literature: poor descriptions of how the authors collected and analysed their data. For example,

Lough et al. offer no information how they analysed their observational data. Another limitation with interprofessional education studies that include multiple perspectives is that, in general, they capture only learner and tutors' perspectives. Rarely does this type of study obtain a patient's perspective on interprofessional education.

3.2.4.3. Tracking change over time

In assessing the longer-term effect of interprofessional education, like the questionnaire studies discussed (see Section 3.2.1.3), a number of mixed method studies employ a longitudinal approach (e.g. Spratley 1990, Pilon et al. 1997, Young et al. 1998, Wilkinson et al. 2000, Cooper 2005). Kennard (2002) offers an example of this approach in his evaluation of an interprofessional module for nurses, midwives, occupational therapists, radiographers and pharmacists studying for a degree in health studies. The course was evaluated with the use of questionnaires and interviews gathered before, at the end, and five months following the module. Pre-module data initially indicated that participants held generally poor perceptions of one another' professions. Post-module data indicated that participants' positive experiences of interprofessional learning during the module resulted in an increase of positive perceptions. Encouragingly, five-month follow-up data indicated that these positive perceptions of one another's profession had been sustained. Kennard's (2002) paper offers a helpful and well-presented account into the effects of interprofessional education over five months. Indeed, it offers a useful indication of how interprofessional education can positively affect practitioners' perceptions of one another over time.

Tepper's (1997) evaluation of a three-day interprofessional workshop for a team of nurses, occupational therapists, physiotherapists, doctors and psychologists offers another insight into the impact of this type of education over time. Questionnaire and interview data collected five months after the delivery of the workshop indicated that the initial increase in participants' knowledge and skills of teamwork had not only been sustained but they were incorporated into practice. For example, it was reported that team members participated more fully in ward rounds. As Tepper (1997:151) states:

> "[Workshop] participants demonstrated a significant increase in knowledge and self-reported skills. Gains from the workshop were transferred to positive significant behavioural changes on the job as revealed in the five-month follow-up survey".

While providing a useful indication of the longer-term effects of interprofessional education, this work is let down by failing to offer any data extracts to support the authors' claims on the impact of interprofessional education. In addition, the use of questionnaires and interviews when examining changes to practice is problematic, as without triangulating these data with observations one cannot be certain of the credibility of an author's findings.

3.2.4.4. Action research

While most evaluations of interprofessional education do not employ an explicit methodological framework, a small number of action research studies were found (Glennie & Cosier 1994, Lacey 1996, 1998, Bond 1999, Atwal 2002). In contrast to the 'detached' approach taken with most evaluations of interprofessional education, action research is more participative. In essence, action researchers work collaboratively with participants through cycles of action and research: to plan change, guide participants through change and evaluate change. Bond's (1997) study provides a useful example of this approach. After exploratory discussions with four members of a primary care team, it was agreed that the author (as an action researcher) would support the team by providing them with a series of interprofessional seminars where they could discuss and share their ideas on collaboration. Observations, interviews and documentary data were collected after ten months to evaluate the impact of the interprofessional learning. Findings revealed that the use of action research helped support this team from a position of working together in a "fragmented" manner to collaborating in a more "synergistic" way (Bond 1997:97). In doing so, the author notes:

> "They [the team] crossed new boundaries, generated ideas about working together in more proactive ways with service users... they perceived this as professionally satisfying and organisationally beneficial" (Bond 1997:97).

While providing a rare and valuable account of how an action research approach employed within an interprofessional education initiative can achieve changes to practice, the paper provides little information relating to data collection and analysis. In addition, like most studies, it provides no details of the actual processes that occurred to produce these outcomes. Nevertheless, findings from this and the other action research studies (Glennie & Cosier 1994, Lacey 1996, 1998, Bond 1999, Atwal 2002) provide an encouraging insight into how an action research approach can be successful in supporting changes to professional practice.

Summary

This chapter has reviewed the research literature related to the development and delivery of interprofessional education. It found a limited amount of research literature on the development of interprofessional education. In addition, the chapter found a more voluminous amount of research related to the delivery of interprofessional education. Importantly, it was found that the literature generally neglects to focus on the processes related to development and delivery activities. Instead, it concentrates on reporting the outcomes produced from interprofessional education. Therefore, as argued in Section 1.1.1, the literature contains two 'black box' problems, which restrict our understanding of the nature of the development and delivery of interprofessional education. In beginning to open these black boxes and address the study's research aim and objectives (Section 1.2), the thesis describes how the use of an ethnographic approach (see Chapter 5) produced an insight into the processes attached to the development (Chapter 6) and delivery (Chapter 7) of the Training Ward.

Having reviewed the relevant interprofessional education literature and identified how the study aims to address the current shortfalls it contains, the next chapter provides contextual information to provide a detailed picture of the locations and individuals involved in this work.

Chapter 4: Study context

Introduction

This chapter presents details of the locations in which data were gathered and information on the participants who took part in the study. The chapter is divided into three main sections. Section 4.1 presents information on the social and historical backdrop to help provide an understanding of the broader contextual issues associated with the study. Section 4.2 presents information on the steering group who were responsible for the development of the Training Ward and, finally, Section 4.3 presents information on the students and facilitators who participated in the pilot ward that the steering group delivered in early 1999. The aim of this chapter is to provide a "thick description" (Denzin 1989:83) of the study context to help readers judge the relevance of these findings in their own local settings.

4.1. Social, political and historical backdrop

This section describes salient aspects of the socio-political and historical backdrop in which the study took place to provide an insight into the nature of the wider context in which the Training Ward project.

4.1.1. A 'turbulent' inner-city hospital

The Training Ward project was developed and delivered in a large teaching hospital located in a socially and economically deprived inner-London borough. It served an ethnically and culturally diverse local population made up of people from Bangladeshi, Somali, Irish, Afro-Caribbean, Turkish, Chinese and Vietnamese communities. The hospital also had responsibility for one of the largest refugee populations in London.

Due to its social and economic problems, the hospital's local population faced significant health difficulties, particularly in terms of the number of residents affected by tuberculosis, diabetes and heart disease. Consequently, the hospital faced a continually heavy demand for its services. This, in turn, meant that bed occupancy across the hospital operated at around 100 per cent throughout the year. To meet this constant demand for beds, hospital management had a continued focus on increasing patient 'throughout' in order to reduce patient length of stay in the hospital.

The hospital also faced longstanding difficulties with recruitment and retention of nursing and therapy staff, which meant that a number of wards were under-staffed. Consequently, existing members of staff were often over-stretched. In addition, as a teaching hospital, the on-going rotation of students and junior staff through the different clinical directorates of the hospital added further pressures on staff and also contributed to undermining staff stability.

As well as facing these local pressures, hospital management needed to address national pressures created from the government policies for service accountability in providing efficient, safe, high quality care (Department of Health 1997, 1998). A recent study undertaken at this hospital found that these combined (local and national) pressures meant that it should be considered "a turbulent" organisation (Bridges 2004:166). An organisation in which factors such as staff turnover and heavy demand for clinical services impedes the stability required for effective organisational function. (The influence of the pressures created by this turbulent organisational context on the development and delivery of the Training Ward is discussed in depth in Section 9.3.2).

4.1.2. Institutional relationships

In total, staff based at five separate institutions were involved in the development and delivery of the Training Ward: three universities (with representation from schools of nursing, medicine, occupational therapy and physiotherapy) and two hospitals (one acute, one community-based) based within a single NHS Trust. All institutions were located within five-mile radius of one another.

In terms of relationships between the three universities, only the schools of medicine and nursing had an established partnership for joint teaching and learning initiatives before becoming involved in the Training Ward. These two institutions had developed a clinical and communication skills centre in the early 1990s, a shared faculty that provided medical and nursing students opportunities to practice and enhance their clinical and communication skills. In addition, these schools had developed, in 1995, a community-based interprofessional learning experience for first and second year dental, medical and nursing students, which provided opportunities for shared learning on a number of community-orientated initiatives. In contrast, the schools of occupational therapy and physiotherapy did not share such links. Nevertheless, all four schools shared a relationship with the hospital in which the Training Ward project was developed and delivered. This relationship was based on the clinical placements, which the hospital provided to the students from each of the four schools for well over a decade.

In terms of the relationship between the acute and community-based hospitals, as these hospitals both operated under a single NHS Trust, they had formal links with one another. For example, the community hospital provided outpatient clinics for a number of the medical teams based at the acute hospital, therefore these staff often worked across both sites.

4.2. Contextual information on the development of the Training Ward

This section provides contextual information on the steering group who developed Training Ward (their formation, membership, details about their meetings) and information about how the group employed a Swedish model for the basis for their own interprofessional initiative.

4.2.1. Group formation

As noted in Section 1.1.3, the steering group was formed in 1997 after two senior university managers (one from a school of nursing, the other from a medical school) had visited the interprofessional Training Ward at Linköping in Sweden (Sandén & Walhström 1996, Walhström et al. 1996). Enthused by the innovative nature of this practice-based initiative, these managers asked two members of their staff (both with an interest in educational development) to establish a steering group that would develop and deliver a similar initiative in the UK.

Drawing upon their local networks, staff from nearby schools of occupational therapy and physiotherapy and a local NHS Trust hospital were invited to begin discussing the feasibility of initiating this interprofessional project. At this point, the steering group consisted of six members: four educational representatives from each of the schools and two clinical managers from the Trust. Documentary data from steering group meetings[15] indicated that all members agreed that to successfully develop and deliver this

---

[15] Details on data collection methods are presented in the next chapter.

interprofessional initiative in a clinical practice setting, better representation from clinical staff was needed. Therefore, in early 1998 this initial core of six members was expanded to 14 members.

4.2.2. Membership and meetings

In total, over the two-year period of fieldwork for the study, the group consisted of 20 members, made up from 11 clinicians and nine educationalists (see Table 3, page 59).

As noted above, to ensure that the group had good representation from clinical staff, it expanded in 1998 from six to 14 members. Table 4 (page 60) offers details of this and other changes that occurred in steering group from 1997 to 2000.

The 1998 expansion also ensured that the membership between educationalists and clinicians became more balanced. Of the 14 members, half held clinical posts (two doctors, three nurses, one occupational therapist and one physiotherapist) and half held educational posts (one doctor, two nurses, two occupational therapists and two physiotherapists). As Table 4 (page 60) indicates, during 1999 to 2000, eight members left the group and four members joined (to replace some of those who had departed). Two reasons were cited for leaving the group: a change in post or an increase in work commitments. The members who joined the group in this period were clinical staff from either a nursing, medical or physiotherapy background.

4.2.3. Inspiration: the Swedish ward

As previously noted, the inspiration for the Training Ward was an interprofessional initiative based in Sweden. To provide background context, this section outlines the Swedish initiative in more detail and describes the alterations that were made to deliver the ward into the UK.

Developed by staff based at Linköping University and Linköping Hospital, the Swedish ward commenced in January 1996. The ward was sited in a well-resourced hospital that served an affluent local population. Based in a specially created eight-bedded clinical area, which was solely used for the delivery of this initiative, it provided final year students from nursing, medicine, occupational therapy, physiotherapy, social welfare and laboratory technology with a compulsory placement in which they worked together as an interprofessional team.

Name[16]	Details[17]
Ben	Educationalist. Original steering group member. Left the group to take up a post in another institution.
Brigit	Clinician. Joined the group after the pilot. Regularly attended steering group meetings until 2000.
Christine	Educationalist. Original steering group member. Attended steering group meetings until 2000.
Derek	Clinician. Original steering group member. Attended steering group meetings throughout the study.
Edward	Clinician. Joined the steering group in 1998. Left in 1999 due to heavy work commitments.
Elsa	Educationalist. Joined the steering group in 1998 and regularly attended steering group meeting until 2000.
Emma	Clinician. Joined the group to replace Patricia. Periodically attended steering group meetings until 2000.
Janet	Educationalist. Original steering group member. Withdrew from the group in June 1999 due to heavy work commitments
Jean	Clinician. Joined the steering group in January 1998. Attended steering group meetings throughout the study.
Judith	Educationalist. Joined the group in January 1998. Attended steering group meetings continuously throughout the study.
Julia	Clinician. Joined the group in January 1998. Attended steering group meetings continuously throughout the study.
Lucy	Clinician. Joined the group to replace a departing member. Periodically attended steering group meetings until end of study.
Margaret	Educationalist. Joined the group in 1998. Attended steering group meetings continuously throughout the study
Maria	Educationalist. Joined in January 1997. Attended steering group meetings until June 1997. Left due to work commitments.
Matt	Clinician. Joined in late 1999 to replace a departing member. Periodically attended steering group meetings until end of study.
Michael	Clinician. Original group member. Attended a few of the early meetings and withdrew due to heavy work commitments.
Nancy	Clinician. Joined in late 1998 to replace a member who left post. Attended continuously from 1998 to 2000.
Patricia	Clinician. Original steering group member. Attended steering group meetings from 1997 to 1999. Left to take up another post in late 1999.
Sam	Clinician. Joined in late 1999 to replace a departing member. Periodically attended steering group meetings until end of study.
Todd	Clinician. Joined the group in January 1998. Left the group in 1998 shortly before the pilot run to take up another post.

Table 3: Steering group members

---

[16] All names of steering group members have been changed to protect their identities.
[17] Only brief contextual information is given on the steering group members. Due to the unique nature of the initiative, offering more detailed information may result in these individuals being identified.

Year	Membership	Change
1997	Ben, Christine, Derek, Janet, Maria, Michael, Patricia	-
1998	Ben, Christine, Derek, Edward, Elsa, Janet, Jean, Judith, Julia, Maria, Margaret, Nancy, Patricia, Todd	1 member leaves 8 members join
1999	Ben, Christine, Derek, Edward, Elsa, Janet, Jean, Judith, Julia, Margaret, Nancy, Patricia	2 members leave
2000	Christine, Derek, Elsa, Emma, Jean, Julia, Lucy, Margaret, Matt, Sam	6 members leave 4 members join

Table 4: Steering group membership change

Students collaborated to provide care to up to eight orthopaedic patients (with simple orthopaedic conditions such as hip fractures). Supervision was provided by nurse facilitators who worked with the student teams throughout the placement. In addition, students received part-time profession-specific supervision from a consultant (who was also in overall charge of the ward), a medical registrar, an occupational therapist and a physiotherapist. The underpinning educational approach employed on the ward was PBL, which was employed to encourage students to work together to ameliorate patient 'problems'. Wahlström et al. (1997:428) also note that PBL was selected to stimulate "the acquisition of knowledge to [help students] learn to respect different opinions".

While on the Swedish ward, students had to meet the following four learning aims. To:
- Develop skills for co-operation in a team;
- Increase their understanding of each other's professions;
- Increase their understanding of the whole care of the patient;
- Increase their knowledge of practical experience of medical care and rehabilitation (Wahlström & Sandén 1998:227).

Three teams of students covered the ward for a two-week period. During this time, student teams worked two shifts: mornings and afternoons. The bulk of their time was spent on the ward working together to provide care for patients. In addition, students attended team reflection sessions at the end of each morning shift where they reflected upon their individual and team performances. During their placement, students undertook tasks that were specific to their profession and also shared "general care" tasks (Walhström & Sandén 1998:229) such as taking patient observations and washing patients. Each team's ward experience was concluded by an interprofessional 'care conference' where student teams discussed issues relating to delivering collaborative care. This care conference was also used to assess student learning from their ward experience.

4.2.4. Transferring the Swedish model

To assist the steering group with their work in developing and delivering the Training Ward, two short visits to Linköping were undertaken to observe the ward and talk informally to staff and students. The first visit occurred in mid-1997 and involved a small number of educationalists (including two steering group members). The second visit was undertaken in early 1998 and consisted of the six new steering group members.

Documentary data gathered from meetings in 1997 indicated that following the first visit, the group agreed to incorporate a number of aspects of the Swedish model into the UK Training Ward. These were:

- Basing the ward in an orthopaedic setting;
- Adopting the same facilitation arrangements;
- Using student team reflection sessions;
- Employing the same student shift arrangements;
- Concluding the placement with an interprofessional case conference;
- Retaining the model's PBL foundations.

However, the group felt that the Swedish model should be altered in two significant ways. Firstly, it was felt that sharing "general care" (Walhström & Sandén 1998:229) tasks was an unrealistic part of interprofessional practice. It was therefore agreed that students should focus on undertaking their profession-specific work, while the team reflection sessions would offer them time to talk about their interprofessional interactions. Secondly, it was felt that a two-week placement was too short to provide the students with a sufficient insight into the processes of working together to deliver patient care. As existing student placements lasted for four weeks, this was felt to be a more suitable period for the Training Ward.

Following the second visit, the group decided to reverse these two decisions. It was felt that to preserve the strengths of the Swedish ward it should be transferred without alteration. It was therefore agreed to include general care tasks and restrict the Training Ward to a two-week placement. In addition, to understand the impact of this initiative before rolling out it out on a longer-term basis, it was decided to pilot the Training Ward for a four-week period. (The process associated with reversing these decisions is presented in Section 6.2.1, while the impact of these changes during the delivery of the four-week pilot is examined in Sections 7.2.2 and 7.2.3).

4.2.5. Steering group work

The foundations of the steering group's collaborative work on the Training Ward were based upon their formal meetings. Steering group meetings were held on a monthly basis and lasted between one and two hours. These meetings focused on discussions around the range of educational and operational issues connected to the development and delivery of the Training Ward. As noted above, due to a significant amount of effort needed to deliver this interprofessional experience in a practice setting, the group's meetings were initially focused upon the development and delivery of a four-week pilot ward. After the pilot was delivered in early 1999 the group used their subsequent meetings to begin to re-establish the ward to run on a longer-term basis. Ultimately, the group was unsuccessful in this part of their work. (Section 7.2 explores the challenges that contributed to the group's lack of success).

To help foster a sense of 'joint ownership' during their work on the ward, the steering group rotated their meetings between a number of sites. Four locations were used, rooms in the:
- Occupational therapy school (ten occasions);
- Hospital management offices (eight occasions);
- Ward where the Training Ward was based (two occasions);
- Medical school (one occasion).

Steering group members also undertook a number of activities outside the meetings (e.g. negotiating with professional regulatory body representatives to ensure student participation) in order that their work on the ward could progress. In addition to their work planning the Training Ward, a number of steering group members also undertook educational activities designed to support the work of the students and facilitators. In preparation for the Training Ward pilot, three members designed and ran a session for the facilitators to develop their understanding of using PBL. During the pilot ward, seven members of the steering group also facilitated some of the students' learning activities: three members facilitated the students' team reflection sessions; three offered on-ward facilitation of the student teams; one member facilitated an interprofessional ward round and another facilitated the interprofessional care conference.

4.3. Contextual information on the delivery of the Training Ward pilot

As previously noted, the steering group decided to deliver a Training Ward pilot to understand its impact before operationalising the ward on a full-time basis. A four-week pilot was therefore delivered in early 1999. This section outlines contextual information on the pilot and the students and facilitators who participated in the ward.

4.3.1. Location and participants

The Training Ward pilot was located on the second floor of a large Victorian building that formed the main part of the hospital described in Section 4.1.1. Other departments such as outpatients were housed in newer buildings located nearby. The pilot occupied a 12-bedded area within a 27-bedded orthopaedic and rheumatology ward. The ward consisted of three bays that contained five beds in each and a larger 12 bedded area (used for the Training Ward). In addition to these four areas, the ward also had a kitchen, day room, seminar room, patient washroom and a sluice room.

In total, 34 students took part in the Training Ward pilot (11 medical students, 12 nursing students, six occupational therapy students and five physiotherapy students). As Table 5 (page 71) reveals, students worked in teams that consisted of six members (two medical students, two nursing students, one occupational therapy student, one physiotherapy student).[18] The students' were aged between 21 and 31, with the majority in their early twenties. The occupational therapy and physiotherapy students tended to be slightly older than their medical and nursing colleagues, as they had completed undergraduate degrees before entering their respective professional courses. As Table 5 (page 64) indicates, like the membership of the steering group, the students were mostly female: out of the 34 students, 25 were female.

Due to timetabling differences between the four schools, the process of student selection for the pilot ward varied. Occupational therapy, physiotherapy and most medical students were offered the choice by their respective institutions to participate in this initiative.[19] All 12 of the nursing students were, however, randomly allocated by their course leader to participate in the pilot ward.

---

[18] Illness and a family bereavement meant that two of the teams only had five members.
[19] After failing a clinical examination, four of the 12 medical students were required to participate in the pilot ward to gain additional clinical experience.

(The effect of employing these contrasting approaches to student selection is considered in Section 7.2.6).

Team	Members	Profession
Blue team	Fiona, Wasim Kate, Zara Tamsin Tom	Medicine Nursing Occupational therapy Physiotherapy
Red team	Molly, Yvonne Anne, Cathy Marie Deborah	Medicine Nursing Occupational therapy Physiotherapy
Yellow team	Jake Sue, Maggie Andrea Clara	Medicine Nursing Occupational therapy Physiotherapy
Orange team	Jo, Matt Tanya, Barbara Melanie	Medicine Nursing Occupational therapy
Green team	Miriam, Ralph Kelly, Wendy Clare Max	Medicine Nursing Occupational therapy Physiotherapy
Purple team	Jeff, Polly Gwyn, Keith Suzanne Jen	Medicine Nursing Occupational therapy Physiotherapy

Table 5: Student teams

All students were enrolled in full-time pre-qualification courses. Medical, nursing and occupational therapy students were in the final year of their course while the physiotherapy students were in the second year of a three-year course.[20] While medical, occupational therapy and physiotherapy students were studying on a degree-level course, the nursing students were studying on a diploma-level course. All students had regularly undertaken clinical placements as part of their pre-qualification education. However, none of them had previously participated in any interprofessional learning activities. The occupational therapy students had most experience of PBL (their school employed PBL throughout their pre-qualification curriculum). In contrast, the medical, nursing and physiotherapy students had less experience, as their respective schools employed PBL on a less extensive basis. Although students from the same course knew one another, none of the students knew their colleagues from the other pre-qualification courses.

---

[20] Due to timetabling difficulties, it was not possible to recruit final year physiotherapy students into the Training Ward.

Facilitation during the Training Ward pilot was offered by nine facilitators (see Table 6). All nine worked in the clinical area where the Training Ward pilot was based.

Facilitator	Profession
May	Nursing
Carol	Nursing
Val	Nursing
Hal	Medicine
Kit	Medicine
Tony	Medicine
Malcolm	Medicine
Teri	Therapy[21]
Caitlin	Therapy

Table 6: Training Ward facilitators

May, Carol and Val worked with the student teams, providing support on nursing and teamwork issues. May and Carol were both in their late twenties and had around five years clinical experience and worked as senior staff nurses. Val was in her middle thirties, had around ten years' clinical experience and worked as a sister. All three had completed a short nursing course on clinical facilitation and regularly facilitated student nurses during their clinical placements. Medical facilitation was provided by Hal, Kit, Tony and Malcolm who were senior house officers with around three years' clinical experience. All were in their mid-twenties. Occupational therapy and physiotherapy facilitation was provided by Teri and Caitlin who were both were senior therapists with over ten years clinical and student supervision experience. Teri was in her mid-thirties and Caitlin was in her mid-forties. In addition to their facilitation duties, two of the facilitators were also steering group members. One had been a member since 1998 and the other joined shortly after the delivery of the pilot ward.[22]

None of the facilitators had previously facilitated students on an interprofessional basis. In addition, none had experience of using PBL in their facilitation work. To help develop their understanding of PBL, three steering group members offered the facilitators a short course. (See Appendix 3 for details of the PBL training offered to the facilitators).

---

[21] To prevent possible identification of the occupational therapy and physiotherapy facilitators, the exact nature of their professional group has been withheld.
[22] To prevent possible identification, the pseudonyms used in the steering group for these two individuals have been altered.

4.3.2. Participation in the pilot

This section outlines the aims and objectives of the Training Ward pilot and provides details on the activities undertaken by the students during their pilot ward experience.

4.3.2.1. Learning aims and objectives

To structure the Training Ward pilot, the steering group developed the following aims:

- To prepare students by developing an understanding of interprofessional and interagency issues around admission, care, rehabilitation and discharge of patients with musculoskeletal conditions.
- To enable students to develop their team work skills by working together as a team and participating in role sharing.
- To treat patients, staff and students as they would wish to be treated themselves on the underlying principles of respect for individuals.

The steering group also devised the six learning aims for the students.

- To promote and facilitate team working within a real clinical setting.
- To identify outcomes of interprofessional working.
- To promote and facilitate a holistic approach to health and social care through collaboration.
- To clarify roles and responsibilities of individual professionals within the team.
- To gain an insight and understanding into the knowledge, skills and attitudes expected of individual professionals.
- To develop individual professional roles within the interprofessional team.

In addition, a further 19 joint learning objectives and around ten profession-specific learning objectives were developed by the group. (Appendix 4 contains the learning objectives employed in the Training Ward pilot).

4.3.2.2. Student activities

Initially, all students were invited to attend a four-hour induction session held on the Sunday before starting on the Training Ward pilot. These sessions were designed to provide the students with an introduction to the pilot ward, an opportunity to allow them to meet the other members of their team, meet their facilitators and also take a short tour around the hospital. In addition, each student received a Training Ward handbook at this session, which contained the following information:

- The overall aims of the pilot ward;

- Background information on the clinical area that located the pilot ward;
- Student team-orientated learning objectives and their profession-specific learning objectives;
- Information on the role of the facilitators;
- Details of the hospital's health and safety policy;
- An outline of the pilot ward evaluation.

As noted above, six student teams worked on the Training Ward pilot for its four-week duration. Three teams initially covered the pilot ward in its first two weeks, while the remaining three teams covered on the ward for its final two weeks. Students worked on the pilot ward for eight-hour shifts in the morning (7.30am-3.30pm) and afternoon (1.30-9.30pm).[23] While on the ward, students' work centred upon two elements:

- Undertaking tasks that were specific to their individual profession (e.g. occupational therapy or physiotherapy assessments);
- Participating in the delivery of shared 'team duties' (e.g. washing patients, taking patient observations) that were designed to encourage closer working relationships.

The students were provided with two forms of facilitation: team facilitation and profession-specific facilitation. As noted above, team facilitation was provided by May, Carol, and Val. Each of these facilitators was attached to a team and worked with them during their two-week period on the pilot ward, offering them support with their interprofessional teamwork. Profession-specific facilitation was provided by all the facilitators. In addition, student teams also participated in a weekly interprofessional ward round facilitated by one of the steering group members.

To update each other, student teams undertook short (5-10 minutes) interprofessional handovers at the beginning and end of their shifts. In addition, student teams attended reflective sessions after each of their weekday morning shifts where they could discuss their ward experiences. As noted above, these sessions were facilitated by the educational members of the steering group and lasted from 45 minutes to an hour.

The students' experience on the Training Ward was concluded by an interprofessional care conference when the three teams covering the ward came together to discuss and reflect upon aspects of their experiences. Different requirements from the four professional regulatory bodies who validated the different schools pre-qualification

---

[23] Nightshifts during the period the pilot ward was running continued to be covered by qualified staff.

courses meant that, while the pilot ward contributed to the nursing students' course requirements, medical, occupational therapy and physiotherapy students did not receive any accredited clinical time for their Training Ward experience. To help differentiate Training Ward students from clinical staff and promote a sense of team cohesiveness all students wore theatre blues instead of their usual profession-specific uniforms. (The effect of these different approaches to the accreditation of clinical time and the use of a single Training Ward uniform is considered in Section 7.2.6).

Summary

This chapter has provided contextual information for the study in relation to the socio-political and historical backdrop, the participants and locations in which this work was undertaken. Importantly, the chapter described the turbulent context into which the Training Ward project was delivered. It also described how the steering group transferred and modified a model of interprofessional education devised in a Swedish context as the basis for the Training Ward project. In presenting these details the chapter aimed to provide 'thick description' (Denzin 1989) of the study context to allow readers to judge the relevance of the findings from this study to their own settings.

The next chapter presents and discusses the methodology and methods employed in this context to address the study's research aim and objectives (see Section 1.2).

Chapter 5: Methodology and methods

Introduction

This chapter presents a description and discussion of the methodology and methods employed in the study to address its research aim and objectives (see Section 1.2). The chapter is divided into four main sections. Section 5.1 details the process that was undertaken to adopt an epistemological approach and methodology. Section 5.2 describes the methods of data collection employed in the study, while Section 5.3 describes the data analysis process. Finally, Section 5.4 offers a series of methodological reflections. The aim of the chapter is to provide a detailed account and justification of the methodology and methods employed in the study.

5.1. Methodological approach

The need for a sound methodological approach (one with an appropriate epistemology, that informs the selection of a theoretical framework and research method) is a crucial element in producing a high quality study. Indeed, the incorporation of such an approach is essential in ensuring that empirical data can be understood in a comprehensive and systematic fashion. As May (1993:7) argues:

> "If researchers simply content themselves with studying everyday social life, such as conversations and interactions between people, this will distract them from an investigation of the underlying [theoretical] mechanisms which make those possible in the first place".

Furthermore the use of a sound methodology is essential if one wants to avoid the problem of "abstracted empiricism" (Wright Mills 1967:50), a term that describes empirical work that fails to adequately draw upon supporting theory. This problem continues to be a concern within the social research literature (e.g. Rorty 2000, Cooper 2001). Given these issues, this section goes on to describe the process undertaken to select a suitable methodology that could begin to address the study's research aim and objectives.

5.1.1. Interpretivism

As discussed in Chapter 3, the literature contains only a partial examination of the processes attached to both the development (Section 3.1) and delivery of interprofessional education (Section 3.2). Consequently, as argued in Section 1.1.1, there are two 'black box' problems in the interprofessional education literature. In order to 'open' these black boxes and begin to explore and understand their 'contents', I needed an epistemology that could support such an exploratory investigation. I was directed towards an interpretivist epistemology.

Originating from the work of the German sociologist Max Weber, interpretivism emerged as an alternative explanation for social action (*Verstehen*) in a social science heavily dominated by positivistic thought. For Crotty (1998) interpretivism rejects positivism due to its:

- Assumption of the existence of an objective reality;
- Goal of establishing universal laws for human behaviour;
- Focus on proving the existence of causality between independent and dependent variables;
- Use of the hypo-deductive approach to empirical investigation.

Instead, interpretivism is based on processes of negotiation that occur between individuals to create and interpret meanings for their social actions and the social situations in which they exist:

> "[Interpretivism] requires an understanding of the social world which people have constructed and which they reproduce through their continuing activities [...] people are constantly involved in interpreting their world – social situations, other people's behaviour, their own behaviour" (Blaikie 1993:36).

Interpretivism therefore emphases the need for researchers to gain contextually derived and socially situated interpretations of the world:

> "The social researcher enters the everyday social world in order to grasp the socially constructed meanings, and then reconstructs these meanings into social scientific language" (Blaikie 1993:96).

Another key aim for the interpretivist researcher is to understand how they themselves 'fit' into the social world. This allows them to understand the reflexive relationship they share with research participants and also helps them understand the influence of this relationship on their empirical work.

Interpretivism has been criticised in a number of areas. Importantly, Giddens (1984) argues that the emphasis interpretivism places on understanding individual meanings can often result in a neglect of explanations of how social structures can influence social action. In addition, Fay (1974) has argued that interpretivist studies tend to be conservative in nature, as they overlook aspects of social conflict and social change. Despite such criticisms, the stress this epistemology places on exploring interpretation and meaning ensures it provides a sound foundation for this study.

5.1.2. Symbolic interactionism

Having adopted upon a suitable epistemology, I needed to identify an appropriate theoretical perspective to help underpin the work. Given the emphasis on understanding the interactive processes involved in both developing and delivering the Training Ward project, I was directed towards symbolic interactionism (Blumer 1969, Denzin 1970).

Located firmly within interpretivist traditions (Crotty 1998), symbolic interactionism was originally developed by George Herbert Mead in the 1930s and subsequently expanded by his student Herbert Blumer in the 1960s. The aim of this theory was to provide an explanation of how individuals gain meaning from their social interactions. For Blumer (1969:2) symbolic interactionism is founded upon three guiding assumptions:

> "[Firstly] that human beings act toward things on the basis of the meanings that these things have for them; [secondly] that the meaning of such things is derived from, and arises out of the social interaction that one has with one's fellows; [thirdly] that these meanings are handled in, and modified through, an interpretative process used by the person in dealing with the things he [sic] encounters".

Therefore, interactionism has an interest in understanding the meanings individuals develop and modify through their social interactions. As Blumer (1969:5) states:

> "Meaning [...] for a person grows out of the ways in which other persons act towards the person [...] meanings [are] social products formed through activities of people interacting".

Crotty (1998) provides a useful summary of the central role that symbols play within this theoretical perspective. He notes that meaningful interactions are only made possible by the 'symbols' (i.e. language) that individuals share when communicating with one another:

> "Only through dialogue can one become aware of the perceptions, feeling and attitudes of others and interpret their meaning and intent. Hence the term 'symbolic interactionism'" (Crotty 1998:75).

A number of important methodological implications flow from the use of symbolic interactionism. Firstly, to understand the nature of interaction the researcher needs to pay particular attention to behaviour (Schwandt 1994). Secondly, in entering an individual's 'social world' to investigate it, the researcher should aim to capture the situated nature of meanings and interactions related to this context (Denzin 1970). Finally, in order to understand the nature of meaning, the researcher is required to enter the world of the informant to gain their *emic* (personal) perspectives. Once these *emic* understandings have been gathered, the researcher needs to obtain an *etic* insight into the data by analysing them in relation to pertinent concepts and theories (Denzin 1970). On this point, however, Mitchell (1977) notes that in gathering an informant's *emic* perspective view, the researcher needs to be aware that it is the informant's views they are gathering, and not their own:

> "The sociological observer must exercise sufficient discipline on himself [sic] to ensure that it is indeed the actors' meanings that are recorded and not merely his [sic] own" (Mitchell 1977:116, original emphasis).

A number of criticisms have been made about symbolic interactionism. For example, like the criticism aimed at interpretivism, some authors have pointed out that interactionist accounts are preoccupied with eliciting the individual's perspective at the expense of overlooking the impact of wider social structures on interaction (e.g. Silverman 1993). Interactionism has also been criticised for a preoccupation on only uncovering 'underdog' perspectives and therefore neglecting the influence of 'top dog' (managerial) accounts (Dingwall 1980). Nevertheless, as noted above, given the study's aims of exploring interactive processes, symbolic interactionism provides a highly appropriate theoretical framework for the study.

5.1.3. Ethnography

Having chosen an appropriate epistemology and theoretical framework for the study, I needed to select a research method that could help me understand data from the development and delivery of the Training Ward project. Given the choice of selection epistemology and framework, ethnography presented a very suitable research method to employ.

Located within anthropological traditions (Fetterman 1998), ethnography has a focus on understanding the social processes (i.e. behaviours, perceptions) and cultures that occur within groups, gangs, organisations and communities. As Hammersley (1985) states:

> "The task [of ethnographers] is to document the culture – the perspectives and practices – of the people in these settings. The aim is to 'get inside' the way each group of people sees the world" (Hammersley 1985:152).

Indeed, the stress placed on interpretation and meaning within ethnography means there are strong conceptual linkages between interactionism and ethnography:

"Given the emphasis on putting oneself in the place of the other and seeing things from the perspective of others, it is not surprising that interactionism should take to its bosom [a research method] developed within cultural anthropology, that is, ethnography" (Crotty 1998:76).

There is also a long tradition of interactionist ethnographies within the sociological literature, including Strauss' study on the creation of social order in psychiatric hospitals, Becker's (1963) exploration of the illegal use of marijuana and Allen's (1996) study of nurse-doctor relations in acute hospitals.[24]

For Hammersley & Atkinson, ethnography is founded upon by the following central attributes:

"A strong emphasis on exploring the nature of particular social phenomena, rather than setting out to test hypotheses about them; a tendency to work primarily with 'unstructured data', that is data that have not been coded at the point of data collection in terms of a closed set of analytical categories; investigation of a small number of cases, perhaps just one case, in detail; analysis of data that involves explicit interpretation of the meanings and functions of human actions, the product of which mainly takes the form of verbal descriptions and explanations" (Hammersley & Atkinson 1995:248).

Indeed, given the stress placed on exploration and the focus on interpreting meanings, the adoption of Hammersley & Atkinson's approach to ethnography was highly suitable for the study. Another factor in the selection of ethnography for the study was its emphasis on understanding the reflexive nature of social research:

"We are part of the world which we study [...] we act in the social world and yet we are able to reflect upon ourselves and our actions as objects in that world [...] By including our own role within the research focus, and perhaps even systematically exploiting our participation in the settings under study as researchers, we can produce accounts of the social world and justify them" (Hammersley & Atkinson 1995:21-22).

The final factor that guided my selection of ethnography was the location of its foundation within 'subtle realism' (Hammersley 1992). For Hammersley, subtle realism provides a route between the 'extremes' of objectivism (an approach that strives for a single 'truth') on one hand, and constructionism (an approach that stresses the relative nature of knowledge) on the other. In contrast, subtle realism acknowledges the socially constructed nature of knowledge, but also accepts that individuals can obtain a plausible

---

[24] See Rock (2001) for a detailed discussion on the theoretical and empirical linkages between symbolic interactionism and ethnography.

level of agreement over what constitutes 'reality'. As Seale (1999:26-27) outlines:

> "Human communities in practice have created reasonably firm grounds on which plausibility [of knowledge] can be judged".

Nevertheless, ethnography has been criticised in a number of areas. For example, Flick (2002) notes that in an effort to 'get inside' a particular culture, ethnographers can 'go native' (i.e. to over-identify with their research participants) and thus lose their ability for reflexive thought. In addition, Flick (2002:148) argues that many ethnographic studies contain an over-emphasis on both their fieldwork strategies and data presentation, which can result in a "methodological arbitrariness" in their approach to their empirical work. Despite such criticisms, Hammersley & Atkinson's (1995) approach to ethnography provided an appropriate method that linked well with the selected epistemology and theoretical framework and that could help address the study's research aim and objectives (see Section 1.2).

5.1.4. Case selection

Ethnographic research generally does not employ complicated sampling techniques. Indeed, in most studies the selection of case(s) tends to be based upon the researchers' ability to negotiate access for their research. As Silverman (2000:102) points out, "very often a case will be chosen simply because it allows access". Furthermore, as stated above, most ethnographic research tends to be based upon the selection of "a small number of cases, perhaps just one case" (Hammersley & Atkinson 1995:248). This was my approach to case selection. As outlined in Section 1.1.3, the selection of the Training Ward as a single case for the study was largely based on opportunism: being appointed to a research post that allowed access to an research setting in which I could undertake this investigation.

I employed Hammersley's (1992) definition of what a 'case' actually constituted in this work. He states that a case can be regarded as the "phenomenon (located in space/time) about which data are collected and/or analysed" (Hammersley 1992:184). In relation to this definition, I viewed the Training Ward project was the 'case' under study, with the steering group's work developing this initiative and students' experiences of its delivery in a clinical setting as the focus of my investigation.

5.1.5. Generalising from a single case

As discussed above, it is common for ethnographic studies to focus their attention on a single study setting. However, in doing so, ethnographers can face the criticism that their data are not generalisable to others contexts (Flick 2002). Hammersley & Atkinson (1995) recommend the use of two techniques, thick description and theoretical generalisation, to overcome these limitations. I have employed both techniques recommended by Hammersley & Atkinson to help enhance the generalisability of the findings from this study.[25]

5.1.5.1. Two techniques for enhancing generalisability

Typically, ethnographers offer a detailed or 'thick description' (Denzin 1989) of the study context to allow readers to judge the relevance of research findings in their own local settings. In offering such detailed descriptions, ethnographers aim to provide the reader with a sense of 'being there' in the research setting. As Geertz (1988:16) states:

> "Ethnographers need to convince us [...] not merely that they themselves have truly 'been there' but [...] that had we been there we should have seen what they saw, felt what they felt, concluded what they concluded".

In attempting to provide generalisable research findings, I have aimed to provide rich descriptions of the study context in which the Training Ward was developed and delivered (see Chapter 4). In doing so, I aim to provide readers with enough information of the study context to enable them to judge the relevance of this work in their own organisational settings.

Another technique for enhancing the wider relevance of ethnographic research is the use of theoretical generalisation. For Mitchell (1983), this technique aims to produce theoretical principles that can be generalised to other settings. The validity of theoretical generalisation, argues Mitchell, depends not on the typicality of the case, but on the strength of logic of the theoretical reasoning:

> "The inference about the logical relationship between two characteristics is not based upon the representativeness of the sample and therefore its typically, but rather upon the logicality of the nexus between the two characteristics" (Mitchell, 1983:198).

Given the nature of this type of generalisation, Mitchell stresses that it differs from enumerative (quantitative) generalisation, which employs 'probability logic' to make statistical inferences from the sample to a wider population.

---

[25] While Hammersley & Atkinson prefer to use the term 'generalisability', it is important to note that other qualitative researchers find it problematic. For example, Lincoln & Guba (1985) argue that generalisability is too closely aligned to the use of statistical extrapolation to be helpfully applied to qualitative research. They therefore argue that the term 'transferability' is more appropriate.

Hammersley & Atkinson (1995:233) argue that the use of the "comparative method", a process involving a careful comparison of data categories during inductive data analysis, is the main route for developing (generalisable) theory within ethnographic research. In essence, this technique entails an analysis of the data related to a particular phenomenon, whereby data categories are continually compared with one another until saturation occurs (i.e. all data are allocated to conceptually well fitting categories). This process helps to produce a coherent account of that phenomenon on which a tentative theoretical explanation can emerge. Hammersley & Atkinson warn, however, that this generation of theory is not the end point of a study. It is the first step. They go on to argue that "further development and refinement of theory" (Hammersley & Atkinson 1995:236) is then required to test the generalisability of the empirically generated theory.

Through the comparative method (see Section 5.3.2 for an explanation of how this was employed in the data analysis), I have attempted to provide a tentative theoretical explanation of the relationship that exists between the development and delivery of interprofessional education (see Section 9.8), linked to the third of the research objectives for this study (Section 1.2).

5.1.6. Enhancing validity

A central concern of any researcher is that their empirical work is valid. Hammersley & Atkinson (1995) state that reflexivity and triangulation can be employed to help enhance the validity of an ethnographic study.[26] Both techniques have been incorporated into the study to help strengthen the validity of its findings.

5.1.6.1 Reflexivity

Reflexivity is commonly employed in ethnographic research (e.g. Alvesson & Skoldberg 2000, Finlay 2002). It provides the reader with a valuable understanding of how a researcher's personal ideas and experiences may have influenced their empirical work (Hammersley & Atkinson 1995). By offering the reader a detailed account of these ideas and experiences, it allows them to understand their possible impact on the study's findings.

---

[26] Although Hammersley & Atkinson employ the term 'validity', other qualitative researchers find its use problematic. Lincoln & Guba (1985) argue, for example, it is inappropriate within qualitative research, as it reflects the quantitative preoccupation with establishing causality. These authors have therefore developed the term 'credibility' as an alternative.

Despite criticisms that reflexive accounts stress the researcher's interpretation at the expense of other, equally valid, interpretations (e.g. Hertz 1997), Seale (1999) argues that reflexivity plays an important function in enhancing the validity of a qualitative study:

"There is no substitute for presenting the evidence that has led to particular conclusions, giving the fullest possible details about the contexts in which research accounts arise. In the last analysis, writers must then trust in their readers' capacity to make their own judgements" (Seale 1999:177).

In aiming to produce a reflexive account, Sections 5.4.1.1 to 5.4.1.3 offer detailed background information on myself, as well as experiences that have shaped my thinking. In doing so, I have attempted to provide the reader with a transparent account of the range of influences associated with this study.

5.1.6.2. Triangulation

Triangulation is a research technique in which a researcher compares different methods and perspectives to help produce a more comprehensive set of findings. The term is often linked to navigation or surveying whereby people discover their position on a map by taking bearings on two landmarks: where the two lines intersect indicates a person's position. Denzin (1978) outlines four types of triangulation. Firstly, data triangulation, which involves the use of different sources of data to examine phenomenon in several different settings and different points in time or space. Secondly, investigator triangulation, which involves the use of multiple researchers to generate a complex range of perspectives on the data. Thirdly, theory triangulation, where researchers approach data with different concepts and theories to see how each helps to understand the data. Finally, methodological triangulation, which involves the collection of different types of data, such as observations and interviews, to help provide richer insights into the phenomenon under study.

While the traditional use of triangulation relies on the notion of achieving convergence to provide a single plausible version of reality, Hammersley & Atkinson express caution about this use. They state a convergence of findings does not necessarily mean that an analysis is correct:

"It may be that all inferences are invalid, that as a result of systematic or even random error that lead to the same, incorrect, conclusion" (Hammersley & Atkinson 1995:231).

To help overcome the problems of producing an invalid analysis, Seale (1999) argues, from a subtle realist perspective (see Section 5.1.3), that a researcher needs to judge the plausibility of different types of data during the triangulation process. As I go on to describe in Section 5.3.3, in employing this approach, I relied upon my observational data to offer more 'plausible' accounts of interaction (as I had physically witnessed them) than my interview data. In contrast, interviews rely upon an individual's ability to recall events accurately, an ability that may diminish over time. Such a position has been outlined by Strong (1977), who argues that claims about the validity of interview data can be strengthened by collecting related observational data.

5.1.6.3. Structured case comparison

A further technique for enhancing the validity of a single case study is a structured case comparison. According to Silverman (2000:104) this technique involves a close examination of published cases to look for similarities and differences between the findings in one's own case and the findings in other "cognate cases". By undertaking this technique, Silverman (2000:104) argues that one can "make larger claims" about one's research in terms of its validity.

Given that the steering group used the Swedish ward as the basis on which to develop the Training Ward (see Section 4.2.4), the Swedish initiative appeared to provide an excellent case for a structured comparison. However, as Chapter 8 goes on to discuss, a limited amount of comparable data from the evaluation work undertaken on the Swedish ward means that I have not been able to make any claims for the validity of the study's findings by employing this technique.

5.2. Data collection

This part of the chapter offers a description and discussion of the approach taken to collect data from the development and delivery of the Training Ward project.

Data collection was undertaken from January 1998 to April 2000. During this time, observations, interviews and documentary data were collected with the steering group who developed the Training Ward project and the students and facilitators who participated in the pilot of the ward, delivered in early 1999. Table 7 (page 79) provides an overview of the data collected for the study.

The decision to collect these different forms of qualitative data was taken to help ensure that the study would yield a more robust understanding of the processes associated with developing and delivering the Training Ward project.

Data collected	Development of Training Ward	Delivery of Training Ward pilot
Observations	21 (1-2 hour) steering group meetings (1998-2000)	90 hours (15 hours per team) of the six student teams who participated in the pilot (1999)
Interviews	Individual semi-structured interviews with 13 steering group members (1998) Individual semi-structured interviews with 10 steering group members (2000) 20 short informal interviews with steering group members (1998-2000)	6 group interviews with student teams (1999) 9 individual semi-structured interviews with all Training Ward facilitators (1999)
Documents	Minutes of meetings, letters, discussion papers (1998-2000)	Student handbook (1999)

Table 7: Details of data collected for the study

For example, a study that only collected observations may provide useful data on social action, but would lack an understanding of the meanings individuals' attach to their actions, as Seale (1999:55-56) states:

> "The privacy of the interview situation can allow people to say things they would not reveal in natural settings of everyday interaction where significant others might hear or disapprove".

Similarly, a study that only collected interview data may provide good descriptions of the meanings individuals' attach to their actions, but as Strong (1977) notes, an individual's recall of social action can differ from the actual 'action' that took place. It is therefore important to collect multiple forms of data to overcome this limitation.

5.2.1. Access and withdrawal

Obtaining access into a study setting can be problematic for ethnographic work, particularly as people are often reluctant to be 'scrutinised' by researchers (Hammersley & Atkinson 1995). However, gaining access into the steering group and the pilot ward was a relatively uncomplicated process. As I was appointed to work on a two-year funded evaluation of the Training Ward project, I had direct access into this initiative.

While I had access into the Training Ward to undertake the evaluation project, I also obtained agreement from steering group members to ensure I could collect observational and interview data from them for this PhD study. However, as Hammersley & Atkinson

(1995) note, access into the research setting cannot be considered a 'one-off' event. Often access will need to be re-negotiated with the different individuals at different stages of a study. Therefore, although I had access into the project for both evaluation and PhD purposes, I still needed to develop and maintain good relations with all participants to ensure that I did not compromise this access. (This aspect of my fieldwork is discussed in more depth in Section 5.4.2).

Withdrawal from the Training Ward project was undertaken in two stages. In relation to the pilot ward data, as previously noted, after the ward ran for a four-week pilot period in February 1999, it closed and never re-opened. Consequently, no further data collection was possible with students or facilitators. (Section 6.2 provides a detailed description of why the steering group only delivered the four-week pilot ward). In relation to the steering group, after nearly two years of observing the group develop the Training Ward project, reviews of my field notes[27] indicated that I had reached a point of data saturation (i.e. no new insights were emerging from the data). I therefore decided to stop collecting observational data for the study in February 2000. To complete the study, I undertook a final round of interviews with steering group members (between March and April) to explore their views and reflections of working together on the project for over two years. My decision to withdraw from the group was in some senses timely, as in June 2000 the group decided to disband. (The reasons for this decision are presented in Section 6.2.6.2).

5.2.2. Developing the Training Ward: steering group data

This section provides a detailed description of approach taken to collect data from the steering group that developed the Training Ward project.

5.2.2.1. Observations

Observational data were collected from the 21 steering group meetings from January 1998 to February 2000. In collecting these data I adopted the role of a "marginal ethnographer" (Hammersley & Atkinson 1995:115), an approach in which the researcher is a marginal participant in the social action they are observing. In terms of my role within steering group meetings, this was restricted to reporting on the progress of the funded evaluation.

---

[27] I reviewed my field notes on a monthly basis in order to refresh my memory of previous events and also to examine for the emergence of any interesting and possibly illuminating data.

From both a methodological and practical viewpoint, this marginal position was advantageous. Practically, as I was contributing little to the meetings, I could easily record observations directly as they occurred. Methodologically, such an approach was advantageous as it helped to minimise the effects of reactivity, as I was viewed more as another group member rather than an 'outsider'. This role also helped to ensure that there was a 'distance' between the steering group and me. For Hammersley & Atkinson (1995:115) an "intellectual distance" is useful as it limits the possible effects of over-identification with informants.

Apart from briefly updating group members on the progress of the evaluation project, I remained quiet throughout the meetings. This ensured that I could focus on gathering observational data. Initially, I employed an unstructured approach to recording my field notes in an effort to gather a 'holistic' insight into the group's work. However, when I reviewed my early field notes, there was an overall 'messiness' to these data. In attempting to obtain a holistic record of the steering group's work, I felt concerned that I had been gathering a rather general impression of it and thus missing the subtleties. I therefore decided to focus my observations. Three features were beginning to offer an insight into the group's collaborative work, which I decided to focus on:

- Nature of group negotiations and discussions (e.g. subjects discussed during meetings);
- Decision-making (e.g. nature of the decisions, decision-making outcomes, members' reactions to decisions);
- General atmosphere (e.g. the level of formality/informality during meetings).

Like other ethnographies (e.g. Porter 1995, Allen 1997), the use of a participant observation technique meant that I had the opportunity to collect informal interviews in the form of short conversations. These data (I collected 20 such interviews) allowed me to obtain additional insights from steering group members about their collaborative work and clarify any uncertainty I had around events that occurred within the meetings. Typically, they occurred on a serendipitous basis, often en route to or from steering group meetings.

All observational data collected from the steering group were recorded on notepads. While these data were gathered in 'real time' the informal interviews were usually written-up shortly after they occurred. This approach was adopted to preserve the more 'natural feel' of this type of interview.

However, as Fielding & Fielding (1986:32) point out, researchers can have a tendency to select "'exotic' [data] at the expense of less dramatic (possibly indicative) data". To overcome this potential bias, I reviewed my observational field notes at the end of each month to ensure I was collecting both the 'dramatic' and more 'mundane' social action that occurred within steering group meetings.

5.2.2.2. Semi-structured interviews

Individual interviews with steering group members were held in two phases of the study. In 1998, when I joined the group, I interviewed all 13 members to explore their initial views and ideas on developing the Training Ward. Interviews were again undertaken in 2000 with 10 members[28] at the end of the study to explore their views and experiences of working on this project after a two-year duration. (See Appendix 5 for the interview schedules employed in this part of the study).

All interviews were based upon a semi-structured format, an approach that offers the consistency of a structured interview schedule, but allows the researcher freedom to probe additional areas of interest to help illuminate emerging findings. As May (1993:93) notes:

> "Questions are normally specified, but the interviewer is more free to probe beyond the answers [allowing] both clarification and elaboration on the answers given".

Interviews with steering group members were undertaken in their own offices and lasted between 45 to 60 minutes. To obtain accurate data, all interviews were recorded on audio tape and then transcribed by a secretary. To ensure that the transcripts tallied with my recollection of the interview I listened to all the tapes whilst reading the transcripts. This process was useful for two reasons: it helped to familiarise me with the data and helped to ensure that I picked up any minor errors generated by the transcribing process. To ensure anonymity and confidentiality all tapes were destroyed once they had been transcribed. In addition, pseudonyms were used to replace all the actual names of the steering group members to protect their identity. (Section 5.4.3 provides more information on the ethical considerations related to the study).

While these data provided important insights into the meanings and experiences individual steering group members attached to their work developing and delivering the Training

---

[28] As noted in Section 4.2.2, this reduction in the number of interviews collected in the second phase reflected the smaller size of the steering group in 2000.

Ward project, the interviews served another unanticipated function. I found that a number of steering group members used the privacy of these interviews to raise concerns they had about their work that they did not formally raise in steering group meetings. (Section 6.2.1 describes this issue in more detail).

5.2.2.3. Documents

During the study, I also collected documentary data from the steering group. The main source of data was minutes gathered from the group's meetings. In total, I gathered minutes from all the 21 meetings that took place during the fieldwork phase of the study (1998-2000). I also gathered minutes from three of the early steering group meetings held in late 1997 as well as letters and discussion documents circulated during meetings. These data provided a further useful perspective into the processes associated to the development of the Training Ward project and the delivery of the pilot ward.

5.2.3. Data gathered from the delivery of the pilot ward

Observation, interview and documentary data were collected from the four-week pilot ward that was delivered in early 1999. These data were gathered to begin to understand the issues related to the delivery of the Training Ward project.

5.2.3.1. Observations

During its four-week duration, all the six student teams that participated in the Training Ward were observed during their morning and afternoon shifts on both weekdays and weekends. (As noted in Section 4.3.2.2, students were not required to work night shifts, as qualified staff covered these shifts). I observed each team for around 15 hours. In total, I gathered around 90 hours of observational data into the nature of students' interprofessional experiences on the pilot ward.

Like my approach to gathering observational data with the steering group, I adopted the role of a marginal participant while collecting data in the pilot ward. Again, this allowed me to record the students' Training Ward experiences as they occurred. It also provided with the opportunity to talk to students and their facilitators when the ward was quiet, to help clarify aspects of my observations. Building upon the experience gained from my work with the steering group, I organised the collection of observations around:

- Behaviour (e.g. how the students worked together while delivering patient care);
- Verbal interactions (e.g. negotiations and discussions) while working together;

- The general 'flavour' of interactions (e.g. the level of formality/informality during interactions).

Observations of the student interaction focused on four main activities undertaken on the Training Ward: planning sessions; on-ward teamwork; handover sessions and reflection sessions. To capture these different activities, I collected data from three areas of the pilot ward: main ward area; ward corridor and seminar room. In the main ward area, where the students undertook the delivery of care I collected data by sitting at each end of the ward. At one end, there was a desk, telephone and a trolley that contained patients' notes, and at the other end, a table and a filing cabinet. Locating myself in these positions ensured I had a good view of student activity. The ward corridor was where medical students went to look up patient records and where all students went to obtain clinical equipment (e.g. rubber gloves, syringes) for their work. I collected data by sitting at the nurses' station. This position was useful as it was near the computer where the medical students ordered clinical investigations and the trays of clinical supplies that all students used. In addition, as it was located away from the earshot of patients, it formed a natural meeting point for students who had left the ward to talk more informally. The seminar room, located near the Training Ward, was used for student planning, handovers and reflection sessions. When collecting data in this area, I sat in the corner of the room, away from the students and their facilitator. Apart from a brief conversation with the students and facilitators before or at the end of these sessions, I remained silent throughout. This enabled me to concentrate on the content of the student discussions during their planning, handing over or reflection activities.

Although collecting data from student handovers and reflection sessions was unproblematic, as they occurred at specific times and included all the student team members within a small seminar room, trying to observe action that could simultaneously occur in the main ward area and in the corridor was more problematic. Therefore, to cover student interaction in these areas I ensured I spent time sitting in both locations. Nevertheless, the bulk of my time was spent on the main ward area where the most student interaction occurred. My movements between these two parts of the ward depended largely upon what was occurring in the main part of the ward. If things were quiet on the ward I went into the corridor and sat by the nurses' station.

Despite attempting to move regularly between these two areas, I was conscious that I would inevitably miss some action. For Lacey (1976:71) this is a normal fieldwork anxiety, which he called, "it's all happening elsewhere syndrome". Nevertheless, by adopting this approach I felt that at least I had captured an indication of the differing forms of action that occurred in both areas.

All observational data collected from the Training Ward pilot were recorded on notepads. Like my approach with the steering group, during my observations, I also collected short informal discussions with students and facilitators. The data I obtained from these interactions were usually written-up shortly after they occurred in a notepad that I kept with me throughout the study. Like my approach with the steering group, to ensure that I was not concentrating disproportionately on 'exotic' data and overlooking the more prosaic action I regularly reviewed my observational field notes during the delivery of the pilot ward.

5.2.3.2. Student and facilitator interviews

In order to explore the students' views and experiences of the pilot ward, I collected group interviews with all six participating student teams. These interviews were held directly on completion of their two-week placement on the pilot ward. This type of interviewing technique was employed, as it is particularly useful for eliciting data on a shared group experience (Krueger 1994, Ashbury 1995).

To gather a further perspective on the delivery of the pilot ward, I also collected individual interviews with each of the nine facilitators who worked with the students during the pilot ward. These interviews explored facilitators' perceptions of the students' interprofessional experiences. The decision to gather individual interviews with facilitators was based on the need for confidentiality: I felt the facilitators' responses might not be as candid if they were interviewed in a group. (See Appendix 6 for the interview schedules employed in this part of the study).

Student and facilitator interviews were undertaken in the seminar room near the Training Ward and lasted between 30 and 90 minutes. All were recorded on audio tape to ensure accuracy. Like the steering group data, a secretary transcribed all interviews. Again, to ensure that the transcription tallied with my own recollection of the interview I listened to all the tapes whilst reading the transcripts. To ensure anonymity and confidentiality all tapes were destroyed once they were transcribed. In addition, pseudonyms were used to replace all the actual names of the students and facilitators.

5.2.3.3. Documents

To further help understand the issues related to the delivery of the pilot ward, I obtained a copy of the student handbook that the steering group produced for the pilot ward.

5.3. Data analysis

This section describes the approach taken to analyse data collected from the development and delivery of the Training Ward project. While for the purposes of clarity I have separated the data collection and data analysis activities in this thesis, in reality there no clear division, as Hammersley & Atkinson (1995:205) explain:

> "The analysis of data is not a distinct stage of the research. In many ways it begins in the pre-fieldwork phase [...] and continues through the process of writing reports [...] the analysis of data feeds into research design and data collection."

This study was no different. Analysis of data collected in the earlier phase of the study informed subsequent data collection. In addition, analysis of the data continued well into the writing-up 'stage' of this study.

Although the description of the analysis presented below appears to assume a rather mechanical process, progressing through a number of distinctive 'stages' of analysis, there was a good degree of imagination and creativity needed to 'make sense' of the data, an aspect of data analysis that authors have stressed in their ethnographic work (e.g. Hammersley 1990, Porter 1995).

5.3.1. Data handling

For ease of handling, all data were input into a PC word processing package. I used a word processing package as it provided me with a good degree of flexibility to manipulate the data. I kept back-up paper and electronic copies of all the data. To ensure confidentiality, the electronic data stored on my PC were password protected. Hard copies of the data were stored in a locked cupboard. In addition, as noted above, the names of all informants were removed and replaced with pseudonyms.

5.3.2. Inductive thematic analysis

In making sense of my data, I employed an inductive thematic analysis as described by Hammersley & Atkinson (1995). This approach emphasises the inductive emergence of meaning from data. Nevertheless, there is recognition that the analysis also has a deductive element, through the initial development of research aims/objectives and the on-going input of ideas and thoughts that occur during a study.

The first stage of analysis involved an initial 'deconstruction' of the data. This process entailed the generation of a large number of differing conceptual categories. Each of these categories contained interview transcript extracts, observation notes or extracts from documents that were conceptually linked to one another. For example, a category entitled 'resistance' emerged in the Training Ward data set related to the issue of medical students resisting shared team duties. To help frame this initial process of analysis, categories were loosely based around the study's research objectives. The result of this initial fragmentation process produced a tentative thematic framework from which I could then begin a more detailed analysis of the data. (See Appendix 7 for selected themes from this stage of the analysis).

In the second stage of analysis I employed the "comparative method" (Hammersley & Atkinson 1555:233) in which I began to reformulate or 'reconstruct' the loosely connected categories in a more systematic fashion involving a process of data comparison. This work involved undertaking a careful comparison of the data contained in each category in order to ensure that there was a sufficient degree of conceptual similarity between them. If I found that the data compared poorly within a category, they were either re-assigned to a more appropriate category or used to create a new one. The result of this second stage work was to produce a more conceptually rigorous analysis of emergent themes from the data. (See Appendix 8 for selected themes from this stage of the analysis).

The emphasis on the first two stages of analysis is placed on the exploration of common conceptual themes from the data. Nevertheless, an important feature in understanding one's data is to search for 'negative instances: data that offer explanations that run counter to the emerging analysis. For Seale (1999) the search for negative instances offers a useful safeguard against developing an analysis that is too closely associated with a researcher's own preconceived ideas. The third stage of my analysis therefore involved a re-examination of my analytical framework to again compare data categories in order to identify alternative explanations that ran counter to the emerging 'story'. Returning to the example of medical student resistance described above, through the process of searching for negative instances I sought instances where medical students had willingly co-operated in this activity. This analytical approach was repeated across the other themes contained within my framework.

In addition to providing a rigorous analytical framework, as discussed in Section 5.1.5.1, through this process, I generated a tentative theoretical explanation of the relationship that exists between the development and delivery of interprofessional education (see Section 9.8).

5.3.3. Triangulation

As discussed in Section 5.1.6.2, Hammersley & Atkinson (1995) recommend that ethnographers employ triangulation to enhance the validity of their research. I employed methodological triangulation (a technique which involves the collection of different types of data to provide richer insights into the phenomenon under study). In doing so, I triangulated interview, observation and documentary data. This process involved the close examination of emerging analyses from, for example, steering group interview data with the observational data I collected from their meetings. In using this technique, I aimed to produce a more complex and insightful understanding of the development and delivery of the Training Ward project.

In employing this technique, as discussed in Section 5.1.6.2, I relied primarily upon my observational data to offer more 'plausible' accounts of interaction, as I had witnessed them. In contrast, interviews rely upon an individual's ability to recall events accurately, an ability that may diminish over time. I also treated the documentary data I gathered (primarily minutes of steering group meetings) in the same fashion, as these sources provide a highly distilled and possibly sanitised version of social interaction. Nevertheless, during this process I ensured that I searched for both convergence and divergence in the data to help enhance the richness and depth of my analysis. For example, an interesting divergence that emerged was related to a small number of steering group members whose interview data indicated that were critical of the approach being taken to develop the ward, observations of steering group meetings indicated they never formally fed back their concerns to the wider group. (Section 6.2.1 considers this aspect of the steering group work in more detail).

5.4. Methodological reflections

This final part of the chapter offers a series of reflections on the methodology and methods employed in the study.

5.4.1. Reflexivity

As discussed in Section 5.1.6.1, reflexivity is a useful technique to employ to enhance the validity of a study. The following three sections therefore offer detailed background information on myself, as well as key experiences that have shaped my thinking. In presenting this account, I have aimed to provide the reader with an understanding of possible issues that may have influenced the production of the study's findings.

5.4.1.1. Personal biography

The need to recognise the influence of a researcher's own gender, ethnic background and social status on their work is an important aspect in producing a reflexive account (e.g. Silverman 1993, Seale 1999). As Wallerstein (1999:49) argues:

> "We need to understand our personal biographies of race, educational and social status, gender and other identities; how these inform our ability to speak and interpret the world".

For Wallerstein (1999:49) the impact of the researcher's own biography is significant as it can "inform power dynamics within the research relationship itself". To offer an insight into this area, I discuss my position as a young-looking white male researcher. On a macro level, white males occupy a privileged position in society and within the health and social care professions (e.g. Gamarnikow 1978, Witz 1992, Wickes 1998). However, on a micro level, as a junior researcher, gender and ethnicity and did not appear to offer any perceivable advantage to my work with either the steering group, students or their facilitators. Indeed, in relation to steering group members, who all occupied management positions, I occupied a less advantaged position. Similarly, as the Training Ward facilitators were all qualified health professionals, some with over ten years' experience, I again felt disadvantaged.

In relation to the students, while as the project evaluator I could 'officially' access the pilot ward to collect data, this role did not feel as if it had that much 'influence' attached to it. I was aware that the students could easily refuse to co-operate with my work, for example, by not attending a group interview, thereby undermining the quality of both the evaluation and the PhD study. In many respects, therefore, the participants of social research hold much of the 'power', as without their continued support, a research study will collapse.

5.4.1.2. Marginality

As noted in the Section 5.2.2.1, marginality is an important aspect within ethnographic research. Marginality helps limit the possible effects of a researcher over-identifying with their research participants. As Hammersley & Atkinson (1995:115) state:

"There must always remain some part held back, some social and intellectual 'distance'. For it is in the space created by this distance that the analytical work of the ethnographer gets done".

In relation to the study, my sociology background marginalised me from my informants, who were either healthcare professionals or students. Moreover, as I have an undergraduate degree in sociology and a master's degree in social research methods, I had not experienced the usual professional socialisation processes associated with becoming a healthcare professional.[29] Consequently, I did not share a common culture with the either the steering group members, the students or the facilitators, which limited the problem of over-identification. Nevertheless, as I discuss in Section 5.4.2, while I did not share a similar background with the research participants, the development of positive research relations helped ensure that I gathered a candid insight into the processes involved in developing and delivering the Training Ward initiative.

5.4.1.3. Involvement with interprofessional education

I have now been involved with evaluating interprofessional education for nearly eight years. In this time, I have published a number of papers on the subject. These publications fall into three main areas:

- Evaluations of interprofessional education initiatives (Pryce & Reeves 1997, Reeves & Pryce 1998, Freeth et al. 1998, 1999, Pryce et al. 2000, Reeves 2000, Reeves et al. 2000, Freeth et al. 2001, Reeves & Freeth 2002, Reeves et al. 2002a, Reeves 2002, Zwarenstein et al. 2003, Reeves 2004);
- Systematic reviews on the effectiveness of interprofessional education (Barr et al. 1999a&b, 2000, Zwarenstein et al. 1999, 2001, Koppel et al. 2001, Reeves 2001, Hammick et al. 2002, Freeth et al. 2002);
- Discussion pieces on interprofessional education (Reeves et al. 2002b, Reeves & Summerfield Mann 2003, Reeves & Parker 2003, Glen & Reeves 2003, Freeth & Reeves 2004).

As a result of this work I have become familiar with the conceptual, methodological theoretical and practical issues related to interprofessional education. Inevitably, my involvement in this field has also meant that I have developed a personal view of this activity. For me, the use of interprofessional education to improve the problems of collaboration (as discussed in Section 2.2) is a worthwhile aim. Nevertheless, my previous research and thinking on interprofessional education has led me to a view that

---

[29] Both Becker et al. (1961) and Melia (1987) provide excellent accounts of the professional socialisation processes experienced by medical and nursing students entering their respective professions.

developing and delivering interprofessional education is a complex and difficult aim to achieve. In doing so, one may have to deal with a number of individual (e.g. learner scepticism), professional (e.g. negative stereotyping), organisational and logistical factors that can inhibit this type of education. Nevertheless, as a member of CAIPE (and its website manager from 1999 to 2004)[30] I am keen to see interprofessional education activities grow, as I believe it does have potential for improving collaboration and patient care. Indeed, as a researcher interested in interprofessional education, I am keen to undertake further research to understand, in more depth, the nature of this activity.

5.4.2. Managing research relations

Whyte (1981) argues that the creation and maintenance of positive field relations means that a researcher is more likely to elicit candid research insights. Nevertheless, one needs to be mindful of Allen's (1996) argument that managing a research relationship is different to managing a relationship in 'normal' life, and that one needs to pay particular attention to self-presentation and research-related interaction.

5.4.2.1. Steering group relationships

In developing a positive relationship with steering group members, I initially informed them that I did not belong to any health or social care profession. In doing so, I wanted the group members to be aware that I did not have any professional allegiances. Thus in answering Becker's (1967) poignant question related to the nature of research relations, 'whose side are you on?' I had made it clear that I was professionally neutral.

I paid particular attention to the way I dressed in steering group meetings. As all members were either educational or clinical managers, they tended to dress quite formally. I therefore followed a similar dress code. At meetings, I often wore a suit or trousers and a shirt, rather than jeans (my usual mode of dress).

As outlined in Section 5.2.2.1, I collected observational data at steering group meetings by manually recording them in a note pad. While one might consider the sight of a researcher in a meeting writing notes a slightly odd phenomenon, I found that it was not unusual for other members of the steering group to write notes during the meeting. Therefore, recording my observations during meetings did not look 'out of place'.

---

[30] The UK Centre for the Advancement of Interprofessional Education (CAIPE) is a voluntary organisation that promotes interprofessional education and collaboration both in this country and aboard see: www.caipe.org.uk for more details.

I ensured that I was open and friendly in my interactions with all group members. This approach paid a number of dividends in building a good relationship with the group. As the following extract indicates:

> After the meeting, Patricia spoke to me about the possibility of having an office during the evaluation. Of course, I accepted without hesitation! I feel this offer of office space is a positive indication of this research and my role as the project researcher (steering group observation 4/98).

Another example of the constructive relationship I had with steering group members can be seen in an invitation from the chairperson to work with members in the preparation of a bid to help fund of the Training Ward project:

> The group decides that they should submit a bid to a local charity to help support the project. In looking for people to form a small group to undertake this work, the chair asks for volunteers. Three people offer their help. He looks towards me and asks if I would be interested in helping, as someone with experience in bidding for funds. I agree. We then all make a date to meet and work in the bid (steering group observation 11/98).

Encouragingly, my interest in the steering group's work on the Training Ward project was, on occasions, complemented by an interest from steering group members in my work. For example, I was sometimes asked at the beginning or end of meetings how my PhD work was progressing. In addition, members were initially curious about the data I was recording in my field notes. In responding to these enquiries, I ensured I was both open and honest about my work. (Indeed, I actually enjoyed talking about my work to anyone who would listen).

In general, my field notes indicate that I gained a good degree of trust and acceptance within the steering group as time progressed. A useful indication of the nature of these relations can be seen in one of the last exchanges I had with a member at a conference we both attended:

> During the conference, I bumped into Derek who had come for the day. After chatting, he invited me to lunch where we shared a bottle of wine and he reflected on his steering group work (steering group observation 2/00).

Although these field notes do not contain any problematic reactions to my attending steering group meetings, it does not automatically mean that everyone was comfortable with my presence. Steering group members who did feel uncomfortable in my presence may have displayed subtle reactions that I missed.

5.4.2.2. Relationships on the Training Ward

Like the approach taken with the steering group, I informed the Training Ward students and facilitators that I had no health or social care professional affiliation. Again, this answered Becker's (1967) question of 'whose side are you on?' by declaring that I was professionally neutral.

When collecting data on the Training Ward I dressed in trousers and a shirt and wore my university identification badge.[31] This style of dress contrasted with that of the students and their facilitators, who all wore uniforms, unlike the medical facilitators who dressed similarly to me. However, I was never mistaken for a doctor, as I did not wear a tie or carry a stethoscope.

As outlined in Section 5.2.3.1, I collected observations by positioning myself at either end of the ward. Although my presence may have been considered an unusual feature in this environment, my field notes indicate that there appeared to be very little reaction to me. Reflecting on this situation, I felt that in the context of this busy ward where students and their facilitators were attending to the needs of patients, there was little time to notice me. Indeed, as the students spent a good deal of their time writing up notes, another person undertaking this activity may not have appeared an 'unnatural' part of the scenery. Nevertheless, during quieter periods on the Training Ward, I found that students and facilitators occasionally came over to talk to me and discover what I was recording in my field notes. In responding to their enquiries, I was open and honest about my work. As I noted above, I was happy to discuss the work.

As well as observing and talking to the students and facilitators on the pilot ward, my research role evolved into one where I began to assist the student teams. Firstly, when the students were busy with the patients I began answering the telephone and taking messages. Although I had not anticipated undertaking this role, I found it impossible to sit and collect data when the telephone was ringing and no one was going to answer it. Secondly, as a result of spending relatively long periods on the ward gathering observations I found that I was being asked by facilitators and students if I had seen a certain person. Indeed, on one occasion my role extended even further, to wheeling a patient back from using the telephone:

> *While observing by nurses station, one of the patients who had been wheeled by Barbara [nursing student] to the phone, finished her call. The student had gone off to attend to other business. Recognising me, the patient asked if I*

---

[31] I was required to wear identification on the ward at all times.

could push her back to the ward. I, of course, obliged. As I wheeled the patient back to her bed, I received two surprised and amused responses. Val [nursing facilitator] said, 'we'll get you in theatre blues [the Training Ward uniform] soon!' And Melanie [occupational therapy student] said, 'we'll get you to help with the patient washes tomorrow!'" (ward observation, orange team).

Like the research relations I developed in the steering group, my field notes indicate that I gained the trust and acceptance of the students and facilitators. Again, the development of these positive relations helped ensure I could gather candid insights into the nature of the students' experiences of the pilot ward. However, it should be noted that while my observation notes did not contain any 'adverse' reactions to my presence on the Training Ward, this does not mean there were no other 'problems' with my presence. Like steering group members, students and facilitators who felt uncomfortable with my presence may have displayed subtle reactions that I missed.

5.4.3. Ethical considerations

All social research needs to be undertaken in an ethical way, with due care and attention to safeguarding the interests of research participants. Punch (1994) outlines the main ethical issues that researchers need to consider when undertaking a study:

"The avoidance of harm, fully informed consent and the need for privacy and confidentiality" (Punch 1994:89).

Similar views on this issue have been outlined by a number of other researchers (e.g. Kelman 1977, Dingwall 1980b, Blumer 2001). In following the procedure for undertaking safe and ethical health services research, ethical approval was obtained from a local research ethics committee before the study commenced. Furthermore, as a member of the British Sociological Association (BSA), I adhered to the ethical code of practice developed by this organisation.[32] Key elements of this code are discussed below.

5.4.3.1. Informed consent

The BSA (1997:3) states that an important aspect of producing ethical research is that it should be "based on the freely given informed consent of those studied". Therefore, as noted in Section 5.4.2.2, I adopted an overt approach to the data collection activities with steering group members, students and facilitators to ensure that all participants were knowledgeable and informed about my work. Indeed, as noted above, informal conversations with steering group members, students and facilitators during the data

---

[32] A copy of this code can be obtained from the British Sociological Association website (www.britsoc.co.uk/about/ethic.htm). Similar ethical codes are published by other organisations such as the Social Research Association, the British Educational Research Association, the American Sociological Association and the British Psychological Association.

collection phase for this study helped to ensure that all participants were kept fully informed with my work as it progressed (see Sections 5.4.2.1 and 5.4.2.2).

5.4.3.2. Anonymity, confidentiality and privacy

Another crucial aspect in producing an ethical study is the need to respect the "anonymity and privacy of those who participate in the research process" (BSA 1997:5). Information given to researchers by participants should be protected to ensure they are not exposed or placed in a compromising position as a result of being identified in a research study. Where the identification of individuals is possible, the publication of a study can be barred for several years (Meyer 2001).

To ensure that informants' identities could not be recognised in this study, a number of precautions were taken to maintain confidentiality:

- Audio tapes of interviews were destroyed once they were transcribed;
- Informants' real names were changed in transcripts to pseudonyms;
- Hard copies of data were stored in a locked cupboard;
- Electronic copies of data were stored on a PC that was password protected.

Furthermore, the thesis has been written with the aim of safeguarding all informants' identities. Therefore, any information that could identify a participant has been removed or changed. Indeed, it should be noted that as around five years has passed since the steering group disbanded, the threat of individuals being exposed by this study will have diminished.

5.4.3.3. Participant safety

Social researchers "enter into personal and moral relationships" (BSA 1997:2) with the individuals they study. In doing so, they have a responsibility to safeguard the interests of their research participants. However, unlike medical trials, qualitative research does not physically endanger its participants. Nevertheless, this type of research can cause psychological harm (in the form of embarrassment or discomfort). Therefore, a researcher needs to safeguard the interests of participants involved in their work.

In practical terms, to safeguard the interests of the participants in the study, as outlined above, I ensured that all participants were fully informed about the nature of this work. In addition, to ensure that I did not cause embarrassment by breaching their confidences, I protected their identities by anonymising data and storing it securely. Furthermore, I paid particular attention to ensuring that none of the participants felt they were coerced in participating in the study by reminding them that their participation in the study was entirely their own choice and that they were free to withdraw from this research at any time.

5.4.4. Strengths and weaknesses

This section discusses the methodological strengths and weaknesses related to the study to provide the reader with a firmer understanding of the overall quality of this piece of work.

While designing, undertaking and writing up this work, a continual effort has been made to produce a valid research account. I have therefore attempted to enhance its methodological quality by employing a range of approaches and techniques. Importantly, by undertaking a relatively lengthy period of data collection (two years) the study obtained a detailed longitudinal insight into the processes of developing and delivering a practice-based interprofessional education initiative. Indeed, the collection of interview, observational and documentary data during this time has ensured that the study has yielded a comprehensive and multi-faceted understanding of this topic.

An iterative approach to data collection was adopted for the study. Therefore, issues and themes identified during the early stages of data collection were examined in the later stages of data collection. Such a flexible approach is a central feature of qualitative research (e.g. Silverman 1993), as it helps to ensure that research accounts can focus on potentially illuminating issues that arise during the research process.

The use of semi-structured interview and observation schedules has provided a good degree of consistency when collecting these data. As noted in Section 5.2.2.2, a semi-structured interview schedule provides the researcher with both a reliable tool (as the questions are repeated to informants), while the researcher also has the flexibility to explore other issues that emerge when interviewing.

In relation to the data analysis undertaken for the study, the use of a recognised approach to analysing the data (Hammersley & Atkinson 1995) has helped ensure that the analytic process followed a clear, logical and well-tested route. Furthermore, as discussed in Section 5.3.3, the triangulation of methods (interviews, observations and documents) has helped provide a more comprehensive research account. As Denzin (1978:294) argued, the use of triangulation can help "raise sociologists above the personalistic biases that stem from single methodologies". In addition, in attempting to employ a reflexive approach in this work (see Section 5.4.1) I described my background and the major influences I brought to this work, as well as the nature of relationships I shared with research participants. For a number of qualitative researchers (e.g. Hammersley & Atkinson 1995, Seale 1999) the adoption of a reflexive approach helps ensure the trustworthiness of a research account.

I have also attempted to provide thick descriptions of the research context in an effort provide readers with of a sense that they could "experience the events being described" (Denzin 1989:83) to help enhance the wider relevance of this work. In addition, through use of the comparative method of analysis (see Section 5.3.2), I have attempted to provide a tentative generalisable theoretical explanation of the relationship that exists between the development and delivery of interprofessional education (see Section 9.8).

Nevertheless, while I strove to produce a good quality research study, this work inevitably contains a number of limitations. Despite collecting a comprehensive data set from the steering group members, detailing the developmental process they undertook to develop and deliver the Training Ward, the student data set is more limited in nature. As noted in Section 4.3.2, students only participated in a four-week pilot ward. Therefore it was not possible to obtain a more comprehensive amount of data on the students' experiences of the initiative the steering group delivered. Consequently, this imbalance of data sets limits the validity of the study's findings in relation to providing a more detailed insight into delivery factors.

Although the study obtained some illuminating observations of steering group and student interactions during the development and delivery of the Training Ward, these data were restricted largely to formal meetings and scheduled students' teamwork sessions. Therefore, the study failed to gather data on any interactions that occurred between these participants in other settings. This absence of observational data limits the validity of the study's findings in relation to offering a more insightful understanding of the nature of steering group and student collaboration.

While methodological triangulation was undertaken to help strengthen the validity of the findings (Sections 5.1.6.2 and 5.3.3), one needs to acknowledge the limitations of this technique. Importantly, as noted in Section 5.1.6.2, Hammersley & Atkinson (1995) argue that this technique does not automatically guarantee a valid analysis, as a single data set or method may contain some form of error, thus rendering the triangulation process incorrect. Similarly, for Bloor (1997), convergence does not result in a valid set of findings, as the inclusion of a further perspective, at some future point, may potentially contradict one's findings. Despite its shortfalls, Seale (1999:61) maintains that triangulation is still useful in helping to provide "evidence in support of key claims", particularly by comparing interview data with related observational data. For other authors such as Richardson (1991) and Silverman (1993), this use of triangulation overlooks one important issue. Richardson and Silverman both argue that the aim of triangulation is not to adjudicate between perspectives in order to discover 'truthful' (valid) and 'untruthful' accounts. Rather, it should be employed to gain an understanding of how different accounts (multiple realities) are actually produced. Indeed, for Richardson, the term 'crystallisation' is more suitable than triangulation, as it more appropriately describes the process of crystallising the existence of multiple versions of reality.

The absence of member validation is another of the study's limitations. Member validation is a methodological technique in which the researcher feeds back elements of a study (e.g. interview transcripts, research report) to participants to provide them an opportunity to make judgements on the validity of the research (Hammersley & Atkinson 1995). This technique was not employed in the study for the following reason: I did not want to burden participants with additional work. I felt that asking steering group members (who all had demanding jobs) or students (who were about to undertake their final assessments) to read interview transcripts or parts of my field notes was unrealistic and unfair, especially after their had so generously provided data for this study.

While I employed the use of thick description to help enhance the generalisability of findings this study, one should be wary of the limitations in using this technique. In particular, Mehan in Silverman (2000:176) argues that the use of thick description can produce anecdotal research accounts, specifically when a case study only provides "a few exemplary instances" of this type of description, which are also poorly justified in terms of their inclusion. In such cases, the generalisability of findings from such studies remains difficult to establish. To help address this particular limitation, I have ensured that descriptions of the study context are as comprehensive as possible, while also outlining a rationale for their inclusion.

Despite undertaking efforts to enhance the generalisability of the study's findings, including thick description and the use of the comparative method to generate a tentative theoretical explanation of the relationship between the development and delivery of interprofessional education, the use of a single research setting for this study inevitably limits the wider relevance of this work.

Summary

This chapter presents a description and discussion of the methodology and methods of data collection and analysis employed in the study. It has detailed the processes undertaken to adopt a suitable epistemology (interpretivism), theory (interactionism), method (ethnography) and data collection tools (interviews, observations and documentary data) that could begin to address the research aim and objectives (see Section 1.2). Importantly, it has argued that the use of techniques such as thick description and theoretical generalisation can help strengthen claims for the wider relevance of the work, while reflexivity and triangulation help enhance the validity of findings gathered from a single case study.

The next two chapters present and discuss the study's key findings on the development and delivery of the Training Ward project. In doing so, they aim to open the black boxes associated with these two activities and begin to explore their contents.

Chapter 6: Developing the Training Ward

Introduction

This chapter presents findings related to the key successes and challenges encountered by the steering group in their work developing the Training Ward. In this chapter, the first of the study's research objectives contained in Section 1.2 is addressed. The chapter is divided into two main sections. Section 6.1 examines the successes related to the steering group's work developing the Training Ward project, while Section 6.2 presents the challenges related to the group's work on this interprofessional initiative. The aim of this chapter is to offer an in-depth insight into the key factors related to the development of the Training Ward.

6.1. Steering group successes

This section examines the key successes ('a shared enthusiasm for the Training Ward', 'the role of positive group relations' and 'using the evaluation to inform development work') related to the steering group's work in developing the Training Ward.

6.1.1. A shared enthusiasm for the Training Ward

A central success for the steering group was their shared enthusiasm for developing the Training Ward project. Early interviews (collected in the first few months of the study in 1998) indicated that steering group members viewed the prospect of participating in the development of the ward in enthusiastic terms:

> "I am very excited about the Training Ward. I think it has got a lot of potential" (Todd, steering group member interview 3/98).

> "It is the first time that we have got some sort of interprofessional activity [...] I think it [the Training Ward] is of great importance and I would like that to be something which is developed" (Judith, steering group member interview 3/98).

The group's enthusiasm for the ward continued throughout the project. As indicated in their later interviews (collected at the end of the fieldwork in 2000) when they reflected on their involvement in the project:

"I think you will find that the group has been driven by a great enthusiasm for the initiative" (Derek, steering group member interview 5/00).

"I can always just remember people being really enthusiastic about the Training Ward" (Nancy, steering group member interview 4/00).

The group's enthusiasm for the Training Ward manifested itself in a number of ways during the study. In addition to attending steering group meetings, a number of educational members also spent time outside the meetings negotiating with their professional regulatory bodies to ensure that students could participate in the project. Indeed, two of the educational members were required to spend time altering their existing programmes to ensure students were available. Similarly, clinical members spent time outside the meetings preparing the environment and recruiting staff to participate as facilitators. Furthermore, as noted in Section 4.2.5, around half of the group contributed to supporting student activities (e.g. facilitating their on-ward work, facilitating their student reflection sessions) during the ward pilot.

The group's enthusiasm for the Training Ward helped create a shared commitment to the project and an incentive for the members to work together. As one member noted, the group's enthusiasm meant that they *"put a lot of time and effort"* (Nancy, steering group member interview 4/00) into the project. Therefore, the group's enthusiasm appeared to provide them with a 'gelling agent' for their collective work:

"I think we really quite gelled together over the past two years [...] I think we did form quite well together because people were enthusiastic" (Patricia, steering group member interview 4/00).

The steering group's enthusiasm for the Training Ward was crucial. In essence, their enthusiasm helped provide the 'glue' that helped keep the group together to overcome the numerous challenges they encountered in their joint work. The need for enthusiasm within interprofessional education is regarded as a vital ingredient for its success (Shaw 1994, Parsell & Bligh 1998, Roberts et al. 2000, Freeth 2001, Harris et al. 2003). As Lary et al. (1997:68) argue, the success of interprofessional education initiatives depend upon the willingness of individuals "to contribute time and energy" to this type of education. Nevertheless, the interprofessional education literature does not offer any evidence for the effects of enthusiasm. This finding therefore begins to indicate, empirically, the central role of enthusiasm in the development of an interprofessional education initiative. Indeed, Section 6.2 goes on to indicate that although enthusiasm was an important factor in the steering group's work, it also created a number of difficulties in the way they collaborated and problems in the delivery of this interprofessional initiative.

6.1.2. The role of positive group relations

Another key success for the steering group was the development of positive group relationships during their work on the Training Ward project. As Ben and Elsa both pointed out:

> "One of the best things that came out of it [the Training Ward project] was that people were starting to talk to each other and get on with each other to develop something together" (Ben, steering group member interview 4/00).

> "We have brought together people from three universities and four schools and we do get on [...] we get on as a group and I think that in itself is a really tremendous interprofessional achievement" (Elsa, steering group member interview 4/00).

Indeed, observations of steering group meetings indicated that members collaborated in a largely constructive and genial fashion during the years they worked together on the Training Ward project. As the following two extracts (the first gathered from a steering group meeting held in April 1998, the second from a meeting held in October 1999) indicate:

> There are eight steering group members seated around a table. Derek enters just as the group starts the meeting. He is just in time to take a chocolate from Patricia who is passing around a large box of Milk Tray [...] The atmosphere is generally relaxed and jovial [...] As the group is making good progress through the agenda, Ben says 'time for another chocolate'. He takes one for himself and passes the box around [...] On the way out of the meeting Janet mentions 'its like one of the old wards I used to work on where someone comes in with ward goodies to share'. She thought this relaxed approach was good for the group's relations (steering group observation 4/98).

> This is the first meeting after most of the group took their annual leave in August. Before the meeting starts, Derek, Janet, Judith, Christine and Elsa chat about their holiday experiences. They exchange details of the various locations they visited and some of the humorous tales associated with their trips [...] Over the past months of working together on the Training Ward the group has maintained its positive relations, the sharing of their holiday tales provides a good indication of the cordial nature of their relationships (steering group observation 10/99).

For the steering group, the positive nature of their group relationships helped ensure that they worked together in a collaborative fashion on the Training Ward. As the interprofessional education literature does not provide evidence on the nature of group relations during the development of an initiative, this finding begins to illuminate the nature of this issue. Nevertheless, the interprofessional practice literature does support this finding. Research into the development and maintenance of positive interprofessional relations has been found to be crucial for the success of a collaborative venture (e.g. Miller et al. 2001, Onyett 2003). Without such positive relationships, joint project work cannot usually be sustained over long periods of time. (Despite sharing genial interprofessional relations during their formal meetings, Section 6.2 goes on to indicate that there were a number of underlying tensions related to the group's collaborative work).

6.1.3. Using the evaluation to inform development work

Another key success for the steering group's work on the Training Ward project was the inclusion of a funded evaluation. As noted in Section 1.1.3, one of the schools had been successful in securing evaluation funds for a post that ensured the group could understand the impact of the project on students, patients and facilitators.

For steering group members, the incorporation of a funded evaluation meant that the Training Ward project could be examined, understood and modified, if required, to help ensure its future success:

> "We do need to evaluate it [the Training Ward] very carefully to understand its impact and see whether we need to change it to improve it" (Elsa, steering group member interview 4/98).

> "If this ward is a success, what we really want is a good evaluation [...] that is why the evaluation really is important [...] because we could get to the end of two years and not really know if it has worked or not" (Christine, steering group member interview 3/98).

All steering group members welcomed the feedback of findings from the evaluation during their meetings. In particular, the group valued the production of the evaluation report (Freeth & Reeves 1999), which provided them with a helpful insight into the impact of the pilot ward. As the following extracts indicate:

> As steering group members enter, before the meeting starts, they tell me how impressed they are with the report. 'A comprehensive piece of work' says Derek. These sentiments are echoed by Christine, Elsa, Margaret, Judith and Janet as they enter [...] The agenda reaches the subject of the evaluation report. The chair offers 'a formal vote of thanks' for the work on the evaluation. The other members agree. She goes on to say that the report has provided some valuable insights into pilot ward, which can only help their work in re-developing the ward in future (steering group observation 9/99).

> "I think it [the evaluation report] said some things that needed to be said and as a result of that, changes were made to the ward" (Ben, steering group member interview 4/00).

Indeed, observations of the steering group meetings in the months that followed the delivery of the evaluation report indicated that, in an effort to strengthen the initiative, the group went on to modify the Training Ward along the lines recommended in the report. (These modifications are described in Section 6.2.3.3). Nevertheless, while the group welcomed the early feedback from the evaluation project, as Section 6.2.3 discusses, their enthusiasm to deliver the pilot ward resulted in this feedback being largely overlooked by group members.

As outlined above, steering group members regarded funded evaluation and the production of its report as a valuable aspect of the Training Ward. It provided them with empirical data that could be fed back to help them enhance the quality of the project. Given the relatively new and untested status of interprofessional education, it is agreed that this type of activity should be evaluated to understand its positive (and negative) effects on participants (e.g. Cooper et al. 2001, Freeth et al. 2002). It could also be argued that the inclusion of the evaluation generated another benefit. The evaluation report (Freeth & Reeves 1999) and the three papers (Freeth et al. 2001, Reeves et al. 2002, Reeves & Freeth 2002) that were produced provided information to other groups interested in developing similar initiatives.

6.2. Steering group challenges

This section examines the range of internal ('difficulties related to subgroup enthusiasm', 'overlooking the need to discuss group roles and processes', 'a lack of critical assessment when using the Swedish model') and external challenges ('problems associated with turnover and workload', 'the effect of curricula and professional validation constraints', 'the impact of management and organisational change') steering group members encountered when developing the Training Ward project.

6.2.1. Difficulties related to subgroup enthusiasm

Although the steering group's shared enthusiasm for the Training Ward was considered a successful part of their joint work, the data indicated that the enthusiasm of a small subgroup led to a number of members being excluded from making decisions on the development of the project.

As noted in the Section 4.2.2, in early 1998 the steering group expanded its membership to ensure that the views of clinical staff (from the hospital where the Training Ward was going to be located) were represented. To familiarise these new members with the project, they undertook a short visit to the Swedish ward. During their visit, it emerged that four members (three clinicians and one educationalist) who shared "a terrific enthusiasm" (subgroup member 1, steering group member interview 3/00) for the Training Ward and how it should be developed formed a small subgroup:

"When we came back from Sweden, there was a small group of us [...] the practical people who would, could actually initiate the project [...] We were all terribly enthusiastic about it" (subgroup member 1, steering group member interview 3/00).

Members of this subgroup often referred to themselves as the *"doers"* (subgroup member 3, steering group member interview 4/00), the steering group members who could successfully develop and deliver the ward. In contrast, their view of other group members was somewhat dismissive. They were regarded as the *"talkers"* (subgroup member 3, steering group member interview 3/00) and were considered less effective group members.

The subgroup's enthusiasm was influential on the development of the ward. In the meeting that followed their visit, they sought agreement to develop the Training Ward along the Swedish model rather than develop a separate model, as the group had previously agreed:

> *X, X, X and X [subgroup members][33] have been far more vocal about the development of the ward than previously. It seems that their trip has made them great advocates for the Swedish ward. All throughout this meeting, they have been proposing, in particular X and X, that the ward needs to be developed along Linköping lines rather than trying to design a separate model. As X said at one point in the meeting, "this ward works well, what's the point in trying to re-invent the wheel? Lets go for something we know is operational"* (steering group observation 3/98).

In modifying the ward along Swedish lines, the subgroup initiated a change of the ward's design in two important areas: they altered the Training Ward from a four-week to a two-week placement and they incorporated role sharing in the form of team duties into the placement. (The effect of these changes are considered in Sections 7.2.2 and 7.2.3). At this point, their enthusiasm for the Training Ward meant that steering group members supported the subgroup:

> *"At the end of the day the enthusiasm and solidarity of the group that went to Linköping has convinced me that this is the way it should be"* (Janet, steering group member interview 3/98).

Indeed, in the absence of clear leadership within the group (an issue that is considered in more depth in Section 6.2.2.1), steering group members felt that the subgroup could effectively take the project forward and ensure its success:

> *"They [the subgroup members] were the doers in the group [...] the people could actually deliver the ward in a clinical setting"* (Christine, steering group member interview 4/00).

---

[33] Due to the possibility of identifying these four individuals, their pseudonyms have been removed.

However, for some members this viewpoint began to alter when it emerged that in their enthusiasm to progress the project, subgroup members had met *"behind the scenes"* (Ben, steering group member interview 4/00) with senior managers to take decisions on the Training Ward without informing the wider group:

> *I chat to Judith while leaving the meeting, she tells me that she is unhappy about the meeting that the subgroup members had with the senior hospital managers. 'It was initiated without anyone telling us, we were excluded, no one was told about it. How could any of us have input into this meeting if we aren't told about it in the first place?'* (steering group observation 8/98).

Although members conceded that this type of informal work did help to progress the project, it was nevertheless viewed as exclusionary. The key issue was that members felt this behaviour essentially undermined the *"collaborative spirit"* (Jean, steering group member interview 3/00) of the group. Indeed, it was generally felt that all members should be involved in decision making on the Training Ward's development:

> *"I think I feel that those people* [subgroup members] *could have perhaps invited other people to work with them. It was like closed doors though"* (Margaret, steering group member interview 4/00).

In contrast, subgroup members regarded their approach in more pragmatic terms:

> *"There were quite a lot of issues that just had to be done* [...] *and on the whole that's been down to a few members to set up a little meeting with whoever it is relevant to keep the thing rolling"* (subgroup member 3, steering group member interview 4/00).

Observational data indicated that concerns expressed about the *"exclusionary tactics"* (Christine, steering group member interview 4/00) of the subgroup were not formally raised in steering group meetings. Nevertheless, they were discussed during the interviews for the study. When asked why these members did not formally voice their concerns, it was felt that raising this difficulty might have had a detrimental impact on the overall development of the project:

> *"I didn't want to be the person to start complaining about the way the group worked together, to deflect our attention away from developing the ward. Like the other people in the group I was really keen to get on* [...]*"* (Nancy, steering group member interview 4/00).

There was another reason why members withheld their views. Generally, they felt that if they did voice their concerns, the subgroup might withdraw, leaving other members to take the project forward. For these individuals, heavy workloads attached to their jobs made the prospect of this task unwelcome:

> *"Although I wasn't really happy about them* [subgroup members] *meeting without the rest of us, it did seem that they were making good progress with the ward* [...] *I didn't want to interfere as things might fall to me, which would*

have been really difficult with my heavy work commitments" (Jean, steering group member interview 4/00).[34]

While the approach taken by the subgroup members may, at first sight, appear unproblematic, as they were helping to progress the project and relieving members of additional work, as discussed above, many members still felt that the 'covert' approach undermined the collaborative essence of the group's joint work. There may have also been other reasons for their reticence. Firstly, when one considers the dynamics between the subgroup and the wider members of the steering group, observations indicated that when two or more subgroup members were present, they tended to dominate group discussions. Secondly, given the shared their enthusiasm for the Swedish model, subgroup members tended to speak assertively and confidently about the need to incorporate this model into the Training Ward:

> *The subgroup, especially X and X, were again very vocal about how the ward should be developed – essentially along the Swedish model, which they see as essential to the success of the project, given the success this model has achieved in Sweden* (steering group observation 4/98).

In addition, while the subgroup consisted of three clinicians and one educationalist, as noted above, two subgroup members belonged to a 'high status' health care profession.[35] Interprofessional power imbalances may therefore have contributed to the reluctance from other members of the steering group, to challenge the subgroup's exclusionary approach. However, the effect of power dynamics is difficult to establish here, as the issue did not explicitly emerge in the steering group interviews and observations of steering group meetings did not indicate any apparent power inequalities. Indeed, the two most vocal subgroup members did not belong to this 'high status' profession. Nevertheless, given the role of such power dynamics between health and social care professionals (e.g. Hugman 1991, Walby et al. 1994, Porter 1995, Skjørshammer 2001), one needs to acknowledge their existence within in this context.

As discussed above, it appears that the visit to Sweden was the catalyst for the emergence of the four-member subgroup that shared an enthusiasm to replicate the Swedish model. Despite the subgroup's enthusiasm being initially regarded as a positive influence within the wider group, their use of 'behind the scenes' work to develop the project, without informing the other steering group members, created feelings of exclusion.

---

[34] The issue of the effect of heavy workloads on the development of the Training Ward project is considered in more depth in Section 6.2.4.2.
[35] Due to the possibility of identifying these subgroup members, details of their actual profession are withheld.

While the interprofessional education literature, as outlined in Section 6.1.1, discussed the role of enthusiasm, it has not provided evidence for its actual effects. For the first time, this study has indicated that as well as having a *facilitative* side enthusiasm can have a more *problematic* side related to the development of an interprofessional education initiative. While the wider literature does help to understand the importance of 'backstage work' (Goffman 1963), it does stress that an exclusionary approach to work can undermine a core principle of collaboration: the need for equity between group or team members (e.g. Kraus 1980, Drinka & Ray 1987, Drinka & Clark 2000, Onyett 2003). When a group or team is not working together in an equal fashion, it has found that tensions can emerge between members (e.g. Larson & LaFasto 1989, Gibbon 1999). Furthermore, Poulton & West (1999:17) found that health care teams who operated in an open and inclusive manner were more likely "to work together [...] and be more efficient" than those with a more exclusive approach to their collaborative work.

6.2.2. Overlooking the need to discuss group roles and processes

While the steering group's shared enthusiasm for the Training Ward project was a vital ingredient to progress the project, the data indicated that group members neglected to pay attention to the way in which they worked together. In particular, members failed to consider their expectations, group roles or the group processes associated with their collaborative work.

6.2.2.1. Tasks rather than roles

Observations of steering group meetings indicated that members focused their energies on discussing, agreeing and completing a range of tasks connected with developing the Training Ward (e.g. student supervision arrangements and facilitation arrangements). As Table 8 (page 109) helps to illustrate, during the two years of fieldwork for the study the steering group spent the bulk of their meeting time discussing the various practical tasks connected to developing and delivering the ward.

While this focus was vital to development of the initiative, providing its content and shape, it meant that the group failed to spend any time negotiating, discussing and agreeing their group roles. Apart from the role of chairperson and secretary (who took minutes of meetings), there were no other recognisable roles in the steering group. Rather than agree specific roles for members, the group's approach to their work was task-orientated in nature.

Issue discussed[36]	Number of meetings issue discussed
Student supervision	20
Student availability	18
Student handbook	18
Training Ward uniforms	18
Learning objectives	16
Student roles	14
Facilitator training	12
Funding	12
Start date	10
Student selection	9

Table 8: Nature of steering group discussions

In general, members volunteered to undertake the tasks connected to developing the project. However, given the enthusiasm of the subgroup members, this situation resulted in an unevenness of task allocation. Therefore, while the subgroup undertook numerous tasks, other members had less to do. For example, in the three months before the pilot ward ran, two subgroup members were engaged with producing the student handbook, arranging the student induction session, obtaining insurance cover and securing ethical approval for the pilot ward. A few of the members questioned this division of labour in their interviews. For one, it represented another aspect of the subgroup's exclusionary approach to their work within the steering group, for the others it reflected the uncertainty in their collaborative work, as the group did not have clearly established roles:

"Well, what are the roles of the different team members? [...] *Because until you have established that it is very difficult to work together"* (Judith, steering group member interview 3/98).

For these members, it was felt that some attempt was needed to agree clear roles to ensure that there was clarity among members in their collaborative work. However, again, these concerns were only expressed during their interviews for the PhD study. As pointed out above, there was a general unwillingness to voice concerns, as members were fearful of undermining their colleagues' enthusiasm for the Training Ward.

The steering group data also indicated a continuing uncertainty in relation to the role group leader. When asked about this, most members considered that the leadership role belonged to the chairperson:

"The chair needs to offer guidance and leadership to the group in taking the initiative forward" (Derek, steering group member interview 4/00).

---

[36] While the steering group also discussed other tasks related to the development and delivery of the Training Ward project, such as ethical approval for the pilot ward, the students' use of the hospital's computer system, Table 9 presents the ten most frequent topics discussed.

In contrast, however, the two members who occupied this role held a different view. For them, the role of chairperson was regarded with more uncertainty:

"I was never exactly certain what the responsibilities of my role were as chair. We never discussed it so it was up to me to decide" (Chairperson 1, steering group member interview 4/00).

"I never knew what my role was [...] I was much more of a co-ordinator and agenda producer than a group leader" (Chairperson 2, steering group member interview 4/00).

Consequently, there was some concern expressed about the lack of leadership in the group:

"I felt as though the whole thing lacks leadership and direction, which is why it never really got going properly" (Judith, steering group member interview 4/00).

Steering group members, once again, only expressed these concerns about a lack of leadership during their interviews. Nevertheless, as noted in Section 6.2.1, in the absence of a clear leadership role, the group's activities were informally 'led' by the four-member subgroup. To help members with their collaborative work, early findings from the study were used in the evaluation project to feedback to the group (Freeth & Reeves 1999:105). Importantly, this paper outlined the problems the group was experiencing in relation to a lack of clarity around their group roles, as outlined above. However, observational data gathered from the meeting in which this paper was presented indicated that, while the group expressed their gratitude for this work, they only undertook a cursory discussion of this paper.

As presented in this section, a neglect of group roles in favour of a focus on task completion resulted in an imbalance in the way in which the group worked together, as well as creating an uncertainty over who was leading the group. Due to a lack of research within the interprofessional education literature on group processes, this finding offers a new insight. Research into team function, however, helps to explain this finding. It has repeatedly found that the formation of clear roles is an essential element for effective teamwork (e.g. West & Slater 1996, Williams & Laungani 1999, Carpenter et al. 2003b, West & Markiowicz 2004). Where there is confusion in roles within groups or teams, tensions and uncertainties in working relationships emerge (e.g. Brown et al. 2000, Ross et al. 2000, Booth & Hewison 2002). Indeed, the need for a clear leadership role has been found to be crucial to the effectiveness of interprofessional collaboration (e.g. Field & West 1994, Firth-Cozens & Mowbray 2001, Ross et al. 2005). As Øvretveit (1990:287) states:

"The quickest way to establish close and effective teamwork is to start with a clearly defined team leader role".

Leadership within interprofessional practice, however, can be problematic. Separate professional responsibilities and different lines of management of members mean that identifying a single leader is difficult among members (Øvretveit 1993, 1997a, Norman & Peck 1999). Therefore time is needed to negotiate and agree how this role is employed within such groups.

6.2.2.2. Failing to explore expectations

The data indicated that members never took time to explore their expectations of the project either at the start of their collaborative work, or when new members joined the group. While all group members wanted the Training Ward project to be successful, interview data suggested that they nevertheless held a number of competing individual, departmental and profession-specific expectations:

"If one was being very cynical about the whole thing, one could say that this project is a very good opportunity for people to undertake a bit of empire building" (Edward, steering group member interview 3/98).

"We are interested in trying to recruit staff to our department" (Derek, steering group member interview 3/98).

"Our school is very isolated [...] I think it [the Training Ward initiative] *will develop the school's profile within the university and with colleagues in the hospital trust"* (Elsa, steering group member interview 3/98).

"It would be wrong to say that we are not looking to develop our own profession" (Maria, steering group member interview 5/98).

Indeed, for two steering group members, the failure to explore their expectations of the Training Ward meant that the group missed an important opportunity to discuss how the project could meet their different expectations. Moreover, for these members, this oversight also meant the group failed to agree a way in which they might collaborate in a more effective manner:

"We have never clearly identified what our own expectations are of what we are trying to achieve, how we might get there and stuff like that [...] *we need to develop as a cohesive group because we can't do anything until we are"* (Margaret, steering group member interview 4/00).

Although it was crucial that steering group meetings were focused on developing and delivering the Training Ward, it did mean that they failed to dedicate time exploring their expectations of the project. Given the range of expectations held by group members, incorporating this type of discussion into their meeting time could have helped improve the quality of their joint work. This finding offers a new insight into the development of an interprofessional education initiative. The research undertaken into team effectiveness, however, does help to illuminate this issue. Research continues to demonstrate that shared time for teambuilding activities, such as discussing and agreeing expectations, can be particularly effective in enhancing team function (e.g. Larson & LaFasto 1989, West 1996, Opie 1997, Onyett 2003, Pethybridge 2004).

6.2.2.3. Failing to reflect on group process

Like their oversight in discussing their expectations, the data indicated that group members also overlooked the use of shared reflection in their collaborative work. Indeed, while the group ensured that students regularly undertook shared reflection on the pilot ward, observations indicated that the steering group never engaged in this type of activity. As Elsa pointed out:

> "We don't take time out to reflect on how we are working" (Elsa, steering group member interview 4/00).

Given the difficulties the group experienced during their time working together (see Sections 6.2.1, 6.2.2.1 and 6.2.2.2), time spent undertaking this activity could have benefited the overall quality of steering group's collaborative work. Indeed, a small number of members expressed concerns related to their group function:

> "We are totally separate and a different institution and our courses are arranged totally differently and I felt that there wasn't any effort to find out how each other's systems worked" (Judith, steering group member interview 4/98).

> "I think we have gone about it [working together] in a very superficial the way [...] it is too superficial to be effective" (Margaret, steering group member interview 5/98).

> "I really don't think that there has been any real discussion of issues that have arisen" (Margaret, steering group member interview 4/00).

Again, for the reasons discussed in Section 6.2.1, these group members did not formally feedback their concerns to the group. As no research could be located within the interprofessional education literature to help understand this finding, it offers some new light into the development of an interprofessional initiative. Research into interprofessional teamwork has, however, indicated that providing teams with a "reflective space" (Onyett 2003:122) to discuss joint work and negotiate ways of overcoming problems can enhance their collective performance (e.g. Opie 1997, Meerabeau & Page 1999, Borrill et al. 2000, West & Markiowicz 2004). Indeed, for West (1996), the use of regular reflection can result in team becoming reflexive in their work (e.g. they collaborate in an integrated and well co-ordinated manner).

6.2.3. A lack of critical assessment when using the Swedish model

Another challenge that appeared to be closely associated with the steering group's enthusiasm for the Training Ward was a lack of critical assessment of the implications related to the Swedish model they agreed to incorporate into their project.

6.2.3.1. Emerging problems

The steering group data indicated that members overlooked three main problems in the Swedish model being implemented. The first problem was related to difficulties the Swedish medical, occupational therapy and physiotherapy students had in participating in the 'general caring' work (e.g. preparing patients for theatre, bed making), which they perceived as 'nursing oriented' duties. Moreover, these students reported that undertaking this type of work meant they struggled to complete their own profession-specific tasks (Wahlström & Sandén 1998).[37] The second problem that the steering group overlooked was linked to delivering the placement on a two-week basis. It was reported that the students generally considered this time frame too restrictive to develop into an effective interprofessional team and had therefore requested "a further one or two weeks" to achieve this goal (Wahlström et al. 1997:428). The third problem overlooked by steering group members was associated with the learning aims used in the Swedish ward. It was reported that students on the Swedish ward were encountering difficulties meeting all their learning aims (see Section 4.2.3). In essence, these students were finding that they could not fulfil both the profession-specific and team-oriented aims within a two-week placement (Freeth & Reeves 1999).

Despite being given published papers from the Swedish ward (Wahlström et al. 1997, Wahlström & Sandén 1998) and a paper of early findings from the evaluation project (Freeth & Reeves 1999) that described these emerging problems, observational data indicated that the group did not draw upon any of this work in their discussions on the development of the project. For example, data gathered from the meeting where the

---

[37] In an effort to resolve the medical students' reluctance to participate in the general care work (led by the nursing students), it was noted that the placement was altered to allow these students to 'lead' patient care planning meetings (Wahlström & Sandén 1998), thereby allowing both groups of students' reciprocal opportunities for team leadership. Despite this change, subsequent evaluation indicated that most medical students continued to resist this type of work (Fallsberg & Wijma 1999, Fallsberg & Hammar 2000).

evaluation project paper was presented indicated that while the group were grateful for *"an insightful account of the project"* (Derek, steering group observation 11/98), they did not go on to discuss the implications contained in this paper on the problems related to the Swedish model.

In overlooking work that might inform the development of the project, the steering group had a less informed understanding of the model they were transferring. Indeed, it appeared that these oversights led to the emergence three key challenges when the pilot ward was delivered. Firstly, for most medical, occupational therapy and physiotherapy students (like their Swedish counterparts), their participation in shared 'nursing oriented' care duties were a problematic feature of their pilot ward experience. Secondly, again, like their Swedish counterparts, the students generally regarded a two-week placement to be an insufficient amount of time to develop in-depth experiences of interprofessional teamwork. Finally, the creation of 19 team-oriented and around ten profession-specific learning objectives was considered by the students to be too many to meet within a two-week placement. (Sections 7.2.2, 7.2.3 and 7.2.4 go on to present, in more detail, the nature of these issues during the delivery of the pilot ward).

6.2.3.2. Problem-based learning

A further area in which the steering group failed to fully assess the implications of incorporating the Swedish model into the Training Ward was related to the use of PBL. As noted in Section 4.2.3, the Swedish model drew upon PBL principles to inform the design of the initiative. However, while steering group members agreed that the Swedish model's use of PBL would be advantageous in the Training Ward, they overlooked two key aspects when attempting to incorporate this model. Firstly, group members under-estimated the amount of preparation and support the Training Ward facilitators (none of whom had previous experience of using PBL) required to be able to use this approach effectively on the pilot ward. Indeed, the group overlooked that the staff retention difficulties reported in one of the published papers they were given (Wahlström & Sandén 1998) were related to the heavy demands of facilitating PBL within a clinical setting. Secondly, steering group members overlooked the general inexperience of students in using PBL. As noted in Section 4.3.1, whereas the occupational therapy students' course contained a significant element of PBL, medical, nursing and physiotherapy students had more limited exposure to using this approach. In contrast, the Swedish students had used PBL throughout their professional courses (Wahlström et al. 1996), which meant that they were generally more confident about its use while working in their ward.

The data indicated that these oversights had three main effects on the delivery of the pilot ward. Firstly, students generally felt under-prepared to use PBL in their work as an interprofessional team. Secondly, despite receiving a two-day introductory workshop (see Appendix 3) facilitators felt they did not fully understand how to effectively facilitate PBL on the pilot ward. Consequently, they adopted different approaches, which the students reported as adding further difficulties to their pilot ward experiences. Finally, the facilitators felt that their work on the ward was both demanding and exhausting, which could result in 'burnout' if they were based on the ward over a long period of time. (Sections 7.2.1 and 7.2.5 go on to describe and discuss, in more detail, the effects of these issues during the delivery of the pilot ward).

Given the lack of research into the processes associated with the development of interprofessional education, the findings presented in these two sections (6.2.3.1 and 6.2.3.2) offer new insights. Importantly, they indicate that a lack of critical assessment during the development of an interprofessional initiative, specifically around the nature of the educational model being employed can impede the initiative when it is delivered. (Section 9.2.1 goes on to provide a more in depth discussion of this issue).

6.2.3.3. Over time
Following the delivery of the pilot ward, the steering group did, however, go on to incorporate a number of recommendations from the evaluation report (Freeth & Reeves 1999) in an effort to strengthen the design of the Ward. In relation to the two emerging problems associated with the Swedish model (Section 6.2.3.1), the group agreed to:
- Withdraw team duties to ensure that all student could focus on their profession-specific role while working in the team;
- Increase the length of the Training Ward experience from two to three weeks;[38]
- Reduce the numerous profession-specific and team-oriented learning objectives to four key objectives, which aligned the Training Ward experience with the Swedish ward.

In addition, to help overcome the difficulties with using PBL on the pilot ward (Section 6.2.3.2), the steering group agreed to:
- Provide a more comprehensive preparation period for students and facilitators;
- Offer more support to facilitators when involved in delivering the ward;

---

[38] This initial decision was later changed back to a two-week placement, as the four schools' curricula could not accommodate a three-week Training Ward experience.

- Amend the Training Ward model from one that drew upon the principles of PBL to one that incorporated a 'collaborative problem-solving' approach (in which students could jointly plan their work, undertake it and then reflect upon it).

Nevertheless, as the next two sections indicate, despite modifying the Training Ward to strengthen it, a number of external influences combined to inhibit the steering group's work developing the project.

6.2.4. Problems associated with turnover and workload

In addition to the internal challenges encountered by the steering group, the group faced a number of external challenges in their work on the Training Ward project. This part of the chapter examines how external factors associated with group members' jobs affected the development of the Training Ward.

6.2.4.1. Group turnover

Steering group members encountered a regular turnover of members as promotions or job changes meant that a number of members left the group and new ones joined. As pointed out in Section 4.2.2, during the study eight members left and 12 new members joined the group. In general, it was agreed that these changes undermined the cohesion of the group and their ability to collaborate effectively:

> "There have been so many changes [in the group membership]; I think that has made it very difficult to have the cohesion necessary for our work" (Derek, steering group member interview 4/00).

It was also considered that the introduction of new members created a further problem. As time was needed for them to 'get up to speed' with the more established group members' understanding of the project, this further reduced the group's ability to progress the project:

> "I think that is quite a big factor because, it takes a bit of time to get on board and appreciate what the philosophy of the ward is and to value it [...] it just takes a time for you to get adjusted to that" (Christine, steering group member interview 4/00).

While a changing membership is an inevitable part of a project that spans a number of years, it can nevertheless have a detrimental impact on a group's relations and their ability to collaborate in an effective manner. Indeed, as Freeth (2001) notes, a turnover of group members when developing an interprofessional education initiative can be detrimental to its progress:

"The newcomers will not have shared the clarification of roles and objectives, the frustrations, setbacks and early successes of setting up the initiative [...] the changed team may be less cohesive" (Freeth 2001:40).

While the interprofessional education literature provides no other empirical insights into the nature of this finding, research from the teamwork literature indicates that where a group has a stable membership it is likely to work in a more effective way as members will know and trust one another (e.g. West & Slater 1996, Pritchard 1995, Gair & Hartery 2001).

6.2.4.2. Work pressures

The pressures associated with steering group members' full-time educational or clinical posts meant that they all encountered difficulties finding enough time to work on the project:

> "All the people in the group are all doing it on top of their jobs, which really means you can't devote enough time to it" (Nancy, steering group member interview 4/00).

This situation created three main problems for the development of the Training Ward. Firstly, it meant that attendance at steering group meetings was variable. Despite a membership of around 13, only around six or seven members regularly attended meetings (see Table 9, page 118).

Observational data indicated that some members did not attend three or four consecutive meetings. This poor attendance meant that the group's ability to progress the project was restricted, as decisions could not be taken without the presence of certain members. As a result, decisions were regularly deferred. The following extracts (the first taken from 1998, the second from 2000) provide an insight into the nature of this problem:

> "I think at the last meeting [March 1998] we lost track of everything and there was only Derek was there from the trust [...] Todd wasn't there, Patricia wasn't there. And they are the critical people really. We can schedule the students through whenever, but they [the clinical staff] need to be ready" (Elsa, steering group member interview 4/98).

> "If there has been nobody there at all from the directorate, as there has been the last couple of times, then nothing can really go on. You need management there, really, to tell the group exactly what is happening with the directorate and what is going to happen with the ward" (Christine, steering group member interview 4/00).

Meeting	Number of members
1998	
January	11
February (early)	13
February (late)	9
March	9
April	9
June	5
July	7
September	5
November	11
1999	
January	11
February	6
March	10
May (early)	5
May (late)	7
June	5
July	7
August	9
October	5
November	7
December	5
2000	
January	5
February	8

Table 9: Attendance at steering group meetings

Secondly, heavy workloads attached to the steering group members' jobs also meant that members encountered difficulties undertaking tasks between meetings:

> "Our workloads meant there was a sort of reluctance to do things in between meetings so that you kept coming to meetings and saying you were going to do things and maybe one or two people had done it and the rest hadn't" (Ben, steering group member interview 4/00).

A particular problem created by this situation was that the group had to wait for six months until the educational members had obtained details of student availability for the pilot ward, a difficulty that reoccurred in the months which followed the delivery of the pilot ward when the group was attempting to re-establish the project. Given the lack of time steering group members had to work on the Training Ward, it was suggested that they needed a *"project manager"* (Christine, steering group member interview 4/00) who could have dedicated time (one or two days a week) to devote to the project. While there was general agreement at this suggestion, limited funds meant that this post was never created.

As indicated in this section, steering group members' workloads meant that they had little time to contribute to the project. Variable attendance at meetings and problems completing tasks between meetings limited the group's progress. As the development of an interprofessional education initiative is usually undertaken on top of a full-time workload, it has been acknowledged that progress can be slow. Consequently, finding extra time and energy for this type work can be difficult (Chapman et al. 1995, Carpenter 1995c, Freeth et al. 1998). As the data has indicated (see Section 6.1.1), while enthusiasm is a vital component for developing interprofessional education, a full-time workload can nevertheless physically restrict the amount of time people have available for this type of project work.

6.2.5. The effect of curricula and professional validation constraints

The development of the Training Ward was also affected by two further external challenges: differences between the four schools' curricula and the differing requirements of the professional validation bodies associated with the four participating professional groups.

Firstly, as stated in Section 4.3.2, timetabling differences between the curricula of the four schools involved in the project meant that steering group members employed two different methods to select students for the pilot ward. Secondly, different requirements of the four professional regulatory bodies meant that the students were offered different types of accreditation for completing the pilot ward. Cumulatively, these factors created imbalances between the student groups that undermined the quality of their interprofessional experiences on the pilot ward.

In relation to the first factor, data indicated that selecting students by use of contrasting methods was problematic, as it undermined the sense of equality within each of the student teams. In relation to the second factor, student findings indicated that employing different approaches to the accreditation of their Training Ward experiences was also problematic, as again, it undermined the sense of equality within the student teams. (Section 7.2.6 goes on to examine the students' views of both theses issues in more depth).

6.2.6. The impact of management and organisational change

Steering group data indicated that two management changes and one organisational change had an additional constraining effect on the steering group's work developing the Training Ward.

6.2.6.1. Management change

The first management change occurred in early 1998 and involved a senior school manager, who was committed to the project, leaving to start work in another institution. Unfortunately, this individual's successor was more ambivalent about the Training Ward. This effectively meant that the group lost a key senior management supporter. An indication of this ambivalence was that early assurances given to the steering group to release students for the project were withdrawn. This again restricted the progress the group could make with the Training Ward:

> *I talk to Derek on the way back from the May meeting. He tells me how the situation with one of the schools* [where a management change has resulted in little senior support for the ward] *is a frustrating one for him and the other members of the group as it is again holding up progress on the ward* (steering group observation 5/98).

Nevertheless, a series of negotiations between subgroup members and the new senior manager resulted in senior support being regained for the project and students being released for the pilot ward.

The second management change occurred around a year later, in the months that followed the delivery of the pilot ward. A reform of the hospital management structure[39] meant that one of the members (the manager of the directorate where the pilot ward had been delivered) left the group to begin another post elsewhere in the hospital. To ensure that management views could be represented, this individual's replacement was invited to join the group. It quickly became clear, however, that the new manger did not share the same level of enthusiasm for the Training Ward as her predecessor. During the only meeting she attended, she raised a significant objection against re-establishing the Training Ward:

> *The meeting is going well with the group looking at how to re-establish the Training Ward when X* [the new directorate manager] *who has been sitting quietly raises an objection about the ward. She is concerned that the Training Ward will be too costly to run in the directorate. Derek and Elsa defend the ward by saying that these costs should be offset by an increased visibility for the directorate, which in turn should improve recruitment and retention problems in the directorate. The manager does not look convinced and says she will keep a close eye on the costs of this initiative* (steering group observation 6/99).

---

[39] This reform was initiated by senior hospital managers following the publication of the government's white paper on clinical governance (Department of Health 1998), which aimed to enhance the quality of care through the introduction of new professional governance systems.

For Derek, as this new manager lacked the shared history of developing the ward, she therefore did not have the same level of enthusiasm as the more established group members:

> "X [the new directorate manager] *has no particular knowledge about it, wasn't involved in any of the formative years of it and, therefore, doesn't see it as a vital part of her work"* (Derek, steering group member interview 4/00).

There was therefore a general agreement that this management change (and the associated loss of enthusiasm), again, inhibited the group's progress in establishing the ward:

> "The change in the directorate management has made it ten times more difficult [to establish the ward] [...] now we have lost X who was a key force in speaking on behalf of the ward [...] but X [the new directorate manager] hasn't got the same enthusiasm for it" (Elsa, steering group member interview 4/00).[40]

Despite an initial lack of managerial interest in the Training Ward, the new manager did later display support for the steering group's work by delegating the work of re-establishing the ward to member of her staff.

As indicated in this section, the management changes experienced by the steering group underlined the need for management support in the development of an interprofessional initiative. The loss of managerial support meant that the steering group's work on the project was restricted. In relation to the literature, it has been argued that senior management support for setting up and sustaining interprofessional education initiatives is vital to their success (e.g. Satin 1987, McCarey & Mires 2002, Carpenter et al. 2003a). On this issue, Casto (1994b:100) argues that management commitment is required from all participating organisations to ensure that "funds, personnel and physical facilities" are made available for the development and delivery of interprofessional education.

6.2.6.2. Organisational change

In the months that followed the second of the management changes described in Section 6.2.6.1, the steering group encountered a further, more significant organisational change. Due to the continued pressures for beds (see Section 4.1.1), senior hospital management decided that the clinical area earmarked for the Training Ward was needed for an acute admissions unit. This change meant the group needed to find another ward within the hospital. However, due to a hospital-wide shortage of beds there were no suitable

---

[40] Pseudonyms of these steering group members have withheld to prevent possible identification.

replacements. Steering group members viewed this change as the *"final straw"* (Derek, steering group member interview 4/00) for their work on this initiative:

> *"We obviously can't move forward operationally because there is massive problem with the waiting list for patients. That is why they* [senior hospital managers] *have actually turned the ward into an acute admissions ward"* (Nancy, steering group member interview 4/00).

Like the problems the group encountered with management changes, these organisational changes highlighted a central problem with steering group: its lack of senior management influence:

> *"The group had absolutely no control over Trust issues because the membership from the Trust weren't those that had that level of control* (Margaret, steering group member interview 4/00).

Reflecting on the nature of this organisational change, Elsa pointed out that the group's efforts in attempting to re-establish the Training Ward was significantly affected by the normal pace of change in clinical service settings:

> *"The project has been hit by things that they cannot do anything about. The ward closing, the change of managers; there is nothing we could have done to predict that. That is just one of those things that can happen at any time in the NHS. It could all reorganise in another six months"* (Elsa, steering group member interview 4/00).

Without any other possible locations for the Training Ward, shortly after these organisational changes were implemented, the steering group decided to disband.[41]

As indicated, while the steering group coped with the impact of a number of group and management changes, the loss of the physical space for the project, due to the need for acute admissions beds, proved to be an external challenge they could not overcome. In effect, this organisational change ultimately caused the end of the Training Ward project. The interprofessional education literature does not offer an empirical insight into the nature of organisational change on the development of an initiative. This finding helps to illuminate the significance that organisational change can have on undermining the success of an interprofessional initiative.

---

[41] After a dormant period of around one year, another steering group was set up (containing one original steering group member) to develop and deliver another practice-based interprofessional initiative in a separate hospital. This new initiative commenced in October 2003 and included students from two of the original schools. However, educational and professional constraints have meant that this new initiative does not allow students to collaborate around the planning and delivery of patient care. Instead, they work together on paper-based patient scenarios and interview patients to obtain their experiences of the care delivered by qualified staff.

Summary

This chapter has presented a detailed account of the key successes (Section 6.1) and challenges (Section 6.2) related to the development of the Training Ward project. Importantly, it indicated that that while enthusiasm helped ensure the steering group worked together, it also created a number of challenges in the way in which they functioned as a group, and challenges for the design of Training Ward itself. The chapter also indicated how number of external factors such as curricula constraints, work pressures, management and organisational change played a significant role in undermining this practice-based project. In presenting this account, the chapter has addressed the first of the study's research objectives (to explore the factors – roles, relations, interactions, processes – that influenced the development of the Training Ward, see Section 1.2). In doing so, it has provided an insight into some of the contents of the black box related to the development of interprofessional education.

Having explored the processes related to the development of the Training Ward project, the next chapter explores the processes involved in the delivery of this initiative.

Chapter 7: Delivering the Training Ward pilot

Introduction

This chapter presents and discusses findings related to the key successes and challenges encountered in the delivery of the Training Ward pilot. In this chapter, the second of the study's objectives contained in Section 1.2 is addressed. The chapter is divided into two main sections. Section 7.1 examines the key successes related to the delivery of the pilot ward in a clinical setting, while Section 7.2 presents the key challenges related to its delivery. The aim of this chapter is to offer an in-depth insight into the key factors related to the delivery of the Training Ward.

7.1. Delivering the pilot: key successes

This section of the chapter examines the four key successes ('delivering a four week pilot', 'a valuable interprofessional experience', 'the rewards of sharing time and space', 'the benefits of off-ward work') related to the delivery of the Training Ward pilot.

7.1.1. Delivering a four-week pilot

In considering the successes of their work, steering group members felt that the delivery of the four-week pilot ward was a key achievement. Margaret offers a typical response on this issue:

> *"I think the main success, that we actually got it* [the Training Ward] *to work* [...] *we actually managed to get four weeks out of the Training Ward"* (Margaret, steering group member interview 5/00).

The delivery of the pilot ward was regarded by the steering group to be a success for a number of reasons. Importantly, it was the first interprofessional learning initiative of its kind to be implemented in the UK:

> *"This was the first ward of its type in this country, we were on the cutting edge"* (Patricia, steering group member interview 3/00).

Secondly, it also offered pre-qualification students a unique practice-based interprofessional learning experience:

"The Training Ward provided students with a type of experience that they never had had before" (Christine, steering group member interview 4/00).

Thirdly, the pilot ward provided the facilitators who worked on the pilot ward with a valuable opportunity for professional development:

"It is a unique opportunity for them [Training Ward facilitators], *it will look great on their CVs, it will develop them in many, many ways"* (Todd, steering group member interview 3/98).

In addition, it was agreed that the pilot ward should be considered particularly successful given the timetabling and professional regulatory body difficulties the group overcame to deliver this pre-qualification practice-based interprofessional initiative:

"There were three universities and four professional bodies involved and that's not easy, tackling the timetabling issues and the professional regulations. Its really hard" (Ben, steering group member interview 4/00).

Another of the group's successes was delivering the pilot ward within a busy clinical directorate without compromising the overall quality of its clinical service:

"We delivered it [the pilot ward] *in a large and busy hospital, and the overall standards of care provided in the Training Ward was good"* (Jean, steering group member interview 3/00).

Furthermore, the steering group felt a particular sense of achievement as the pilot ward was delivered on top of their existing (heavy) workloads. Finally, as noted in Section 6.2.6, the group delivered the pilot in the face of continuing changes to membership and the loss of a key senior management supporter.

Given the range of difficulties and barriers to be overcome, steering group members felt that the delivery of the pilot was *"a major achievement"* (Julia, steering group member interview 4/00). It was also agreed that the delivery of the pilot ward in February 1999 was an important factor in sustaining the group's efforts on the project for another 15 months:

"It [the Training Ward pilot] *was an achievement and I think it kept the group together. If that hadn't happened, I don't think we would be talking about it going at all. It* [the Training Ward project] *would just have become a non-entity really"* (Derek, steering group member interview 5/00).

The steering group's efforts in delivering the four-week pilot ward should be hailed as a key success, especially given the number of problems they overcame. In general, the delivery of pre-qualification interprofessional education is considered a difficult goal due to the need to overcome a range of logistical difficulties such as inequalities in student numbers and differences in curricula (Tope 1996, Pirrie et al. 1998, Roberts et al. 2000). Indeed, as noted above, in delivering this initiative, the steering group not only overcame these hurdles, but they also ensured that the pilot was implemented in a ward within a busy inner-city hospital environment without adversely affecting patient care.

7.1.2. A valuable interprofessional experience

One of the key successes for the students was that the pilot ward provided them with a valuable practice-based teamwork experience. In working together on the pilot ward, students reported that they had gained a beneficial insight into the nature of teamwork in a busy acute hospital setting:

> "It provided us with an really useful insight into how an interprofessional team operates in an acute ward" (Tamsin, occupational therapy student, blue team interview).

The data also indicated that the pilot ward provided students with some valuable insights into the pressures and roles attached to different professional groups working in an acute care setting:

> "It [the pilot ward] gave us an insight into the work of other professions such as OT, physio and medicine" (Cathy, nursing student, red team interview).

For the students, their experiences of teamwork on the pilot ward also helped them develop an understanding of delivering patient care from the perspectives of other professional groups:

> "The ward helped me develop a global, holistic outlook on caring for patients; looking at it from other professional perspectives" (Sue, nursing student, yellow team interview).

Students particularly valued the 'real life' experience the pilot ward offered them, which, when compared with their traditional clinical placements, was considered more effective, as the students were more active in their learning:

> "You're immersed into the thing [...] and it sticks to you and you remember it, it's not like learning from a lecture" (Ralph, medical student, green team interview).

Indeed, students considered the 'real life' experience of organising and providing patient care was one of the most beneficial aspects of their ward placement. In particular, they valued the increased levels of responsibility and autonomy they had, an experience which allowed them a better opportunity to *"think through"* (Clara, physiotherapy student, yellow team) and decide how they could best care for patients. The Training Ward was therefore regarded as offering a striking contrast to their normal clinical placements, in which their supervisors tended to lead in patient care.

These views were supported by the facilitators, who also felt that the pilot ward provided the students with a range of helpful interprofessional experiences:

> "It [the pilot ward] *provided the students with some really good experiences of what its like working as a member of a multidisciplinary team"* (May, facilitator interview).

Observations of the students working together on the pilot ward indicated that their interactions were positive and constructive in nature:

> *Kelly* [nursing student] *and Clare* [occupational therapy student] *are making beds together. They are chatting and smiling while working. Wendy* [nursing student] *and Val* [facilitator] *are doing the drug round. Miriam* [medical student] *is on the phone. She puts the receiver down and walks across to Ralph [medical student] and Max* [physiotherapy student] *who are talking together while looking at some patient notes. Miriam appears to be feeding back the information from her phone conversation into the discussion* (ward observation, green team).

The positive nature of student relationships was also evident in their off-ward planning and reflection sessions:

> *The team has been discussing how they could enhance their teamwork on the ward. There is a short pause. In breaking the silence, Tamsin* [occupational therapy student] *says that one of the patients thought Wasim* [medical student] *was a nurse.*[42] *On hearing this Wasim goes on, 'yeah, the patient said, 'so you're a doctor then, I thought you were a nurse' and I said to her, 'well, don't tell the nurses, they might be offended." This comment produces a good deal of laughter from the students* (reflection session, blue team).

Overall, it was felt their practice-based teamwork experiences on the pilot ward provided the students with a helpful preparation for their future practice:

> "I feel I got a lot of confidence and responsibility which really prepared me for when I qualify, so that has been a valuable part of it" (Yvonne, nursing student, red team interview).

> "Getting the students to work together can only help with their practice, as they now have an excellent insight into the ups and downs of teamwork" (Malcolm, medical facilitator interview).

The opportunity to work together to develop a firmer understanding of the nature of practice-based interprofessional collaboration was important and rewarding for the students. They valued their Training Ward experience as it provided them with insights into how professionals work together in a busy clinical environment. It also provided them with an understanding of the pressures and roles of different professions in the delivery of care. In addition, observations of the students' collaborative work on the ward indicated

---

[42] As noted in Section 4.3.2, to help promote a sense of team cohesiveness all students wore theatre blues instead of their usual uniforms.

that they interacted in a positive and enthusiastic manner when caring for patients. Providing students with insights into teamwork is a central aim of interprofessional education (e.g. Gill & Ling 1995, Gilbert et al. 2000, Morison et al. 2003). Indeed, research has indicated that students value such insights as they feel it can prepare them for their future clinical practice (e.g. Mires et al. 1999, Guest et al. 2002, Johnson 2003).

7.1.3. The rewards of sharing time and space

Another rewarding aspect of students' pilot ward experience was the amount of time and space they shared. As indicated in Section 4.3.2, during the pilot students worked together in eight-hour shifts, during which students shared both on-ward and off-ward time. For many of them, this amount of shared time was considered helpful in ensuring that they had immediate interaction with one another:

> "We've been spoilt, as we can just ask the physio to pop along and take a look at something, or catch the nurses in the middle of a drug round" (Jake, medical student, yellow team interview).

In general, it was felt that sharing the same time and space also allowed the students to work in an effective interprofessional manner:

> Keith: It was good to have large space as you can see all other members of the team [...]
> Gwyn: Yeah, we can see each other, we can see what's going on and liaise. I think it makes teamwork a lot easier (nursing students, purple team interview).

Facilitators agreed with these views:

> "The sharing of time together on the ward has allowed the students to talk and update one another. It has helped them work together" (Hal, medical facilitator interview).

Locating the students together in the same space and time during their on-ward and off-ward activities was considered a valuable experience on this placement. In particular, this form of sharing was viewed as advantageous in ensuring interaction between students was immediate. For the students, this meant their collaborative work could be undertaken more effectively. As the interprofessional education literature generally overlooks the processes associated with delivery activities, this finding offers a new insight into this issue. Research into the nature of health and social care teams does help to understand this finding, as it indicates that time and space for regular interaction is one of the essential elements of effective interprofessional collaboration (e.g. Gregson et al. 1991, Elywin et al. 1998, Annandale et al. 1999, Molyneux 2001, Allen 2002), as a team can more easily meet, plan and agree their collaborative work.

7.1.4. The benefits of off-ward work

A further rewarding aspect of the students' pilot ward experiences was their off-ward activities (team planning, handover and team reflection sessions). These activities, undertaken in a seminar room near the ward, were considered helpful in allowing students time away from the pressures of delivering patient care to plan, exchange information with other teams (during handover) and reflect upon their interprofessional experiences. In relation to their team planning sessions, students felt they provided valuable opportunities to organise their collaborative work before entering the ward to care for patients:

> "We took ten minutes to sit and plan our work. We looked at each patient and wrote a list of what their problems were, whether they were OT, physio, nursing or medical and then we said, 'right that's your job, that's my job and agreed who is going to do what to manage the patient" (Yvonne, medical student, red team interview).

Observations of these sessions indicated that they were useful in allowing students to negotiate and agree a collaborative approach to their ward-based teamwork:

> In their planning session the students consider what tasks need to be undertaken with each patient and agree who will complete these tasks. Kate [nursing student] says that Mrs X is about to be discharged, Zara [nursing student] agrees to sort out transport. Tamsin [occupational therapy student] says she will arrange a home visit for Mrs X, Wasim and Fiona [medical students] agree to chase up outstanding test results and order some sputum tests, Tom [physiotherapy student] says that Mr X needs a physiotherapy assessment which he will do this morning. The students go on agree the division of labour for the team duties. Tom and Tamsin both offer to help Kate and Zara, while Fiona and Wasim complete their profession-specific work (planning session observation, red team).

As noted in Section 4.3.2, at the end of their shift, the out-going student team handed over salient information on patient progress to the in-coming team. For the students, this off-ward activity was considered another successful part of their pilot ward experience:

> "It was good to link up with students from the other teams for a short while when doing handover, just for a quick update of patient progress and some idea of what we needed to do before we entered the ward" (Andrea, occupational therapy student, yellow team).

In relation to their team reflection sessions, the data indicated that students also valued these sessions in providing them with a regular opportunity to reflect upon their teamwork experiences and also explore ways of enhancing their collaborative efforts:

> "It was great to take time away from the ward to reflect on our work and discuss where we went wrong and how we could improve things for the next shift" (Gwyn, nursing student, purple team).

Observations revealed that student teams covered a variety of issues connected to their collaborative work during their reflection sessions:

> Jo [medical student] *points out 'I didn't think we organised ourselves on the first day.' Barbara* [nursing student] *agrees, 'we didn't spend enough time together discussing teamwork and how we do things.' Agreement from the group. Tanya* [nursing student] *says, 'we all worked every individually'. Again, agreement from the group. Melanie* [occupational therapy student] *says, 'it's about organising your workload together'. Jo says, 'we are now working as a team. On Monday we all ran off and did our own thing. The biggest problem we had was lack of communication'* (reflection session observation, orange team).

As outlined above, in addition to providing the students with the time to reflect upon their ward-based work, team reflection sessions provided them with opportunities to explore how they improve their teamwork. For example, many student teams decided to introduce a system whereby they agreed a list of jobs they needed to undertake and *"ticked them off"* (Tanya, nursing student, orange team) as they were completed. Importantly, these sessions were used to help overcome some of the challenges the students encountered with undertaking their shared team duties. (See Section 7.2.2 for information on this issue).

While the students regarded their planning and reflection sessions as important off-ward opportunities that enhanced their interprofessional work, their interviews indicated that they also used other locations, specifically the hospital canteen and the local pub to *"talk about teamwork and team issues"* (Molly, medical student, red team). However, it was noted that these more informal settings were only occasionally used, as following their shift most students preferred to *"get home and relax"* (Deborah, physiotherapy student, red team).

As indicated above, off-ward activities provided the students with valuable opportunities to plan, reflect and attempt to improve the quality of teamwork. In doing so, it helped the students to work more collaboratively while delivering patient care. Once again, as the literature overlooks the processes related to the delivery of interprofessional education this finding begins to shed light on this issue. Research into the nature of teamwork does, nevertheless, indicate that time spent together discussing and reflecting upon collaborative work can improve team functioning (e.g. Antoniadis & Videlock 1991, Meerabeau & Page 1999, Onyett 2003). For example, as Larson & LaFasto (1989:135) found in their interview study undertaken with 32 teams drawn from industry, sports, health and the armed forces:

"A positive collaborative climate is more likely to develop within teams that spend considerable time and energy in examining and seeking ways to improve their own working relationships."

Similarly, in her study of health care teams, Opie (1997:275) found that where a team takes time to reflect upon their work its members are more likely to "fuse together" their different knowledge bases and perspectives. A fusing process can ultimately provide a richer form of collaboration and a "more complex level of functioning" (Opie 1997:275).

7.2. Delivering the pilot: key challenges

This section of the chapter examines the key challenges ('poor student preparation', 'problems of mucking in and role overlap', 'lack of time for team development', 'confusing and competing objectives', 'inconsistent problem-based facilitation' and 'student inequality and confusion') related to the delivery of the Training Ward pilot.

7.2.1. Poor student preparation

In general, students felt under-prepared for their work as an interprofessional team on the pilot ward. Despite receiving an induction session before starting their placement,[43] this session contained no preparation on how they should organise themselves as a newly formed team to care for patients using a PBL approach. Consequently, when the students started on the ward pilot, they felt poorly equipped for their collaborative work. Anne, a nursing student, provides a typical reaction into the nature of this issue:

"There were a couple of hours on the first shift when everything was up in the air [...] it was hectic; no one was sure about how we work together" (Anne, nursing student, red team interview).

Students' concerns were exacerbated by their facilitators. In general, facilitators viewed their role in using PBL as one in which they needed to stand back and offer the students little direction on how they could work together as an effective team. (The difficulties associated with the role of facilitator are considered in Section 7.2.5). Due to this lack of preparation, students felt their initial time on the ward was unnecessarily stressful. The students felt their early experiences could have been made more productive if they had had time to prepare for their collaborative work:

"I just think it would have been more advantageous if we had had some time together as a team, looking at what we needed to do" (Kate, nursing student, blue team interview).

---

[43] As outlined in Section 4.3.2, all students attended an induction session that introduced them to the members of their team and their facilitators, reviewed their handbooks and provided them with a tour of the ward.

However, as noted in Section 7.1.4, the students' off-ward activities did help alleviate this problem, as during their planning and reflection sessions they discussed their division of labour, agreed team roles and planned a collective approach to their teamwork.

In connection to the problems generated by a lack of preparation time, unfortunately, the interprofessional education literature offers no empirical accounts into this issue. The teamwork literature, in contrast, is more helpful. Research into teamwork has revealed that initial team training is an important factor to successful collaboration (e.g. Pritchard 1995, Øvretveit 1997b, Meerabeau & Page 1999, Borrill et al. 2000). As Jaques (1998:29) points out, members of a new group need initial time to get to know each other, to understand the group's task and map out ways of working together:

> "Members of a new group coming together for the first time may have to devote much early energy to getting acquainted with one another and with the group's task, as well as establishing ways of working together".

Without this initial type of input, Jaques goes on to argue that a group's ability to function effectively is impaired, as there is likely to be confusion over their tasks and how they can function together. Øvretveit (1993) holds a similar position. He argues that teams need preparatory time to discuss and agree how they are going to collaborate. During this process teams need to agree aims, roles and responsibilities. An important outcome of this process for Øvretveit is the production of a mutually agreed 'team policy' that provides an explicit framework detailing how that team will collectively work together.

7.2.2. Problems of 'mucking in' and role overlap

As noted in Section 4.3.2.2, to provide students with opportunities to work closely together while on the Training Ward, they were required to participate in shared team duties (e.g. bed making, patient washes, patient observations). However, the inclusion of these activities created a number of problems for the students. In particular, the medical, occupational therapy and physiotherapy students shared a perception that team duties represented low status work, and tended to be described these duties in terms relating to 'dirt' and 'muck':

> *"I'll muck in and help with the team duties"* (Deborah, physiotherapy student, red team reflection).
>
> *"I help with the washes, I don't mind getting my hands dirty"* (Matt, medical student, orange team reflection).
>
> *"Do we all muck in and to do team duties?"* (Suzanne, occupational therapy student, purple team planning session).

Given the nature of these caring activities, most students regarded them as 'nursing-oriented' work. While most nursing students and nursing facilitators considered team duties as an essential *shared* activity, which ensured that ward-based work could be completed, some of the nursing students viewed these tasks in more problematic terms. By equating elements of their role with low status, 'mucky' work it was felt that the other students would develop an unrepresentative view of nursing:

> *"People will think nursing care is just giving someone their dinner or giving them a bowl of water or washing people; that isn't nursing"* (Tanya, nursing student, orange team interview).

Most medical, occupational therapy and physiotherapy students also saw that participation in team duties meant an increase in their workloads, as they had to complete both shared and profession-specific duties:

> *Max* [physiotherapy student] *says there is a problem doing team duties all morning as it meant he did not complete his physiotherapy work "as I kept being called away to make beds." Clare* [occupational therapy student] *agrees. Like Max, she was doing team duties and therefore "did not much time to do my occupational therapy [...] we are both doing work outside our role" she complains* (reflection session, green team).

However, while occupational therapy and physiotherapy students generally felt that undertaking team duties allowed them to collect information for their own professional work, medical students viewed team duties in far less useful terms. For these students, team duties were considered *"not relevant"* (Fiona, medical student, blue team interview) to their professional work. In addition, medical students faced a further difficulty with participating in team duties. Due to the high number of medical teams with patients on the pilot ward,[44] medical students were often busy participating in medical ward rounds while the other students undertook team duties. As one student noted:

> *"There were three* [medical] *teams all wanting us to do individual rounds and so you're supposed to split yourself three different ways"* (Yvonne, medical student, red team interview).

Given this situation, most medical students tended to resist team duties. The following extract provides a typical Training Ward scene in relation to medical student involvement in team duties:

> *I arrive on the ward and I see both Tanya [nursing student], Melanie* [occupational therapy student] *and Barbara [occupational therapy student] either washing patients or making beds. While these students are engaged in team duties, Jo and Matt [medical students] are sitting together reading and*

---

[44] In total, the ward pilot had responsibility for the patients of eleven medical teams. At any one time there were around four or five different medical teams' patients on the ward.

writing up notes and making phone calls to chase up test results (ward observation, orange team).

As well as openly resisting team duties, the data indicated that medical students employed a more subtle form of resistance. This usually involved them leaving the ward, without informing any of their team members, in periods when team duties were being undertaken. For the other members of their team 'disappearances' were noted:

> *When talking to Jen* [physiotherapy student] *and Gwyn* [nursing student] *about the medical students, Jen pointed out that their two medics did not help them with the team duties during the week, as they were preparing for medical team rounds. She went on to say that during the weekend, one of them was particularly good at "drifting away" when this work needed to be undertaken* (ward observation, purple team).

Inevitably, the medical students' non-participation in team duties was a source of friction in the student teams. In general, students felt it undermined the notion of equality with their interprofessional teams. Nevertheless, as noted in Section 6.1.4, through on-going discussion in their reflection sessions, student teams agreed how to manage this issue. For example, in one of the student teams, instead of undertaking team duties, the medical students agreed to provide more help in co-ordinating the discharge of patients.

The data indicated a further problem with the use of shared team duties. As two of the facilitators highlighted, this type of working arrangement was seen as an artificial way to work as a team:

> *"The students are all expected to work together and muck in and help each other. That is not how teams work in reality"* (Val, nursing facilitator).

> *"We have created a very artificial situation for most students except the nurses. All the others found it hard* [...] *this is not normal practice"* (Carol, nursing facilitator).

Empirical work undertaken on the Swedish ward provides some support for the problems related to role sharing (Fallsberg & Wijma 1999, Fallsberg & Hammar 2000). Similarly, this work indicated that the Swedish students also struggled with overlap into the nursing students' role. In addition, research into team function has indicated that sharing professional roles can be particularly problematic (e.g. Øvretveit 1993, West & Slater 1996, Elywin et al. 1998, West & Markiowicz 2004). Indeed, it is generally agreed that team members need separate roles to work effectively. Where role sharing occurs, friction between group members has been found to arise due to role overlap and an uncertainty around their division of labour (e.g. Ross et al. 2000, Tye & Ross 2000, Parker 2001, Booth & Hewison 2002). However, the Swedish evaluation work fails to offer an insight into the issue of medical student resistance. This resistance may be a facet of the unequal power and status relations shared between the health and social care professions, given that medicine is generally regarded as a high status profession in relation to nursing, occupational therapy and physiotherapy (e.g. Hugman 1991, Willkinson & Miers 1999).[45]

7.2.3. Lack of time for team development

Most students felt that a two-week placement did not provide a sufficient amount of time to develop an informed idea of how interprofessional collaboration undertaken in a clinical setting. Indeed, most students felt that by the end of the second week they were only just beginning to perform together as an effective team:

> "We have just warmed up and got into our stride and three more shifts and it's over" [agreement from other students] (Clara, physiotherapy student, yellow team interview).

Generally, students felt that the placement should be extended to three or possibly four weeks to allow them more time to understand how an interprofessional team can work together:

> "I think about three weeks because you have got your first week to establish yourself [in the team], your second week to really start to get to know everything and your last week which would be like, I've got it, I'm doing this right" (Zara, nursing student, blue team interview).

Facilitators echoed the students' views on this issue:

> "I think for it to work well, the students have got to have time to go through their group forming process, which within a two week period they didn't really have time to do" (May, nursing facilitator interview).

It was also noted that a two-week placement was an insufficient length of time if the students encountered problems in their teams. For students in one team, two weeks meant there was little time to find a shared resolution to the problem they encountered in relation to non-participation of team duties:

> "There was no point making an issue of it [medical student resistance of team duties], we only had four more shifts to go" (Barbara, nursing student, orange team interview).

Once again, facilitators shared a similar view:

> "I began to hear people saying toward the end of the second week, 'oh well there is no point in dealing with that [interprofessional team friction] because

---

[45] Although it is generally acknowledged that these traditional power relations are shifting between the health and social care professions with nursing, for example, increasing it standing in relation to medicine (Porter 1999). Useful illustrations of these changes can be seen with the growth of higher status, more influential posts of advanced nurse practitioner and clinical nurse specialist (Zwarenstein & Reeves 2002).

we will be finished on Sunday', and people kind of shelved issues really rather than bang away at something they felt weren't going to get anywhere with" (Caitlin, therapy facilitator).

As indicated above, time was an important factor in the students' experience of the Training Ward. Given that the interprofessional education literature has overlooked this issue, the study offers a new insight into this area. In helping to understand the nature of this finding the teamwork literature offers some help. While it does not provide an exact time frame on how long a team needs to work together to be effective, there is general agreement that a longer rather than a shorter amount of time together is desirable (e.g. Kelly & McGrath 1985, McGrath 1990, Douglas 1996). For example, Douglas (1983) argues that good group cohesion and communication requires trust and openness, which needs time to develop:

"Time spent working together obviously increases the familiarity... more time can bring an increased knowledge and a more realistic level of expectation among group members" (p130).

Douglas (1983) goes on to argue that groups who have a limited life span tend to 'rush' through their development, a factor that can often producing poorer quality inter-team communication and team member support.

7.2.4. Confusing and competing objectives

As discussed in Section 6.2.3.1, steering group members developed around 10 profession-specific and also 19 team-orientated learning objectives for the students to meet during their two-week pilot ward experience. (See Appendix 4 for a list of these objectives). Student and facilitator data indicated that these different objectives created further challenges. Firstly, the students were uncertain about meeting both their profession-specific and team-orientated objectives during their two-week placement:

"There were just so many objectives for us, it was confusing, so we weren't certain what the real aim of the ward was" (Max, physiotherapy student, green team interview).

In addition, the use of two contrasting sets of learning objectives appeared to produce some tension between whether the ward was focused on providing students with a profession-specific or team-orientated experience, a tension that was not always cleared-up by the facilitators, as one of the medical students pointed out:

"X [medical facilitator] told me 'you're not there to do nursing roles [team duties], you're there to do medicine" (Matt, medical student orange team interview)

There was another issue associated with the students meeting both sets of learning objectives. In general, the students complained they were too busy coping with their profession specific roles to attempt to meet both sets of objectives:

> "We were too busy surviving our own role" (Zara, nursing student, blue team interview).

> "It's difficult to learn your own role, let alone someone else's role" (Yvonne, medical student, red team).

This was a particular problem for the medical and nursing students, who, due to their heavy profession-specific workloads, felt they had to spend most of their time on the ward carrying out these duties:

> "We have done the jobs we normally do and we haven't had much input into what anyone else does" (Tanya, nursing student, orange team interview).

The creation of a large number of competing learning objectives appeared to generate further challenges for the students' pilot ward experience. This finding is supported by the interprofessional education literature, which has found that difficulties can emerge when students need to meet both profession-specific and collaborative learning objectives. In general, students prefer to focus on the objectives which aim to develop profession-specific knowledge and skills over those that aim to develop collaborative competencies (Dienst & Byl 1981, Reeves 2000, Fallsberg & Hammar 2000).

7.2.5. Inconsistent problem-based facilitation

As noted in Section 7.2.4.2, none of the facilitators had prior experience of employing a PBL approach. Therefore, steering group members organised a two-day introductory workshop on PBL (see Appendix 3). However, the data indicated that despite this preparation, all the facilitators experienced difficulties with using PBL on the pilot ward.

A key difficulty related to this lack experience was that students were largely unaware that they were employing PBL. For example, one student noted that there was a only "brief mention" (Sue, nursing student, yellow team interview) about PBL during one of her team's reflection sessions. Another student queried its use within her Training Ward experience, she asked "PBL? where did that appear?" (Fiona, medical student, blue team interview). In addition, one of the occupational therapy students (whose school used PBL extensively in their curriculum) pointed out that her team never generated or reviewed any learning objectives. Indeed, observations of the team reflection sessions, where it was anticipated the students would generate and review their learning objectives, indicated that this only happened once during the delivery of the pilot ward.

Another central difficulty facilitators encountered with PBL was *"a general uncertainty"* (Carol, nursing facilitator interview) around how much support they could offer to students. Facilitators' understanding of PBL differed: for some it was an approach in which allowed the students to lead, without much facilitator input; for others it was a more 'hands on', directive activity. As a result, facilitators admitted that they approached their work in contrasting ways:

> *"We were working in very different ways. We all seemed to have different ideas about exactly what our roles as facilitators were* [...] *I saw some of the other facilitators just doing their normal* [didactic] *style of teaching with the students"* (May, nursing facilitator interview).

Observations indicated that medical and physiotherapy facilitators tended to employ a more didactic approach when working with the students, often telling them how to solve their on-ward problems. For these facilitators, a concern about the lack of progress the student teams were making with organising patient care often meant that they took the decision to intervene. As Kit, one of the medical facilitators explained:

> *"I would get exasperated* [by the lack of progress student teams were making] *and I would just say, 'ok the rest of the ward round is going to be entirely didactic'"* (Kit, medical facilitator interview).

In contrast, the nursing facilitators employed a different approach. In general, these facilitators offered students little direction when working in their teams:

> *After the handover, May* [nursing facilitator] *offers the students little input into how students work together as a team on the ward. All she says is "you need to allocate tasks between you. How you do it is up to you* [...] *it's up to you to organise your workload"* [...] *on the way out, after the students have left, I say to her, 'I'm not clear what the students are going to do." She replies, 'me too. I'm just going to let them get on with it and discuss it later with them'* (ward observation, blue team).

These inconsistencies caused two difficulties for the students. Firstly, it created further confusion over the use of PBL on the ward:

> *"Maybe you'd ask a question and sometimes they* [the facilitators] *would throw it back at you, sometimes they would take a lead. So there was uncertainty"* (Keith, nursing student, purple team interview)

> *After about an hour of working on the ward Fiona* [medical student] *comes up to me and complains that she is not sure what to do as nursing facilitator offers no help, but her medical facilitator "is telling us what to do"* (ward observation, blue team).

Secondly, as most students had limited experience of PBL and no experience of working together as an interprofessional team, they were anxious about how they could employ this approach to collaborate in an effective manner. Despite voicing these anxieties, the nursing facilitators, in particular, continued to offer student teams little input:

> "She [nursing facilitator] did let us drown [...]; I thought she could have maybe turned round to and called us together and said, 'look team, you need to prioritise this and get this sorted out'" (Kate, nursing student, blue team interview).

Upon reflection, some of the facilitators also felt this 'hands off' approach was problematic:

> "I don't supposed we had done anything to turn them into a unit [...] It might have been helpful if we had done some sort of team building exercises, in some sort of way, rather than putting them under fire straight away" (Kit, medical facilitator interview).

Responding to these anxieties, one of the medical facilitators began to offer advice to the student teams over how they could organise themselves. This type of input usually took the form of 10 to 15 minute off-ward planning sessions in which he offered ideas organising their workload. Students welcomed these medical facilitator-led sessions:

> "We had that session with Hal [medical facilitator] where he sat us down and said get your patients, make a list of problems, divide up the jobs and that's what you need to do, it was just what we needed" (Fiona, medical student blue team interview).

Two of the nursing facilitators also began to make minor modification to their initial 'hands-off' approach following student feedback. For example, Val encouraged the students to use the ward diary to help their team co-ordination, and May advised that the students should consider in more depth their team-orientated learning objectives. Nevertheless, these facilitators tended to offer minimal direction over student teamwork during their on-ward work.

Students in these teams generally felt that a lack of direction on how to work as a team was the main cause for their poor collaboration:

> "We needed to have someone to say to our team, way back in the beginning, these are your roles and this is how you work together... If we go back to the beginning and look at what we have to do [...], everyone's got their profession specific role but on this particular project, for two weeks, we are working on this as a team" (Keith, nursing student, purple team interview).

In contrast, the third nursing facilitator amended her initial 'hands off' approach to offer the students more direction over how they work in their teams. For example, she suggested to both her teams that they should elect a team co-ordinator to ensure that teamwork processes were emphasised within the student teams:

> "I sort of advised them [the student teams] that it may be a good idea to have a team leader, you know, I said because, and I put the emphasis on lunch

breaks, having tea breaks and things like that. So one person could make sure the rest of the group had a break" (Val, nursing facilitator interview).

This facilitator was also keen to stress to her teams the importance of negotiation over how to solve problems:

"I said to them you need to say, 'ok, I could give you two hours of my time today to help tidy up the ward, or whatever', after that two hours they wouldn't bother you again. That is what teamwork is, negotiating with one another and everybody gets to do what they need to do" (Val, nursing facilitator interview).

Data gathered from the teams facilitated by this nursing facilitator indicated that students tended to work in a more integrated manner, compared to the first two teams facilitated by the other two nursing facilitators. Over time, however, facilitators' initial uncertainties with the use of PBL diminished, as opportunities to share their experiences and informally learn from one another helped to them to provide a more consistent approach to their facilitation.

On reflection, despite encountering difficulties using PBL, all the facilitators enjoyed their pilot ward experiences. However, it was agreed that none of them had anticipated the heavy demands associated with using this type of learning in a clinical setting. In addition to the challenges of coping with PBL, the nursing facilitators found that providing continual facilitation of the student teams during their eight-hour shifts was *"mentally straining"* (Carol, nursing facilitator interview). Furthermore, profession-specific facilitators faced the problem of managing both the demands of their 'normal' role while providing the pilot ward students with sufficient levels of support.

In general, the role of interprofessional facilitator is agreed to be pivotal in creating and maintaining high quality interactive learning (e.g. Parsell & Bligh 1998, Hammick 1998). Furthermore, given the demands of facilitating different professional groups of students, it is generally agreed that facilitators need to be well prepared to successfully undertake this type of work (e.g. Thomas 1995, Van der Horst et al. 1995, Lary et al. 1997 Clay et al. 1999). While this literature provides some discussion on the nature of facilitation, it does not provide any empirical accounts into this activity. This study has, for the first time, provided evidence into the processes related to facilitating interprofessional student teams. Importantly, it has indicated that despite employing a complex educational approach (PBL) during the delivery of the Pilot Ward, none of the facilitators had prior experience using this type of approach. (Section 9.3.1 goes on to discuss, in more detail, the successes and challenges related to using PBL within the Training Ward).

7.2.6. Student inequality and confusion

As discussed in Section 6.2.5, the steering group's work developing the Training Ward was affected by school curricula and professional validation constraints. This section considers the effect of these two issues on the delivery of the pilot ward. The section also discusses the steering group's decision for students to wear a Training Ward uniform rather than their normal profession-specific uniforms.

Different course timetables between the four participating schools resulted in the steering group having to recruit students into the pilot ward by different methods. Consequently, while medical, occupational therapy and physiotherapy students were allowed to choose whether they participated in the ward,[46] nursing students were randomly selected to participate (and therefore had no choice). The data indicated that these contrasting methods of selection were problematic for the students. In general, it was felt that these differences undermined the sense of equality within each of the students' teams:

> *When chatting to Gwyn and Keith* [nursing students] *one of them brings up the issue of student selection. Both are annoyed that they had not been given the choice to volunteer for the ward like the other students in their team. Gwyn says, "the other guys volunteered, we were made to do this* [...] *we are supposed to be adults and have choice". "It's just not fair. We are meant to be working together on this as equal members of a team and that hasn't happened here" says Keith. The others agree. Both go on to say neither of them would have opted to come on to the ward if they had been given the choice* (reflection session, purple team).

Nevertheless, despite these feelings of frustration, all the nursing students took an active part in their team's work during the placement. In contrast, the four medical students who had not volunteered for this placement were some of its main critics, as one of the nursing facilitators pointed out:

> *"Some of the medical students were actually forced to come on the ward, so the result was that they were not happy to come, they were not going to do anything"* (Carol, nursing facilitator interview).

Observational data also indicated that these students tended to interact poorly with the other members of their teams. For these teams, it was felt that this inequality had a distinctive detrimental effect on the quality of their collaboration:

> *"For once you were all trying to work as a team* [...] *all caring for the patient, but if you get one student who doesn't want to be there it can ruin it for the others". All students need to be ready to help out the other students"* (Tanya, nursing student, orange team interview).

---

[46] As noted in Section 4.3.1, after failing a clinical examination four medical students were required to participate in the pilot ward.

It was therefore agreed that only students who had volunteered for the Training Ward should be included, as they would be more enthusiastic and committed to undertake interprofessional education.

Different requirements of the regulatory bodies that validated the schools pre-qualification courses also resulted in the steering group having to accredit the students' pilot ward experience in contrasting ways. For the nursing students, unlike the medical, occupational therapy and physiotherapy students, the placement provided them with *"legitimate"* (Wendy, nursing student, green team interview) clinical learning time for their course. For the other students, participation in the pilot ward meant they effectively 'lost' two weeks accredited clinical hours (that would need to be 'made up' elsewhere in their course). Understandably, for these students, this issue was considered unfair:

> *"It was unfair that we worked hard on this ward and none of it counts for anything really"* (Tom, physiotherapy student, blue team reflection session).

Indeed, students felt that these differences, again, undermined the notion of equality within their teams. Many also felt these imbalances were generally disruptive for students involved in interprofessional education, as they could set up differing incentives and levels of commitment for participating in this type of education.

As noted in Section 4.3.2, in order to differentiate Training Ward students from clinical staff and promote a sense of team spirit, all students wore theatre blues as the 'official' Training Ward uniform. In general, students felt the uniform was helpful in promoting team cohesiveness. However, it was also acknowledged that the uniforms also caused some confusion, as many people were uncertain the students' professional affiliation. Indeed, this issue was considered a particular problem for some of the medical students, who complained that it was *"difficult to tell people apart"* (Fiona, medical student, blue team interview). Nevertheless, observations indicated that medical students could be distinguished from the other students, as they nearly always wore stethoscopes around their necks. Indeed, in one team, a medical student wore a white coat over his uniform. While one could argue that the uniform encouraged a sense of team identity, the higher status medicine occupies over the other health and social care professions (e.g. Hugman 1991, Willkinson & Miers 1999) means that it was not surprising to discover that some of the medical students differentiated themselves from the other students, as a way of reinforcing their enhanced status.

As indicated above, curricula and professional validation factors undermined the quality of the students' interprofessional experiences. In relation to the literature, it has been recommended that equality within all aspects of interprofessional education (e.g. recruitment, assessment and accreditation) helps to ensure that students are equally motivated to engage with this form of education (e.g. Boyer 1977, Gill & Ling 1995, Lary et al. 1997, Reeves 2000). Indeed, given the traditional hierarchical relationships between the health and social care professions (e.g. Hugman 1991, Porter 1995, Wilkinson & Miers 1999) ensuring equality between the different groups of students is a central element to the success of an interprofessional education initiative. However, as the Training Ward was delivered on a pilot basis, it should be remembered that such problems are likely to arise. Indeed, as noted in Section 4.2.4, the decision to initially deliver a pilot ward was taken to identify and assess the nature of problems in order to resolve them in the longer term. Over the longer term, had this initiative become embedded into all four schools' curricula, such problems should have generally diminished.

Summary

This chapter has presented an in-depth account into the successes (Section 7.1) and challenges (Section 7.2) related to the delivery of the pilot Training Ward. Importantly, it discussed how valuable the students found the ward was in offering them shared time and space to work together as a team. In addition, it has discussed the importance of off-ward activities in enhancing the students' collaborative work. The chapter also indicated that the steering group overlooked a number of key factors while developing the project, which resulted in a number of challenges, which undermined the students' experience. In particular, it described how the steering group's oversights while developing the ward (Section 6.2.3) resulted in a number of difficulties for the students and the facilitators. In presenting this account, the chapter addressed the second of the study's objectives (to explore the factors that influenced the delivery of the Training Ward, see Section 1.2). In doing so it has offered an insight into some of the contents of the black box associated with the delivery of interprofessional education.

Given the acknowledged limitations of undertaking a single case study (see Section 5.1.6), the next chapter discusses the use of a structured case comparison, a technique that can be employed to help enhance the validity of case study findings.

Chapter 8: Findings from a comparison of cases

Introduction

This chapter presents details concerning a structured case comparison of this study with the published work from another similar case: the Swedish ward. Initially, Section 8.1 offers information relating to the rationale for and process of undertaking a comparison of this case with case study material from the Swedish ward. Section 8.2 presents the outcomes from the comparative process in relation to context and findings from these two cases. Finally, Section 8.3 provides a discussion of the implications from this technique.

8.1. Rationale and process

As discussed in Section 5.1.6, a structured case comparison, with published findings from one or more similar cases, is a technique that can help enhance the validity of findings from a single case study (Silverman 2000). Therefore, all the published material from the Swedish ward from which the steering group developed the basis of the Training Ward was obtained. In total, six papers were located from the Swedish ward (Sandén & Wahlström 1996, Walhström et al. 1996, 1997, Wahlström & Sandén 1998, Fallsberg & Wijma 1999, Fallsberg & Hammar 2000).

In terms of the process employed for this case comparison, a close reading and re-reading of each of the papers was undertaken, noting the key issues contained in each relating to context and findings. These notes were then compared with the contextual information gathered for the present study and each section of the findings contained in the thesis. The aim of this process was to identify key points of similarity between both cases.

144

8.2. Outcomes from the comparison process

Close scrutiny of the Swedish papers revealed that despite providing some useful descriptive information about the nature of their ward, most were unsuitable for use in a structured case comparison. Specifically, it was found that:

- Four of the papers (Sandén & Wahlström 1996, Walhström et al. 1996, 1997, Wahlström & Sandén 1998) contained no empirical data on the Swedish ward. Instead, they offered descriptions about the nature of the placement and a few author impressions of student reactions about this ward.

- Of the two evaluation papers, one (Fallsberg & Wijma 1999) provided quantitative findings from a questionnaire study that reported changes in students' attitudes, which offered little data for comparison with the findings from this study. The other (Fallsberg & Hammar 2000) offered qualitative data (semi-structured interviews exploring the students' experiences of the Swedish ward) that provided a firmer basis for a case comparison.

Consequently, the comparison of findings between cases has had to be restricted to the two evaluation papers (Fallsberg & Wijma 1999, Fallsberg & Hammar 2000). Nevertheless, the chapter does offer a comparison of contexts, in terms of location, evolution, design and contents of both placements, to help provide a better insight into the points of convergence and divergence of the two study settings.

8.2.1. Comparing contexts

This section provides a comparison of contexts related to the location, evolution, design and contents of these two placements. In terms of location, as discussed in Section 4.2.3, the Training Ward was sited in a large, busy inner city hospital, which served a socially and ethnically diverse, economically deprived local population. The hospital faced continually heavy demand for beds, which meant pressures on management to lower patient length of stay to increase throughout. The location of the Swedish ward was somewhat different. It was based in an affluent Swedish city, Linköping, which faced none of these social or economic pressures. As the following extract, taken from a visit I made to the ward in 1998 for the evaluation project, indicates:

> "There is a sharp contrast between Linköping Hospital and the [the Training Ward] in terms of health care resources. The Training Ward at Linköping is well resourced (staff, space, equipment, training)" (Freeth & Reeves 1999:109 original emphasis).

Despite being able to identify a striking difference between the ward locations, a comparison of the development processes related to the Swedish ward was more difficult. Indeed, only one of the papers (Wahlström et al. 1996) provided a brief description of how the placement was developed:

> "A planning group was formed with the aim of describing a model of a ward for patients needing care and rehabilitation provided by all categories of professions educated at FHS [Faculty of Health Sciences]. Staff representing the Department of Orthopaedics as well as the different educational programmes participated in the planning of the ward. The student-manned ward was subsequently implemented as a collaborative project between FHS and the University Hospital of Linköping." (Wahlström et al. 1996:264).

While it was possible to identify that the Swedish development group, like the Training Ward steering group, contained both educational and clinical staff, it is not possible to obtain any further comparative insights on this issue.

Given the relatively large amounts of description of the design and contents of the Swedish ward (Sandén & Wahlström 1996, Walhström et al. 1996, 1997, Wahlström & Sandén 1998), better comparisons of the initiatives can be made. As described in Section 4.2.3, the Sweden ward consisted of the following features:

- A compulsory two-week placement for final year students from nursing, medicine, occupational therapy, physiotherapy, social welfare and laboratory technology;
- Students worked together on an eight-bedded ward as an interprofessional team to provide care to orthopaedic patients;
- Students undertook both general caring and profession-specific work;
- Nurse facilitators worked with the student teams throughout the placement providing supervision. Students also received part-time profession-specific supervision from a consultant, a medical registrar, an occupational therapist and a physiotherapist;
- The placement had four learning aims (to develop skills for co-operation in a team; to increase their understanding of each other's professions; to increase students' understanding of the whole care of the patient; increase students' knowledge of practical experience of medical care and rehabilitation);
- The underpinning educational theory of the ward was PBL;
- Students worked two shifts: mornings and afternoons;
- Student teams attended team reflection sessions;
- Student learning was assessed by an interprofessional 'care conference', where students discussed issues relating to delivering team-based care.

As Section 4.2.4 discussed, the Training Ward developed by the steering group incorporated a number of aspects of the Swedish ward, which helped retain its essential character. These were:

- Basing the Training Ward in an orthopaedic setting;
- Adopting the same student working patterns and facilitation arrangements;
- Using student team reflection sessions;
- Concluding the placement with an interprofessional case conference;
- Retaining the ward's PBL approach.

One can, however, identify four main differences between the two initiatives. Firstly, as the steering group could not obtain an eight-bedded clinical area for the exclusive use of the Training Ward project, a 12-bedded area located the end of an orthopaedic ward was used. Secondly, due to professional validation restrictions, the Training Ward was a voluntary placement for most students, except the nursing students (who were randomly selected for the placement) and a handful of medical students (all of whom had failed a recent clinical examination). Thirdly, student participation in the Training Ward was restricted to four professional groups, as steering group members did not have links into schools of social welfare or laboratory technology. Finally, steering group members were keen to develop a comprehensive range of learning objectives for the Training Ward. Therefore they produced around ten profession-specific learning objectives for each student group and a further 19 team-oriented learning objectives for all student groups (see Appendix 4).

8.2.2. Comparing empirical data

As noted above, only two of the six Swedish papers (Fallsberg & Wijma 1999, Fallsberg & Hammar 2000) provided an empirical insight into the students' experiences of the ward. Based on the findings contained in these papers, one can identify the following salient points of comparison.

In relation to the first paper (Fallsberg & Wijma 1999), while its use of a before-and-after questionnaire design provides little basis for a comprehensive comparison with this study, the authors' discussion of their findings have a resonance with this study. Fallsberg & Wijma's (1999) evaluation indicated that, like this study (see Section 7.2.2), the use of both general caring duties and profession-specific duties were considered problematic by a number of the Swedish students. These authors note that many students saw general care work as "the goal of nursing" (Fallsberg & Wijma 1999:580). This activity was therefore viewed as having little resonance for the profession-specific development of the non-nursing students.

The most recent paper (Fallsberg & Hammar 2000) offers a more helpful basis for comparison. In this paper, the authors provide findings from a qualitative evaluation of the students' perceptions of the Swedish ward based on a small number of individual interviews with the students. A key finding from this study was that students felt they worked well together on the ward, planning and discussing their collaborative approaches to delivering patient care. Indeed, most stated that the ward had provided them with an "enjoyable time" (Fallsberg & Hammar 2000:346). Nevertheless, the data indicated that despite the ward's overarching aim of developing a more team-oriented approach among the students, this had limited success. In general, this evaluation found that a number of students tended to prioritise the development of profession-specific knowledge over the development of teamwork knowledge. As the authors noted, "a wish to obtain profession-specific knowledge dominates" (Fallsberg & Hammar 2000:346). Due to this emphasis on profession-specific development, it was unsurprising to find that the problem related to participation in general care work, again, emerged in the data:

> "A certain degree of resistance [to participating in general caring work] has been expressed mainly by the medical students [...] these students reported a feeling of being used as unpaid labour and did not see any benefits" (Fallsberg & Hammar 2000:338)

The authors go on to note that the nursing students felt they benefited most from participating in this type of work. Indeed, Fallsberg & Hammar (2000:348) argue that for the non-nursing students, undertaking general care work "seem to conflict" with their own profession-specific development. These authors conclude that such a conflict could be effectively overcome by removing the use of general caring work to provide students with a more realistic view of teamwork (i.e. one where students' professional roles do not overlap).

8.3. Implications from the case comparison

As described in Section 8.1, through the process of comparing one case study with another similar study, the case comparison technique can help to enhance the validity of the findings from a single case study. In relation to context issues between the two cases, despite the differing locations of the two initiatives, both shared a number of similarities in terms of their design and content. Indeed, given that the steering group directly transferred the Swedish model into the UK, it is not surprising to discover that both initiatives compare well in these two aspects. In relation to a comparison of findings between the cases, it was only possible to identify two main areas where empirical data offered a good comparison. Firstly, both the Swedish ward and the Training Ward provided students with a rewarding and enjoyable interprofessional experience. Secondly, the use of shared tasks ('general caring' in the Swedish ward, 'team duties' in the Training Ward) produced similar effects for students in both cases. Like the findings reported in Section 7.2.2, most of the Swedish students also viewed generic caring duties in poor terms and felt they interrupted their own profession-specific work.

Although the structured case comparison technique can help to enhance the validity of findings of a case study, as discussed above there was a limited amount of comparable data from the Swedish ward. Consequently, it has not been possible to make any claims for the validity of the study's findings by employing this particular technique.

Summary

This chapter has presented a comparison of findings from this case with findings from the Swedish ward. The chapter indicated that while there was a good basis for contextual comparison between the two initiatives in terms of design and content. However, limited comparable empirical data from the Swedish ward meant that it was not possible to make any claims for the validity of the study's findings by employing a structured case comparison.

The next chapter presents a discussion of the key findings discussed in Chapters 6 and 7 to provide a more informed understand of the successes and challenges related to the development and delivery of interprofessional education.

Chapter 9: Developing and delivering interprofessional education - understanding the successes and challenges

Introduction

This chapter discusses key findings related to the development and delivery of the Training Ward project to provide a more in-depth understanding of the study's findings. Initially, Section 9.1 provides a summary of the study (its emergence, main findings and limitations) to help frame the subsequent discussion. Section 9.2 begins to discuss the study's findings in relation to three key areas: how PBL was used in the Training Ward; the organisational context in which the Ward was developed; broader aspects related to the successes and challenges of implementing innovative projects like the Training Ward. Section 9.3 then presents an overview of the central argument of the thesis, which is expanded in Sections 9.4 to 9.8. Finally, Section 9.9 outlines how the study makes an original contribution to the interprofessional education literature. The chapter aims to provide an insight into central factors related to the development and delivery of practice-based interprofessional education. In doing so, the chapter addresses all the study's research objectives (Section 1.2).

9.1. Emergence of study, key findings and limitations

As discussed in Chapter 1, the study emerged from an empirical concern related to the interprofessional education literature. Specifically, an over-reliance on reporting outcomes in the research literature has meant that processes related to development and delivery activities have been overlooked. Consequently, as argued in Section 1.1 the literature contained two black box problems related to both the development and delivery of interprofessional education. Given the need to explore the nature of these factors, Chapter 5 described how symbolic interactionism (Blumer 1969) and ethnographic methods were employed to help open these two black boxes and begin to explore their contents.

Findings indicated that the steering group encountered the following successes and challenges during the development and delivery of the Training Ward project.

Developmental successes and challenges (Chapter 6)

- A shared enthusiasm for the Training Ward among steering group members provided a 'glue' that helped keep them together while they developed and delivered the project.
- Group members developed a positive interprofessional rapport, which helped support their joint work.
- The incorporation of a funded evaluation project into the Training Ward meant that members could understand the impact of this initiative in order to strengthen it.

Despite these successes, the steering group encountered the following challenges:

- The emergence of a four-member subgroup, whose enthusiasm for the Training Ward resulted in other members being excluded from making a number of key decisions on the development of the project.
- A shared enthusiasm for the Training Ward was also found to inhibit critical discussion on the design of this initiative and discussion of their group roles and processes, which resulted in problems in the design of the Ward and difficulties in steering group collaboration.
- Heavy workloads and a regular turnover of steering group members restricted the group's ability to work together in an effective manner.
- University timetabling, professional regulatory body restrictions and management change combined to restrict the development of the project. In addition, the loss of a clinical area in which to deliver the Training Ward due to organisational changes, resulted in an agreement that the steering group should disband.

Delivery successes and challenges (Chapter 7)

- A number of educational, professional and organisational difficulties were overcome to deliver an innovative four-week practice-based interprofessional education initiative.
- Students found that the pilot ward offered them a valuable practice-based teamwork experience, which provided them with a number of opportunities to share time and space together while working together.

- Students' off-ward team-based activities were considered another successful element of their pilot ward experience, as these activities helped support their on-ward patient care work.

However, oversights in the design of the pilot ward related to the incorporation of the Swedish model resulted in a number of challenges for students and the facilitators:

- Students felt poorly prepared to work as an interprofessional team. They also considered the incorporation of team duties created further difficulties in their collaborative work.
- Most students found a two-week placement an inadequate length of time for them to develop into an effective team. They also felt there were too many learning objectives to address during the placement, which created further anxiety.
- Students and facilitators struggled to employ PBL during the delivery of the pilot ward due to a lack of adequate preparation and support.
- Timetabling constraints and different validation requirements of the various professional bodies resulted in inequalities for student recruitment and assessment.

As discussed in Section 5.4.4, the study contains a number of limitations. Firstly, as it was only possible to gather four weeks' worth of data from the pilot ward, the insights related to the delivery of the Training Ward are inevitably less extensive than the insights gathered from two years with the steering group. Secondly, although the study generated some helpful observations of steering group and student interaction, these data were restricted to formal meetings and scheduled students' teamwork sessions. Therefore, the study failed to gather data on the interactions that occurred between these participants in other settings. While the study employed triangulation to help enhance its validity, one needs to acknowledge that this technique has its limitations. For example, its use does not necessarily guarantee that an analysis is correct (e.g. Hammersley & Atkinson 1995). Furthermore, to ensure that the research participants were not over-burdened with extra work, member validation was not employed in the study. Despite attempts to enhance the appropriateness of the study's findings by the use of thick description and theoretical generalisation, these techniques cannot overlook a key limitation: the research was undertaken in a single setting. This inevitably limits the claims one can make about the wider relevance of this work.

9.2. Successes and challenges: unpacking the issues

This section begins to discuss the study's findings to help understand the successes and challenges of developing and delivering the Training Ward, three key areas are considered. Firstly, Section 9.2.1 examines the successes and challenges associated with the use of the PBL model that underpinned the Training Ward. Secondly, Section 9.2.2 discusses how the organisational context in which the Training Ward project was located influenced the successes and challenges it encountered. Finally, to help understand the broader issues related to the development and delivery of the Training Ward, Section 9.2.3 considers the wider literature related to the success and challenges of implementing innovation.

9.2.1. Theoretical underpinnings of the Training Ward

As indicated in Section 4.2.3, staff in Sweden drew upon PBL to underpin the creation of the Linköping ward. Section 4.2.4 went on to describe how the steering group drew upon the design of this Swedish model to underpin the Training Ward. However, steering group data indicated that the steering group generally failed to fully assess the implications of implementing this PBL model when developing the Training Ward (Section 6.2.3). In particular, members overlooked two key features: the general lack of experience students had with using PBL and the amount of preparation and on-going support clinical staff (all new to PBL) required in order to facilitate effectively using this approach. The data indicated that these oversights constrained the delivery of the pilot ward in three ways. Firstly, students generally felt under-prepared for their work as an interprofessional team using PBL to support their learning (Section 7.2.1). Secondly, facilitators felt they did not fully understand how to effectively employ PBL on the pilot ward and adopted contrasting approaches, which the students reported as adding difficulties to their pilot ward experience (Section 7.2.5). Finally, the facilitators felt that their role was an exhausting one, which could result in burnout if they worked on the Training Ward over a longer period of time (Section 7.2.5).

Despite the challenges that emerged with in relation to overlooking the implications of employing the Swedish PBL model in the Training Ward, the steering group's use of a theoretically derived model should be regarded a success. As discussed in Section 3.1, it is rare that theory is explicitly employed to underpin an interprofessional initiative, as most initiatives employ theory on an implicit basis (e.g. Barber et al. 1997, Edward & Preece

1999, Alderson et al. 2002). However, as discussed above, in 'borrowing' this model from Sweden, group members did not pay close enough attention to operationalising it in their own initiative. This oversight is surprising for three reasons. Firstly, steering group members were offered information from Sweden on both the high levels of experience Swedish students had of PBL and the heavy demands made on the facilitators working on the ward (Wahlström & Sandén 1998). Secondly, apart from Sweden, no other interprofessional education initiative employed a PBL approach to support pre-qualification students in 'leading' the organisation and delivery of care to patients with real clinical needs. Typically PBL is a classroom activity. It is employed in the delivery of learning activities where students work together on 'solve' paper-based patient problems (e.g. Mann et al. 1996, Hughes & Lucas 1997). Thirdly, during the period the steering group was developing the Training Ward there was no empirical data on the Swedish model. Rather, there were only papers containing authors' descriptions of the initiative and some brief impressions of the impact of the initiative (Wahlström et al. 1997, Wahlström & Sandén 1998). Therefore, one could argue that given the lack of evidence for this model the steering group should have been more cautious, especially as the model employed PBL in an innovative fashion.

However, as argued in Section 6.2.3, the group's shared enthusiasm for progressing the Training Ward played a key role in overlooking potential challenges with this PBL model. (The nature of the steering group's enthusiasm is discussed in more depth in Section 9.4). Despite the steering group's oversights with this model, one should remember that the problems it generated were not fatal to the project. Indeed, as discussed in Section 6.2.6, the main cause of the demise of the Training Ward was an organisational change, which resulted in the withdrawal of a viable location for the Project. (The next section discusses the organisational context in which the Training Ward was located to understand the nature of its influence on the project).

9.2.2. Contextual influences on the Training Ward

As outlined in Section 4.1.1, the Training Ward project was delivered in a large, busy inner-city hospital, which faced heavy demands for beds. These pressures were combined with staff retention and recruitment problems and also the need for hospital managers to meet national political pressures to provide efficient, high quality care. Given the nature of this context, a key success for the steering group members was that they developed and delivered an innovative interprofessional pilot ward experience to students from four professions (see Section 7.1.1).

Nevertheless, the study indicated that the group's work was constrained by a number of organisational influences. Firstly, all members worked on the Training Ward while managing heavy workloads associated with their own educational or clinical posts. Consequently, as discussed in Section 6.2.4.2, group members' regularly struggled to find enough time to work on the project. Secondly, a relatively high turnover of steering group members, as reported in Section 6.2.4.1, undermined the cohesion of the group. In addition, a change of senior management in one of the four schools involved in the project resulted in the group losing a senior supporter to be replaced of an individual who was, initially, more ambivalent about the project (Section 6.2.6.1). Furthermore, a hospital-wide reform of its management structure meant the substitution of a steering group member who managed the directorate in which the pilot ward was delivered with someone who was less enthusiastic (Section 6.2.6.1).

In relation to the literature, a number of studies have reported similar challenges when attempting to develop and deliver new initiatives into a changing or 'turbulent' organisational context (e.g. Richards & Horder 1999, Cozijnsen et al. 2000, Lorenzi & Riley 2003, Wildridge et al. 2004, Greenhalgh et al. 2004). As noted in Section 4.1.1, Bridges (2004) undertook a study in the same hospital as that in which the Training Ward was developed and delivered. This study therefore provides a useful insight into the effect of the local organisational context on the project. Bridges' study examined the introduction of a new 'care co-ordinator' role[47] within the general and emergency medical directorate. She found that a key challenge in the implementation of this initiative was the "turbulent [organisational] context" (Bridges 2004:155). In particular, it was found that directorate managers faced a number of pressures, such as turnover of staff and organisational re-structuring, which inhibited the success of the care co-ordinator project. In addition, Bridges found that the introduction of this new role was affected by the need for managers to meet top down (government driven) targets for improvements in the effectiveness of patient care. Importantly, Bridges found that these different pressures contributed to a loss of original vision of the project and the emergence of a 'fuzzy' or unclear view of the innovation among the new staff. Reflecting upon the nature of this local organisational context, Bridges (2004:166) states:

---

[47] The care co-ordinator role was developed to ensure that a patient's stay in hospital is only as long as clinically necessary. Care co-ordinators therefore attempt to reduce the number and length of 'blockages' in the path of patient care and discharge by identifying any potential discharge delays that could occur. They also help to ensure clinical investigations are conducted on time and to begin co-ordinating the patient's discharge.

"A turbulent environment meant that managers and practitioners were too caught up with daily pressures [to attend to the innovation project]".

Given the nature of the literature discussed in this section, and in particular Bridges' study, one can begin to understand the potential impact of a turbulent organisational environment on the introduction of new initiatives. Due to its potential effect, one should to pay close attention to organisational context when involved in the development and delivery of a new initiative. Indeed, as discussed in Section 6.2.6, an on-going organisational turbulence within the hospital in which the Training Ward was due to be re-established after the delivery of its pilot ward played a significant role in ultimately undermining the project. Specifically, a continued pressure on beds resulted in senior hospital management agreeing to change the clinical area earmarked for the Training Ward into an acute admissions unit. Due to a hospital-wide shortage of beds no suitable replacement ward could be found for the project. Ultimately, the effect of this organisational influence was that the group agreed to disband.

9.2.3. Exploring the wider issues related to introducing innovation

To obtain a more informed understanding of the successes and challenges of the Training Ward, this section discusses them in relation to the wider literature on the implementation of innovation (e.g. change management initiatives, educational programmes, CQI/TQM projects).

As discussed in the section above, the turbulent organisational context in which the Training Ward was developed and delivered played an important role in ultimately undermining the project. Indeed, many studies have found that organisational stability, particularly in terms of low turnover of staff, is a key ingredient an achieving success with the implementation of an innovation (e.g. Mattessich et al. 2001, McNulty & Ferlie 2002, Smith 2003, Ross et al. 2005). For example, in a study of the introduction of a new 'tiered' model of care[48] in a mental healthcare setting, data gathered by Kaner et al. (2003) indicated that the absence of a stable environment was a key factor in constraining the success of embedding this innovation into clinical practice.

Another key factor that undermined the success of the Training Ward was the loss of key clinical and educational management supporters (Section 6.2.6.1). In relation to the literature, it has been found that management support helps to ensure that a project has

---

[48] Kaner et al. (2003:520) describe this tiered model as "a framework for matching mental healthcare to need whilst balancing service constraints".

sufficient resources (funds and time) to achieve success in its implementation (e.g. Mattessich et al. 2001, Lorenzi & Riley 2003, Wildridge et al. 2004). For Lajara et al. (2003:64) organisational management also have a role to play in explicitly demonstrating their "commitment and enthusiasm" for a project, which in turn demonstrates that the innovation is important and worthy of support by all staff.

As discussed in Section 6.2.3, the steering group's enthusiasm for developing and delivering the Training Ward resulted in them failing to pay close enough attention to the complex nature of implementing an innovative interprofessional education model in a busy clinical environment. Kaplan & Shaw (2002) argue that group members need to share an awareness of the complex nature of implementing innovation. Under-estimating its complexity can often result in failure, as staff are poorly prepared to manage the complicated range of issues connected with this activity. Indeed, in their review of the implementation of innovation within health care organisations Greenhalgh et al. (2004) found that such projects were often constrained by complexity. This often meant that groups needed to work in a flexible manner, with movement:

> "Back and forth between initiation, development and implementation, punctuated variously by shocks, setbacks and surprises" (Greenhalgh et al. 2004:16).

While the steering group overlooked the complex nature of employing an innovative model in a clinical setting, as Section 7.1.1 discussed, they were successful in navigating a route through a range of 'setbacks and surprises' that led them to deliver the four-week Training Ward pilot. Nevertheless, the group encountered continued organisational complexity while attempting to re-establish the Training Ward, which ultimately undermined the viability of the project.

The steering group also collectively failed to explore their expected aims and goals of the Training Ward, which resulted in group members having a range of differing and competing visions about the project (Section 6.2.2). In relation to this issue, the literature maintains that groups implementing innovative projects need to hold a clear, shared vision of the aims and goals of the project to ensure it success (Mattessich et al. 2001, Wildridge et al. 2004, Couchman & Fulop 2004). In addition, Section 6.2.2 indicated that the steering group neglected to consider their group roles and group processes. This oversight resulted in the emergence of tensions between group members. The literature indicates that members involved in implementing innovation need pay particular attention to such issues. In particular, the need for effective group leadership had been found to be a key factor in the successful implementation of innovation (e.g. Cozijnsen et al. 2000,

Mattessich et al. 2001, Kaplan & Shaw 2002). Furthermore, the literature has found that groups involved in innovative work need to pay attention to their collaborative processes to achieve success in these shared activities (e.g. Mattessich et al. 2001, Lajara et al. 2003, Eales-White 2004). For Wildridge et al. (2004:7) a crucial part of this collaboration is that all group members assume joint ownership and responsibility for their innovation:

"Joint ownership of decisions and collective responsibility for the direction and activities of the collaboration are required"

In helping to distil the various factors linked to success in the development and delivery of innovation, Smith's (2003) paper analysing the implementation of such work within 59 different organisations offers the following findings:

"[Successful innovation was] kept small and manageable, a dedicated, capable team was assigned to the project, there was vision and support from the sponsor [senior management] throughout the project" (Smith 2003:256).

In relation to Smith's findings, the steering group in this study did not meet most of these requirements. For example, they were a rather large group (usually consisting of around 12 to 14 members). In addition, group members' vision of the project was not consistently shared, as they never discussed their expectations of the project. Nor did the group have stable management support during the period in which they worked on the Training Ward. Nevertheless, all members were dedicated to the development and delivery of the project, and worked hard in attempting to achieve this goal. Moreover, the group demonstrated a range of capabilities in overcoming many of the numerous organisational challenges they encountered while working together on the project.

Given the complex range of factors involved in the development and delivery of innovative projects like the Training Ward, it is unsurprising to discover that a relatively high proportion of projects are ultimately unsuccessful. For example, in his review of the implementation of work-based learning initiatives, Carr (1996) found that between 20-30 per cent of all projects resulted in failure. Similarly, in their examination of the introduction of innovative change management initiatives within 50 commercial organisations Cozijnsen et al. (2000) found that 39 per cent of projects were unsuccessful.

As discussed above, the literature on the implementation of innovation indicates that this type of activity involves the need to navigate around a complex range of factors. Success is therefore difficult to achieve, as both macro (structural) and micro (group-based) factors can impede the development and implementation of such innovative project work. Having begun to unpack the successes and challenges associated with developing and delivering the Training Ward, the subsequent sections of this chapter draw together the study's key findings. In doing so, the chapter discusses, in depth, the influence of the four key elements (enthusiasm, backstage work, negotiation and group development) on the development and delivery of the Training Ward.

9.3. Central argument of the thesis

Despite the many successes achieved by the steering group (Sections 6.1 and 7.1), the numerous internal and external challenges they encountered (Sections 6.2 and 7.2) conspired to undermine the Training Ward and ultimately resulted in its failure. In understanding these factors related to the development and delivery of the project (research objective one – to explore the factors that influenced the *development* of the Training Ward; and research objective two – to explore the factors that influenced the *delivery* of this initiative), the thesis argues that:

- Enthusiasm had a both facilitative and inhibitory effect on the development and delivery of the project.
- Pre-arranged 'overt' informal backstage work played a crucial role in the overall success of the project. However, the effect of using 'covert' backstage work was more mixed: despite supporting the development of the Training Ward, it also undermined the quality of steering group relationships.
- While the steering group's use of 'outcome-orientated' negotiations were vital to achieving their collective goals in the development of the project, unlike the students, the group neglected to employ 'process-orientated' negotiations (focused on supporting their shared work), which contributed to a poorer quality of collaboration. In addition, a number of structural factors, such as organisational change and professional regulations, constrained the effects of the negotiations undertaken by the steering group.
- A lack of time together for both steering group members (during their developmental work) and students (during the delivery of the pilot ward) meant that there was insufficient time to develop and perform together as an effective team.

In addition, the thesis argues that to begin to understand the relationship between the development and delivery of the Training Ward (research objective three – to examine the relationship between the development and delivery of this initiative):

- Course planning groups need to manage the effects of the four factors (enthusiasm, backstage work, negotiation, group development) during the development of an initiative. A failure to manage these factors when developing an initiative is likely to result in the emergence of problems when delivering it, as development and delivery activities are closely entwined.

9.3.1. Using theory to illuminate the issues

As discussed in Section 3.1, there is a limited use of theory within the interprofessional education literature. When theory is employed, it is done so for two reasons. Firstly, to underpin the development of an initiative, adult learning (mostly used on an implicit basis), organisational learning and social psychological theories (most notably contact theory) are drawn upon. Secondly, to help make sense of findings related to the delivery of an interprofessional initiative, a handful of sociological, psychodynamic and groupwork theories have been employed. While these theories have helped to support the development of interprofessional education and have helped explain empirical data related to its delivery, they are unhelpful in beginning to understand the key findings from the current study. Therefore, theoretical work from the sociological and social psychological literature has been drawn upon to examine the four factors that emerged from the study. The search for theories was restricted to these two bodies of literature as they offered the richest seam of work that helped explain the nature of team/group processes and interactions. Importantly, these perspectives provided the 'best fit' in terms of offering new insights into the development and delivery of a practice-based interprofessional education initiative. The following four perspectives were selected:

- Janis' (1982) theory of groupthink is employed to help understand the inhibitory effects of the steering group's enthusiasm on the development and delivery of the Training Ward project.
- Goffman's (1963) concept of backstage performance is drawn upon to help illuminate the uses and 'abuses' of informal work within the development and delivery of the Training Ward project.
- Strauss' (1978) negotiated order perspective is used to help understand the role of steering group and student negotiations in achieving success within the Training Ward project, and how structural factors can constrain the effects of negotiation.
- Tuckman & Jensen's (1977) model of group development is employed to help illuminate how a lack of time together for both the steering group and students, undermined their ability to develop and perform together in an effective manner.

Sections 9.4 to 9.7 provide detailed descriptions of each perspective, a rationale for their selection and a critical discussion relating to their use in the thesis.

9.4. Enthusiasm: a double-edged sword

This section examines how enthusiasm was both a facilitative and inhibitory factor in the development and delivery of the Training Ward project. It also discusses how Janis' (1982) theory of groupthink can help explain the problems generated by the steering group's enthusiasm for the project.

As indicated in Section 6.1, the steering group's shared enthusiasm for the Training Ward was one of the project's key successes. In particular, it provided a 'glue' that helped keep group members working together for over two years. Indeed, the group's enthusiasm helped them overcome a variety of internal and external challenges they encountered during their collaborative work. For example, it helped ensure that they contributed to the project while managing heavy workloads associated with their clinical or educational posts. The group's shared enthusiasm also helped them to cope with a regular turnover of members that undermined their cohesion as a group. Furthermore, it helped them to navigate their way around school curricula (e.g. timetable restrictions) and professional regulatory body limitations (e.g. different requirements for student assessment) that constrained the project.

However, the steering group's enthusiasm also caused a number of problems for their own collaborative work and for the pilot ward they delivered. Firstly, as indicated in Section 6.2.1, following their return from a visit to the Swedish ward, the enthusiasm of a four-member subgroup led all members to reverse their initial decision, and create a Training Ward experience that contained the emerging problems associated with the Swedish model (Section 6.2.3). Indeed, the subgroup's enthusiasm for this model encouraged other group members to accept its use within the project. Consequently, as discussed in Section 7.2, the group delivered a pilot ward that contained similar problems (overlap into the nursing students' role, insufficient team development time, competing learning objectives) that were found in the Swedish ward. In addition, a shared enthusiasm for the development of the Training Ward appeared to result in a lack of critical assessment concerning the Swedish model's use of PBL. This, in turn, resulted in problems for the students and facilitators during the delivery of the pilot ward. The group's shared enthusiasm also appeared to result in members failing to agree group roles and expectations that could have enhanced their collaborative work (Section 6.2.2). Furthermore, unlike the students, the steering group failed to undertake shared reflection activities that could have improved their own collaborative work (Section 6.2.2). Group members' enthusiasm was, however, tempered by the production of the evaluation project, which outlined the problematic nature of the model in relation to poor preparation, the sharing of roles and a limited time for team development (Section 6.2.3.3). Nevertheless, their enthusiasm to progress the Training Ward project meant that most members continued to overlook any of the possible problems in the way they worked together (Section 6.2.2).

Given the facilitative and inhibitory nature of enthusiasm within the Training Ward project, it can be argued that enthusiasm within interprofessional education is a 'double-edged sword'. Although it provided a vital ingredient for steering group members in their work developing and delivering the project, it led the group to become uncritical, which generated problems in their own collaborative work and problems in the pilot ward they delivered. The notion of a duality within enthusiasm provides a new insight into the nature of enthusiasm. To date, both the interprofessional education literature (e.g. Lary et al. 1997, Harris et al. 2003) and in the wider literature (e.g. Seel 1994, Illeris 2003) has viewed enthusiasm in positive terms. In contrast, the study has indicated that enthusiasm is a more complex phenomenon, having both a constructive and disruptive side.

9.4.1. Groupthink theory to illuminate the problems of enthusiasm

To help illuminate the problems created by the steering group's enthusiasm, Janis' (1982) theory of groupthink is drawn upon. This theory was selected as it highlights the problems that can occur when groups, like the members of the steering group, work together without adopting a critical stance. Indeed, as the literature has not explored the 'darker side' of enthusiasm, this theory is particularly effective in beginning to view it in a more problematic manner.

Janis developed his theory from an analysis of documentary materials from a number of well-publicised political incidents, including the Bay of Pigs crisis (where America almost bombed Cuba with nuclear missiles in the late 1960s) and the Three Mile Island nuclear disaster in the early 1970s. Janis found that in each case, the group managing the situation appeared to 'lose' their ability for critical analysis in their discussions and decision making. In addition, each group 'closed ranks' around (erroneous) decisions they had made, as they assumed their decisions were correct. Furthermore, all group members rejected information that contradicted their shared view. Drawing upon data from each of these cases, Janis identified seven *antecedents* that played a part in the development of groupthink: high group cohesion; high stress from outside threat; the fear of failure; a lack of impartial leadership; insulation from outside expertise; a lack of methodical decision making and homogeneity of members. Janis also went on to identify seven *indicators of defective decision-making* resulting from groupthink: the poor search for information; selective bias in processing information; incomplete assessment of objectives; incomplete assessment of alternative ideas; failure to examine preferred choice; failure to re-examine rejected alternative ideas and failure to develop contingency plans. Summarising the effects of groupthink, Watts & Bennett (1983:317) state that when this phenomenon occurs:

> "[A group] ceases to pay attention to information that conflicts with its general assumptions, and strong social pressures are brought to bear on any members who challenge these assumptions".

Research into the nature of decision-making in groups, particularly in management settings, continues to employ Janis' theory to help explain problems that emerge when a group fails to adopt a critical stance (e.g. Hart et al. 1996, Schafer & Crichlow 2002). Nevertheless, while Janis' theory remains generally well regarded by social psychologists (e.g. Raven 1998), it does have several critics who claim that Janis was inconsistent in his use of research and theory in the formation of groupthink. For example, McCauley (1998) argues Janis' claim that high cohesion between group members' results in poor quality decision making is not supported by the empirical literature, which indicates that cohesion can be a helpful factor. In addition, Mullen et al. (1994:200) point out that while research indicates group size to be "a potent predictor of group phenomena", Janis neglects to pay any attention to the possible effects of this factor in his theory.

9.4.2. Groupthink in the Training Ward

Despite such limitations, Janis' theory helps to illuminate the problems that enthusiasm caused within the steering group when members failed to adopt a critical stance. Indeed, in the absence of a literature that regards enthusiasm to have a detrimental effect, this theory can begin to provide an insight into its potentially problematic side.

In relation to Janis' theory, as previously indicated, the steering group's shared enthusiasm for the Training Ward resulted in them becoming uncritical of both the model they were aiming to implement and in their collaborative work. In doing so, the group displayed one of the main characteristics of groupthink: an absence of critical analysis in their decision making. Indeed, when the group was offered feedback produced from the evaluation project and the Swedish ward, they overlooked the potential problems this work highlighted, thus displaying another of the main characteristics of groupthink: an unwillingness to accept alternative (contradictory) viewpoints. On this point, when a small number of members expressed concerns about the problems they saw in the group's approach to working together, they only fed these views into the study. The reason for this behaviour was that they did not want to be considered a 'doubting Thomas' in the face of the group's, especially the subgroup's, enthusiasm for the project.

However, while the steering group appeared to contain most of the antecedents required for the emergence of groupthink, two were seemingly missing: 'high stress from outside threat' (the group did not experience high stress from an external threat) and 'homogenous group membership' (as members were from different professional and clinical backgrounds).   Nevertheless, the group did contain most antecedents. Importantly, the (informal) 'un-impartial leadership' offered by the subgroup appeared to be a key factor in the development of an uncritical view of the Swedish model. In addition, given the group's enthusiasm for the Training Ward project, all members were anxious to see it succeed. Therefore, it could be argued that members shared a 'fear of failure'. Similarly, it could be argued that the group were 'insulated from outside expertise', as they overlooked emerging the feedback they were given on their collaborative work and published work on model they were aiming to deliver.   Furthermore, while 'high group cohesion' was, at times, somewhat absent from the main steering group, due mainly to a turnover of group members, for certain periods they did work together in a cohesive manner. Indeed, the four members of the subgroup did collaborate in a highly cohesive manner.

Similarly, while the steering group appeared to contain most of the indicators of defective decision-making linked to groupthink, two were absent. The first, 'incomplete assessment of objectives' was absent, as the group were clear around the objectives to develop the Training Ward along Swedish lines. The second, 'failure to develop contingency plans' was absent, as the group did initiate a number of contingency plans to help navigate the project around a number of challenges they encountered (e.g. a change of senior management, differing professional regulatory body requirements).   Nevertheless, it could be argued that the group contained five of the indicators of groupthink described by Janis. For example, in relation to the 'poor search for information', the group tended to use one main source of information for the development of the Training Ward: impressions gathered from the subgroup's visit to the Swedish ward. Similarly, in relation to an 'incomplete assessment of alternative ideas', the enthusiasm within the subgroup for the Swedish model played an influential role in the wider group accepting it. Thus they overlooked alternative interprofessional education models.

However, as noted above, the production of the evaluation report (Freeth & Reeves 1999) following the pilot ward did result in the group becoming more critical of the model they had delivered. They therefore began modifying it before attempting to re-establish the project. Nevertheless, in the group's shared enthusiasm to re-establish the Training Ward, they continued to display a lack of critical analysis concerning group roles and collaborative processes, an oversight that continued for another 12 months, until the group disbanded. Therefore, while the relevance of groupthink within the steering group diminished in one area, it persisted in another.

While one could argue that the absence of some of Janis' antecedents and indicators mean the use of groupthink is problematic, given the uncertainties expressed about this theory (e.g. Mullen et al. 1994, McCauley 1998), such absences do result in a flexibility over the application of this theory. For example, further research into the nature of groups may indicate that enthusiasm emerges as another antecedent of groupthink. Similarly, while no account of the emergence of subgroups and their role in contributing to the development of groupthink has so far been offered, future work may indicate that such alliances are influential. Moreover, one needs to consider the argument presented by Rosander et al. (1998:81) who maintain that groupthink should not be regarded as a "variance" theory (one which attempts to explain what causes an outcome), but more as a "process" theory (one which tells a story of how a phenomenon might develop). Given this argument, the use of groupthink does not strictly depend on a group meeting all of Janis' 14 different criteria. Therefore, the emergence of groupthink may still occur without all of the original antecedents and indicators being met.

Despite its shortcomings, Janis' theory provides a useful tool to begin to illuminate the problematic effect that enthusiasm can have on the development and delivery of an interprofessional education initiative. In particular, its use has indicated how enthusiasm for interprofessional education may contribute to the emergence of effects of groupthink.

9.5. Backstage work: uses and abuses

This section examines how informal backstage work, like enthusiasm, both facilitated and inhibited the development and delivery of the Training Ward project. It also discusses how Goffman's (1963) concept of backstage performance can be employed to illuminate the role of 'behind the scenes' work in the Training Ward.

While the use of front stage work was central to both steering group members (for their formal meetings) and students (to deliver care to patients), the use of backstage work played an equally, if not more important role in supporting the Training Ward. As discussed in Section 7.1.4, during their pilot ward placement the students regularly undertook pre-arranged *overt backstage work* during their team planning, handover and reflection activities. The students regarded this use of informal work as a valuable and beneficial element of their pilot ward experience, as it helped to ensure that they worked together in a co-oriented fashion during front stage work on the ward. Similarly, most steering group members undertook backstage work on a pre-arranged overt basis. For example, after agreement, members spent time outside meetings undertaking backstage negotiations with their respective professional regulatory bodies to ensure that students could participate in the project (Section 6.1.1). In addition, members spent time outside the meetings preparing the clinical environment and recruiting clinical staff to participate in the project. Consequently, like the students, steering group members viewed overt backstage work as a valuable aspect of their work. Indeed, without the use of this type of informal work, it is unlikely that group members could have delivered the Training Ward pilot. However, as outlined in Section 6.2.1, in their enthusiasm to progress the Training Ward members of the subgroup also undertook *covert backstage work*. Without informing the rest of the group, subgroup members informally met with senior school and hospital managers to help secure the delivery of the project. Despite agreeing that this type of backstage work contributed to the development of the Training Ward, its covert nature was nevertheless viewed by most members as problematic. In general, it was felt that this type of backstage work excluded them from making key decisions on the project. Consequently, it was felt that the use of covert backstage work undermined the quality of steering group members' relationships.

Given the constructive and more disruptive effects of backstage work, the use of these activities within interprofessional education, like enthusiasm, should be considered as having two dimensions. While the use of overt and (to some degree) covert backstage work supported the development and delivery of the Training Ward, the use of covert work within the steering group also had a detrimental effect on the quality of their relationships. Although the interprofessional education literature offers no insight into the use of informal work in the development and delivery of an initiative, the wider literature provides a more helpful picture. This work reveals that backstage activities can be employed to support more formal activities (e.g. Hyland & Morse 1995, Schlomann 1996). For example, Krogstad et al. (2002) revealed how health professionals working in hospital settings used backstage discussions to support their formal decisions on patient care. The literature fails, however, to provide any account of the possible problems associated with this type of informal work. Therefore, the emergence of backstage work as having two separate dimensions provides a new insight into the nature of backstage group work.

9.5.1. Backstage performance: understanding informal work

Goffman's (1963) concept of backstage performance is employed to illuminate how the informal work undertaken by both the steering group and the students was crucial to their formal work. Goffman's concept was selected as it provides a unique account of the central role informal activities plays in social interaction.

Backstage performance is one of the core tenets of Goffman's (1962) theory on the presentation of self. Goffman developed this theory from his anthropological fieldwork exploring the nature of social interaction within a small rural community. Goffman's data indicated that communication between individuals took the form of linguistic (verbal) and non-linguistic (body language) gestures employed when individuals present their selves to others. In general, Goffman found that individuals over-communicate gestures that reinforce their desired self and under-communicate gestures that they wish to detract from themselves. Goffman called this process 'impression management', whereby impressions of self are actively managed by individuals during their social interactions. For Goffman, the presentation process was regarded as a 'performance', which was undertaken in two distinct areas:

- Public "front region performances" (Goffman 1963:109) such as meetings between work colleagues or professional-patient consultations;
- Private "back region performances" (Goffman 1963:114) such as interactions between friends and family members.

Goffman argued that front region performances were formal and restrained in nature. In contrast, back region performances were more informal, allowing the individual to "relax [...] and step out of [their front region] character" (Goffman 1963:115). Importantly, Goffman viewed backstage regions as key locations where individuals could prepare for their front stage performances. Goffman therefore regarded the activities that took place in private settings as crucial in supporting the activities that occurred in public settings. Joseph (1990:316) provides a useful summary of this work:

> "There is a back 'region' where the show is prepared and we rehearse our parts; and a 'front region' where the performance is presented to an audience".

Research on the socialisation of nursing students (Melia 1987) and medical students (Sinclair 1997) has indicated the significance of front and backstage performances in the socialisation processes of these students. Both studies found that all students employed backstage regions to practice a 'professional' front stage performance, in readiness for their work as qualified practitioners. In addition, Hodges (2003) has employed Goffman's theory to begin to understand the nature of the performances given by the various individuals (student, examiner, patient) involved within a objective structured clinical examination (OSCE), an assessment that forms a key role within the training of medical students. However, Goffman's (1963) theory has been criticised in a number of areas. For example, Collins (1980) argues that Goffman's over-emphasis on micro-level interactions has resulted in a theory that neglects the influence of social structures on individual interactions. Goffman has also been criticised for offering a Machiavellian view of social life, one in which backstage preparations can be viewed as helping to create a "false [front stage] impressions" (Tanner & Timmons 2000:978).

9.5.2. Employing backstage work in the Training Ward

Despite these limitations, Goffman's (1963) concept of backstage performance can help to illuminate the importance of informal work in the development and delivery of the Training Ward project. Furthermore, as noted above, no other perspective could be located in the literature that helped to explain the nature of informal work in such compelling terms.

In relation to Goffman's theory, as discussed above, the students' use of backstage work during their team planning and reflection sessions was considered a valuable element of their pilot ward experience. It helped ensure that they worked together in a co-oriented fashion. Similarly, steering group members' use of backstage work in their negotiations with senior managers, professional regulatory body representatives and clinical staff was also considered a valuable aspect of their work in developing the Training Ward. The subgroup's use of exclusionary backstage work was, however, viewed in a more cautious way. While it assisted the development of the project, it also undermined the group's relationships.

Although Goffman's work helpfully illuminates the significance of backstage work in the Training Ward, importantly, this study also indicated that backstage work can be divided into two subsets: pre-arranged 'overt' and more exclusionary 'covert' backstage work. As noted above, the use of overt backstage work made a positive contribution to the development and delivery of the Training Ward. In contrast, the use of covert backstage work had a more mixed effect. Although it supported the steering group's work on the project, its use also had a detrimental effect on the quality of the group members' relationships. In many respects, one could argue that the 'behind the scenes' work that was undertaken by steering group members was a 'normal' element of committee groupwork, as information is regularly exchanged between members before a committee formally meets. Nevertheless, this study helped to shed empirical light, for the first time, on the 'uses' and 'abuses' that can occur when informal groupwork is undertaken in the development and delivery of an interprofessional education initiative.

In summary, the use of Goffman's concept of backstage performance provides a new insight into the nature of backstage work undertaken in an interprofessional education context. Unlike previous research, which has found the use of backstage work to only have a facilitative effect in supporting front stage work (e.g. Melia 1987, Sinclair 1997), the study has indicated that it can produce both positive and more problematic effects on a group's work. While overt backstage work can facilitate a group's front stage work, covert backstage work can be damaging on a group's relationships.

9.6. The uses and limitations of negotiation

This section examines, on one hand, how negotiation was crucial to both steering group members and students, and on the other, how the effectiveness of steering group negotiation was impeded by a variety of external constraining factors. It also discusses how Strauss' (1978) negotiated order perspective can be employed to illuminate the uses and limitations of negotiation in the Training Ward project.

As discussed in Sections 6.2.5 and 6.2.6, steering group members employed negotiation in attempting to achieve their main outcome: the successful development and delivery of the Training Ward project. In doing so, steering group members undertook a series of *outcome-oriented negotiations*. This type of negotiation was employed in their backstage work with:

- Senior managers (to obtain students, staff and ward space for the project);
- Representatives from the different professional regulatory bodies (to obtain their agreement for student involvement in the project);
- Clinical staff (to ensure they would work as facilitators on the ward).

Steering group members also employed outcome-oriented negotiation during their monthly meetings, to ensure the creation of the project and agree its parameters. In general, therefore, this type of activity produced the project's aims and objectives, generated roles and activities for project participants and secured the location for the pilot ward. In addition, steering group members employed outcome-oriented negotiation to problem solve a range of difficulties they encountered on the Training Ward project. For example, this form of negotiation played a central role in gaining the support of a new (initially ambivalent) senior school manager. Only through a process of negotiation with the new manager did the group obtain the support needed for the school's continued participation in the project.

Negotiation also played an important role for the students who, in contrast to the steering group, employed both outcome-oriented and *process-orientated negotiation* (a form of negotiation which focused on supporting the collaborative processes involved in the students' joint work). As indicated in Section 7.1.4, students regularly undertook outcome-orientated negotiation during their work both on the ward and during their backstage team planning sessions. In addition, students used process-orientated negotiation within their reflection sessions, where they discussed the processes of their ward-based teamwork and explored how to improve their collaborative work. Collectively, both forms of negotiation helped the students to achieve a balance in achieving their collective goal of delivering patient care and paying attention to their collaborative group processes. Such a balance was, however, absent from the steering group. Indeed, as discussed in Section 6.2.2, in their enthusiasm to progress the Training Ward project the group failed to consider the processes of their collaborative work, which appeared to produce a number of difficulties in the way in which they worked together.

Although the steering group's negotiations supported the development of the Training Ward project and the delivery of the pilot ward, they were constrained by three main external factors. Firstly, the four school's curricula and professional regulatory body inflexibility resulted in inequalities in student recruitment into the pilot ward (some students volunteered, others were 'requested' to participate), and inequalities for student assessment (for some students the placement contributed to their course completion criteria, for others it did not). While the group was successful in accommodating these educational and professional constraints in the Training Ward pilot, it was done so at the unavoidable expense of undermining the overall quality of students' interprofessional experiences (Section 7.2.6). Secondly, a lack of available time, due to workload pressures, meant that members regularly missed meetings and failed to complete tasks in between meetings. Inevitably, this restricted progress on the Training Ward. Finally, a 'turbulent' organisational context, specifically a heavy demand for hospital services and a lack of available beds meant that it was not possible to re-establish the project following its pilot phase. The group therefore decided that further negotiation would be fruitless. Indeed, it was agreed that efforts to find another suitable clinical space for the project would take too much additional time and effort. Consequently, the group agreed to cease work on the project and disband the steering group (Section 6.2.6).

The use of both outcome-oriented and process-oriented negotiation within the Training Ward project were key elements to its success. While outcome-oriented negotiation provided a focus on attaining collective goals, the use of process-oriented negotiation helped ensure that collaborative processes were also considered. However, the effects of educational, professional and organisational constraining factors impeded the influence of the steering group's outcome-orientated negotiation and ultimately contributed to the failure of the Training Ward project. Although the teamwork literature has found that a focus on both shared team goals and attention to team processes is vital for the successful function of health and social teams (Øvretveit 1993, Williams & Laungani 1999, Onyett 2003), the explicit role of negotiation in this type of work is generally overlooked. Similarly, while it could be argued that negotiation is implicitly used during the development of an interprofessional education initiative through the discussions undertaken by course planning groups (e.g. Stanford & Yelloly et al. 1994, Richards & Horder 1999), this literature also fails to recognise the explicit role of outcome-oriented and process-oriented negotiation.

9.6.1. Negotiated order perspective: understanding individual interactions and external constraints

Strauss' (1978) negotiated order perspective is used to help illuminate how negotiations can achieve change within organisations and how negotiation can also be constrained by external (structural) factors. Strauss' theory was selected as the continued use of negotiation in both the steering group and students' work in the Training Ward project meant that it had a direct relevance for the study's findings. In addition, no other theoretical work was found that could be employed to help explain the uses and limitations of negotiation.

Drawing upon interactionism, the negotiated order perspective was developed by Strauss et al. (1963) from their research into the nature of staff relations within psychiatric hospitals. For these authors, previous explanations of social order within organisations tended to stress formal structures and rules, and neglect the influence micro-level

171

negotiations. For Strauss and his colleagues, negotiation between individuals (through bargaining, compromising, mediating, etc) essentially creates and shapes organisational rules and structures. Consequently, micro-level negotiation contributes to the development and maintenance of social order that exists within an organisation.

Strauss (1978) modified this theory following criticism that it failed to pay sufficient attention to the influence of structural factors (e.g. Day & Day 1977, Benson 1977). He subsequently argued that although micro-level negotiation was central to creating and maintaining organisational life, negotiations were also constrained by the existence of structural influences. However, in keeping faithful to his interactionist roots, Strauss continued to argue that while macro influences provided the parameters for relationships, micro level negotiations still played the pivotal role in forming and shaping organisational life.

Research using Strauss' negotiated order perspective has revealed that this theory can be usefully employed to understand how micro-level negotiations shape organisational life (e.g. Busch 1982, Hall & Spencer-Hall 1982). It has also been employed to explain how individuals use negotiation to secure the outcomes they desire, such as gaining advantage and control of others (Levy 1982 in Allen 1996). In addition, this perspective has been employed by Svensson (1996) to explore the nature of nurse-doctor negotiations around their patient care decisions. Despite Strauss' modifications, the negotiated order perspective has still been criticised for over-emphasising the influence of micro level interactions and underplaying the role of social structures (e.g. Lee & Newby 1984). In addition, Allen's (1997) use of the negotiated order perspective in an acute hospital setting indicated that nurses' difficulties contacting doctors meant they would often undertake medical tasks, such as initiating a clinical investigation, themselves. Therefore, Allen argues that a 'non-negotiated' order existed between these professions, a dimension that was overlooked by Strauss.

9.6.2. Using Negotiation theory in the Training Ward

Despite these limitations, the negotiated order perspective helps to illuminate the central role negotiation played in the development and delivery of the Training Ward. In addition, this theory provides an insight into how structural, organisational and professional factors effectively limit the influence of these negotiations. Furthermore, as noted above, no other theory was located that offered a detailed explanation of the relationship that exists between micro-level negotiation and wider macro structures.

In relation to Strauss' theory, it is possible to see how the micro-level negotiations undertaken by both steering group members played a central role in formulating and shaping the Training Ward project. For example, as discussed above, steering group negotiations ensured the creation of the Training Ward project, secured senior management and professional regulatory body commitment for the project and resulted in the successful delivery of the pilot ward. In addition, these findings support the stress Strauss placed on the influence of external structures in constraining the effects of negotiation. Indeed, while steering group negotiations were influential in the development of Training Ward project and the delivery of the pilot ward, education, professional, organisational and ultimately financial constraints restricted the influence of these negotiations.

As discussed above, while the steering group's use of outcome-oriented negotiation contributed to achieving the collective goals of the group in the development of the Training Ward project, their neglect of process-oriented negotiation resulted in a number of problems related to the way they worked together. In contrast, the students' use of both forms of negotiation ensured that they were focused on achieving their collective goals and also paid attention to their collaborative teamwork processes. This finding therefore provides an additional dimension to Strauss' negotiated order perspective. While previous research employed this theory to explore the influence micro-level negotiations have on organisational structures (e.g. Busch 1982, Hall & Spencer-Hall 1982) and interprofessional relationships (Svensson 1996), this study has revealed that micro-level negotiation can be separated into outcome and process-orientated negotiation. In addition, the study has indicated that the use of both outcome-orientated and process-orientated negotiation is needed to achieve a group's collective goals and pay attention to the processes linked to their collaborative work.

9.7. The need for group development

This section examines how a limited amount of time to work together inhibited the steering group and students' ability to develop and perform in an effective manner. It also discusses how Tuckman & Jensen's (1977) model of group development can be employed to help understand how a lack of time for interaction impedes a group's collaborative work.

Despite encountering problems in their collaborative work, as discussed in the three preceding sections, steering group members valued their shared time working on the

Training Ward project. Indeed, it was agreed that during the years they worked together, group members developed generally positive relationships with one another (Section 6.1.2). However, while they valued their shared time, the actual amount of time they had to work together was limited by the heavy workloads attached to their respective clinical and educational posts. Consequently, group interaction was largely restricted to their one-to-two hour formal monthly meetings. In addition, workload pressures meant that a number of members regularly missed these meetings (Section 6.2.4). A regular turnover of members (nine members left and 12 members joined the group during the duration of the study) also meant that members had little time together to form into a stable and cohesive group (Section 6.2.4). Similarly, as indicated in Section 7.1.3, the students placed a high value on their time together during the pilot ward. However, in developing the Training Ward project along the Swedish model, the steering group failed to consider the emerging problems linked to the use of a two-week placement contained in this model. Consequently, like their Swedish counterparts, most Training Ward students felt that a two-week experience was too short to provide them with a comprehensive insight into the nature of practice-based teamwork. Therefore, most requested a longer (three or four week) placement.

Collectively, the lack of time experienced by both the steering group and students for their respective interprofessional activities restricted their ability to develop and function together in an effective manner. While the steering group worked together for a three-year period, their time together was disjointed in nature, with monthly breaks between their short (one-to-two hour) meetings. Indeed, due to the problem of poor attendance at meetings, some members experienced up to four months apart before working together. In contrast, although the students worked together for eight-hour shifts on the pilot ward, the limited two-week nature of the experience frustrated them. Most felt they were only beginning to function in an effective manner as their placement ended.

The effects of time upon teamwork are well established within the wider literature (e.g. Kelly & McGrath 1985, McGrath 1990, Douglas 1996). Specifically, this work has indicated that a lack of time for groups to work together can undermine their ability to function in an effective manner. However, the interprofessional education literature fails to provide any account of the effects of time on staff or students involved in an interprofessional initiative. The thesis therefore offers a new insight into this literature by describing how limited time together can undermine the ability of course planning groups *and* student teams to develop and function together in an integrated manner.

9.7.1. Group development: the need for time

Tuckman & Jensen's (1977) model of group development is employed to help illuminate the problems related to the limited amount of time for group development within both the steering group and the students restricted their ability to collaborate effectively together. While there are several similar models of team development (for example, Jaques (1998) presents 11 such models, all containing similar stages of development), Tuckman & Jensen's model was selected as it is one of the earliest developed and most widely applied.

Tuckman (1965) originally developed a four-stage model of group development to help explain the effects of time on groupwork. Following a review of over 70 studies of groupwork, Tuckman devised a group development model that contained four distinctive stages which groups pass through:

Stage 1 - Forming: characterised by ambiguity and confusion as the team members struggle to begin working together;

Stage 2 - Storming: friction is generated between members as they begin to adopt roles and negotiate how they can work together;

Stage 3 - Norming: team members begin to find some consensus on the division of labour within the team;

Stage 4 - Performing: in which members understand one another and work together in a well co-ordinated fashion.

At the core of the model is the assumption that groups pass through the first three stages before they can effectively perform together in stage four. Thus, groupwork issues need to be addressed (through forming and storming) before group norms can be established and the group can perform in an integrated manner. Following another review of studies into groupwork, 12 years later, Tuckman & Jensen (1977) concluded that while the original model was still generally supported by research, it required a fifth 'adjourning' stage. This final stage explained the point where a group concludes its work, usually by completion of their joint task or by membership disruption.

While some authors have found that this model has provided a helpful insight into the effects of time on groups (e.g. Farrell et al. 1986, 2001, Janicik & Bartel 2003), most studies have indicated it provides a simplistic view of group development (e.g. Poole 1981, Poole & Roth 1989, Rickards & Moger 2000). Such research has found that groups rarely progress in a linear fashion along the five stages described by Tuckman & Jensen.

Often, teams can experience 'breakpoints' (discontinuation in their development), which halt their progress and can mean they repeat some stages of the model. In addition, groups undergo periods of disorganised activity where no discernible 'stage' can be identified. Due to these problems, Buchanan & Huczynski (1997) argue that the model should be regarded as offering an 'idealised' view of group development, rather than an exact predictor of time on group behaviour. For these authors, the processes that groups experience during their collaborative work are more complex than passing through a series of well-defined stages.

9.7.2. The importance of group development on collaboration

Despite these limitations, Tuckman & Jensen's model provides a helpful device to assess how time can effect a group's collaborative work. A good example of the usefulness of Tuckman & Jensen's model can be found in a recent study undertaken by Birmingham (2002) who found that teams which had passed through all stages of the model were more likely to perform effectively and attain their goals than newly formed teams.

As discussed above, a limited amount of time to work together on the Training Ward project and a relatively high turnover of members constrained the steering group's ability to function in an effective manner. In relation to Tuckman & Jensen's model, it could be argued that the steering group never fully completed the fourth (performing) stage (where members work together in a well co-ordinated fashion) before reaching the fifth adjourning stage (due to the closure of the clinical area set aside for the Training Ward). Indeed, it could be argued that the group moved back and forth between fully completing both stage three (norming) and fourth stage (performing), due to the on-going problems around group turnover and a lack of clarification of group roles and group processes. While it is difficult to assess how much more time the steering group would have needed to reach the performance stage of Tuckman & Jensen's model, indeed, given the workload pressures all members faced, it may be unrealistic to expect them to find more time for group development. Nevertheless, the incorporation of process-oriented negotiation in their existing meeting time (Section 9.6), could have helped them reach this fourth stage before reaching the final adjournment stage.

Compared to the members of the wider group, it appeared that the four-member subgroup did complete the performance stage of Tuckman & Jensen's model. As indicated in Sections 6.2.1 and 6.2.5, subgroup members worked closely together to undertake covert backstage meetings with senior management and they also worked together in informally directing the rest of the steering group's work on the project. However, as revealed in Section 9.5, the effectiveness of the subgroup's teamwork was achieved at the expense of undermining the quality of their relations with the other group members.

In contrast to the steering group, the students had just entered the performance stage of Tuckman & Jensen's model when they reached the end of their two-week placement. Indeed, as indicated in Section 7.2.3, the students' collaborative work was characteristic of the fourth stage of the model. For example, through their team planning and reflection sessions, the students had overcome their initial difficulties around working together as a newly created team (forming, storming, norming) and were beginning to effectively work together on the pilot ward. However, unlike the steering group who agreed to adjourn, the students' could not make this decision, as the adjournment stage of the model was reached prematurely (before they completed stage four) at the end of their two-week placement. Again, while it is difficult to provide an accurate estimate of how much more time the students would have needed to complete the fourth stage of Tuckman & Jensen's model, the students' suggestion of an additional one or two weeks is likely to improve this problem. However, further research into this issue is ultimately needed to provide an empirical insight into the most effective length of time for this type of interprofessional education experience.

Although Tuckman & Jensen's model continues to be employed to understand the effects of time on team development (e.g. Farrell et al. 1986, 2001, Birmingham 2002, Janicik & Bartel 2003), it has not been applied to the processes associated with course planning groups and students involved in development and delivery of interprofessional education. The use of this model has made it possible to understand how a failure to reach and complete the fourth performance stage of the model can undermine the ability of both staff and students to collaborate in an effective manner during the development and delivery of an interprofessional education initiative. In addition, the study has indicated that a small subgroup can reach the performance stage of Tuckman & Jensen's model while the members in the larger group struggle to achieve this level of development. Although the formulation and function of subgroups within larger groups is established in the wider literature (e.g. Jaques 1998, Douglas 2000), research employing Tuckman & Jensen's model focuses on how a team *collectively* passes through the different stages of the model. It therefore overlooks the separate development processes that can occur between subgroup members and between members of the wider group.

9.8. Managing the effects of the four issues

Having discussed the four key factors that emerged from the study and how they affected the development and delivery of the Training Ward project, this section explores how course planning groups need to manage their individual and collective effects. The section also goes on argue that a failure to manage or 'balance' these factors when developing an initiative is likely to result in the emergence of problems when delivering it, as development and delivery activities are closely entwined. Finally, the section outlines how this thesis provides an original contribution to the interprofessional education literature.

9.8.1. Balancing individual and collective influences

As outlined in the Sections 9.4 to 9.7, the development and delivery of the Training Ward project was affected by four inter-linked factors. However, while each individually affected the project, it is important to state that they also combined to *collectively* affect the development and delivery of the Training Ward. Figure 1 presents an idea of the individual and collective influences of these four issues.

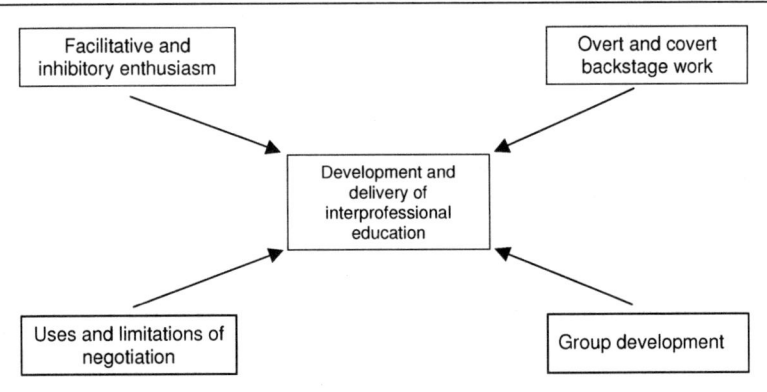

Figure 1: Individual and collective influences on the development and delivery of interprofessional education

As indicated in Figure 1, course planning groups need to be mindful that when developing and delivering an interprofessional initiative they need to manage the individual and combined effects of:

- *Enthusiasm.* Course planning groups need to keep a balance between a level of enthusiasm that positively contributes to the development and delivery of an interprofessional education initiative, while ensuring that their enthusiasm does not result in them becoming uncritical in their work (Section 9.4).

- *Backstage work.* Course planning groups need to ensure that they, and their students, have regular opportunities to undertake overt backstage work to support their more formal activities. In addition, course planning groups need to guard against the possible problems that can arise (e.g. exclusion) from the use of covert backstage work (Section 9.5).

- *Negotiation.* Course planning groups need to ensure that they, and their students, employ both process-orientated and outcome-oriented negotiation. The use of both forms of negotiation can help enhance group relations and ensure that shared goals are achieved. Course planning groups also need to manage the different challenges (e.g. educational, professional and organisational) that arise in the development and delivery of practice-based interprofessional education. In addition, groups need to be aware that while some challenges will only restrict their progress, others can ultimately undermine an initiative (Section 9.6).

- *Group development.* Course planning groups need to ensure that there is time for group development for themselves and their students to form, storm, norm, perform and adjourn. The failure to reach and complete the performance stage before adjourning can compromise the ability of course planning groups and students to function in an effective manner (Section 9.7).

In essence, course planning groups are required to 'balance' the effects of these issues on the development and delivery of interprofessional education. As these two activities are closely entwined, a failure to achieve this balance during the development of an initiative is likely to result in problems when attempting to deliver it. In practice, however, the complexity of the issues means that it is difficult to obtain such a balance. Indeed, as indicated in this chapter, steering group members achieved limited success in balancing these different issues. Figure 2 provides illustration of the successes and challenges encountered by the steering group when developing the Training Ward project. As Figure 2 indicates, the challenges faced by the steering group during their work developing the Training Ward outweighed the successes they achieved.

While the group's shared enthusiasm, their use of overt backstage work and their use of outcome-oriented negotiation were successful elements of their work, the group was undermined by five challenges.

179

Firstly, a shared enthusiasm for the Training Ward resulted in group members being uncritical about their group roles and processes, and uncritical about the design of the model they were developing. Secondly, the subgroup's use of covert backstage work further undermined the quality of the group's collaborative relationships. In addition, a limited amount of time together restricted the group's ability to develop and function together in an integrated fashion. Furthermore, a lack of process-orientated negotiation was another factor that inhibited the quality of their collective work. Finally, organisational and financial constraints ultimately undermined their work on the Training Ward project.

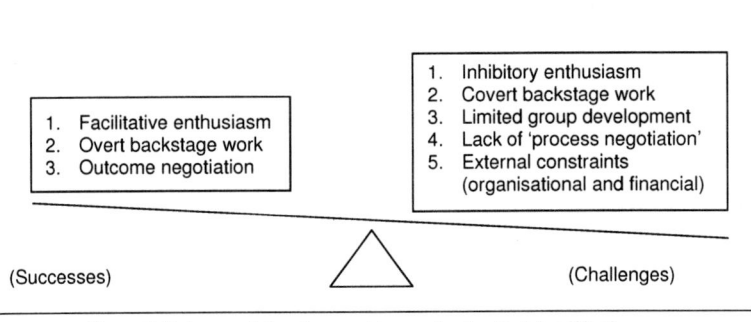

Figure 2: Balance of development issues for the Training Ward

Similarly, the pilot ward the steering group delivered also contained a number of related successes and challenges (see Figure 3).

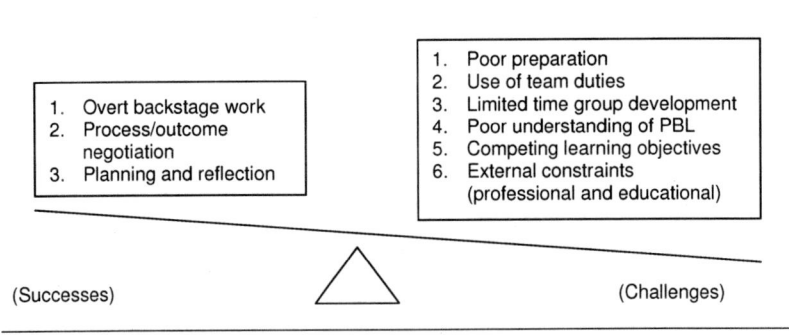

Figure 3: Balance of issues for the delivery of Training Ward pilot

These delivery successes centred on the following areas. Firstly, regular opportunities for overt backstage work helped ensure that students' front stage work was undertaken in an effective fashion. Secondly, opportunities for process and outcome-oriented negotiation helped ensure that the students were both focused on achieving their shared goals and also paid attention to their group maintenance needs. Finally, student team planning and reflection activities supported and enhanced the quality of their interprofessional teamwork. However, a range of factors undermined the students' experiences of the pilot ward. Specifically: a lack of preparation before they started on the ward; the use of team duties (where an overlap into the nursing students' role occurred); a lack of time for the students to reach the 'performance' stage of Tuckman & Jensen's (1977) model; a poor understanding of PBL (resulting in an inconsistency over its use); and a large number of competing learning objectives and external (professional and educational constraints), which created a number of inequalities between the students.

As discussed above, a complex range of issues underpin the development and delivery of interprofessional education. The process of managing the individual and collective effects of these issues on the development and delivery of this type of education is therefore a difficult task. It requires a 'balance' of issues for course planning groups during their development and delivery activities. While securing this balance is problematic, groups involved in this type of work nevertheless need to attempt the best balance of issues and influences they can practically achieve. In doing so, course planning groups can enhance the quality of both their development processes and the interprofessional initiative they deliver to their students.

9.9. How this study contributes to the literature

As discussed in Chapter 3, the empirical literature provides only scant information related to the processes of developing and delivering interprofessional education, resulting in two 'black box' problems. In opening these black boxes and providing a more informed understanding of the nature of these activities, the study makes an original contribution to the interprofessional education literature in the following areas:

- Enthusiasm within interprofessional education can have both facilitative and inhibitory effects. While it is vital to the successful development and delivery of an interprofessional initiative, enthusiasm can produce a lack of critical discussion and debate within a course planning group. This in turn can lead them to overlook their own group processes and fail to critically assess the design of the initiative they are developing and delivering.
- Backstage work plays a crucial role in the successful development and delivery of interprofessional education. However, like enthusiasm, backstage work can have a dual effect within an interprofessional initiative. While pre-arranged overt backstage

work can positively support the formal front stage activities of both course planning groups and students, the effects of covert backstage work are more mixed. Although it can help support the development and delivery of a project, it can also undermine the quality of group relations, as some members are excluded from a group's collaborative work.

- Outcome-orientated and process-orientated negotiation are both central to the development and delivery of interprofessional education. Attention needs to be paid to undertaking both forms of negotiation. Neglect of the former can result in problems achieving project goals, and a lack of attention to the latter can result in poorer quality collaboration for both course planning groups and students. While negotiation is vital to the development and delivery of interprofessional education, external challenges such as professional regulations and organisational restrictions can constrain progress and ultimately cause a project to fail.

- A lack of time together for both course planning groups and students can limit their ability to form, storm, norm and perform. This can result in them struggling to work together in an integrated and effective manner. Sufficient amounts of time to work and learn together are therefore required during the development and delivery of an interprofessional education initiative.

- While these four factors all have an individual influence on the development and delivery of interprofessional education, they also affect these activities in a collective fashion. Groups involved in the development of interprofessional education initiatives need to therefore manage the effects of the four factors. A failure to manage these factors when developing an initiative is likely to result in the emergence of problems when delivering it, as development and delivery activities are closely entwined.

As discussed in Chapter 2, the lack of theoretical work within the literature means that there is a limited understanding of the nature of interprofessional education. The use of theoretical and conceptual work from sociology and social psychology provides new ways of thinking about the development and delivery of interprofessional education. Specifically:

- Janis' (1982) theory of groupthink illuminates the challenges related to enthusiasm. This theory provides an insight into the difficulties that can emerge when a group fails to adopt a critical stance during the development and delivery of an interprofessional education initiative.

- Goffman's (1963) concept of backstage performance provides a novel way of thinking about the uses and abuses of informal backstage work within an interprofessional education initiative. The emergence of *overt* and *covert* backstage work also provides two new subsets of backstage work.

- Strauss' (1978) negotiated order perspective helps to illuminate the potential uses and limitations of negotiations within the development and delivery of interprofessional education. In addition, the emergence of *outcome-oriented* and *process-oriented* forms of negotiation provides two new categories of negotiation.

- Tuckman & Jensen's (1977) five-stage model is a useful tool to illuminate the potentially adverse effects of a lack of time for the development of course planning groups and students. In addition, it provides an insight into how subgroups within wider groups can progress through the model in different time frames to one another.

Summary

This chapter has presented a detailed discussion of the complex range of factors that influence the successes and challenges involved in the development and delivery of interprofessional education. Importantly, it has argued that enthusiasm, backstage work, negotiation and group development were the four key influences on the development and delivery of the Training Ward project. The chapter also drew upon theoretical work by Janis (1982), Goffman (1963), Strauss (1978) and Tuckman & Jensen (1977) to help illuminate the significance of these factors and offer an original way of thinking about the development and delivery of interprofessional education. In addition, it was argued that groups involved in the development and delivery of interprofessional education need to manage the effects of enthusiasm, backstage work, negotiation, group development during the development of an initiative. A failure to manage these factors when developing an initiative is likely to result in the emergence of problems when delivering it, as these two activities are closely interlinked.

Having discussed the key findings in depth and identified perspectives that can helpfully illuminate these findings, the final chapter presents the study's conclusions and implications.

Chapter 10: Conclusions and Implications

Introduction

This final chapter draws together the key factors discussed in the previous chapter in order to provide conclusions and implications for the development and delivery of interprofessional education. The chapter is divided into two sections. Section 10.1 presents key conclusions, while Section 10.2 offers a series of implications for the development and delivery of interprofessional education, as well as for research and policy-making in this field.

10.1. Key conclusions

This section offers a series of conclusions related to the development and delivery of the Training Ward project.

1. The development and delivery of the Training Ward was a complex collaborative venture within which a substantial amount of time and effort was required to manage the array of internal (e.g. group processes) and external challenges (e.g. organisational restrictions). Despite these challenges, the steering group was successful in developing and delivering an innovative practice-based pilot for students from four professions (Section 7.1).

2. Steering group members' enthusiasm for the developing and delivering the Training Ward was a key factor in providing the 'glue' that helped bond the group together while they navigated their way around numerous challenges related to the development and delivery of the Training Ward (Section 6.1.1). Similarly, the positive nature of group members' relations was another important factor for group cohesion in their collaborative work (Section 6.1.2).

3. The funded evaluation and the subsequent the report on the pilot ward (Freeth & Reeves 1999) were considered valuable aspects of the project. In particular, the

steering group valued this work as it provided them with an insight into the impact of the pilot ward they had delivered (Section 6.1.3).

4. While enthusiasm played an important role in supporting the collaborative work of the steering group, it also undermined the group's work on the Training Ward. In general, group members' enthusiasm for the project resulted in them being uncritical of their development work (Sections 6.2.1 to 6.2.3), which led to a number of challenges for the students and staff who participated in the pilot ward (Section 7.2.1 to 7.2.5).

5. Heavy workloads associated with steering group members' clinical and education posts were a continual problem for their involvement in the Training Ward project. In effect, their workloads restricted the time members had to work together, which limited their ability to collaborate in an effective manner (Section 6.2.4).

6. Although the steering group ensured that the students had opportunities for shared team reflection sessions to discuss their collaborative work in order to enhance its quality (Section 7.1.4), they overlooked the need to employ this approach in their own work. This oversight appeared to play a role in the difficulties group members encountered while working together (Section 6.2.2).

7. While developing the Training Ward, steering group members failed to pay close enough attention to the emerging problems attached to the Swedish model they had adopted (Section 6.2.3.1). In doing so, they overlooked difficulties related to role overlap, placement length and competing learning objectives. As a result, the problems that had occurred in the Swedish model re-occurred in the pilot ward when it was implemented in the UK (Sections 7.2.2 to 7.2.4).

8. Although steering group members drew upon the PBL approach used in the Swedish model to underpin the Training Ward, they failed to implement the model effectively when the project was delivered (Section 6.2.3.2). Consequently, the group created a number of challenges for the students and facilitators participating in the pilot ward (Sections 7.2.3 and 7.2.5).

9. Organisational challenges meant that the steering group could not offer the students equality in terms of their recruitment and accreditation (Section 6.2.5). As a result, the students' enjoyment of the Training Ward was undermined (Section 7.2.6).

10. The impact of the organisational context of the hospital in which the Training Ward was developed and delivered into played an important role in inhibiting its success (Section 6.2.6). Indeed, it was found that the hospital's turbulent environment ultimately caused the demise of the Training Ward.

10.2. Implications

This section presents a number of implications arising from this study. Firstly, Section 10.2.1 offers implications for the development and delivery of interprofessional education. Section 10.2.2 goes on to provide implications for future research in this field, while Section 10.2.3 presents implications for interprofessional education policy.

10.2.1. Developing and delivering interprofessional education

The following implications for the development and delivery of interprofessional education are offered:

1. Groups involved in the development and delivery of interprofessional education need to be aware that their collaborative work will contain a number of internal and external challenges. Course planning groups therefore need to be both creative and inventive in order to overcome such difficulties and strive for success in their work.

2. Given the importance of enthusiasm for helping to overcome the array of challenges associated with developing and delivering interprofessional education, course planning groups need a degree of enthusiasm for this type of education. Nevertheless, groups should be watchful of their levels of enthusiasm in order to prevent the emergence of its more detrimental side during their collaborative work.

3. Course planning groups need to agree their expectations, roles and responsibilities in the early stages of their work. Undertaking these activities will help ensure all group members have clear expectations of their work and have clarity around how they will work together. The use of Øvretveit's (1997b) 'team policy' model, which outlines the 'ground rules' needed to be taken to develop effective teamwork, could provide a helpful resource to course planning groups.

4. Given the benefits students derived from undertaking regular shared team reflection activities, particularly in discussing and then resolving problems related to

collaborative work, course planning groups should also aim to engage in this type of activity when developing and delivering an interprofessional education initiative.

5. University and professional body inflexibility meant that students on the Training Ward could not be offered equality in terms of their recruitment and accreditation. Given the social and economic inequalities that exist between the health and social care professions, equality between interprofessional learning activities is paramount. Therefore, course planning should aim, as far as organisational restrictions allow, to ensure that any initiative allows students to work together on an equal footing.

6. Heavy workloads will inevitably restrict course planning group members' involvement in the development and delivery of an interprofessional education initiative, which can limit opportunities for group members to work in an effective manner. Senior management should therefore ensure that sufficient time is provided to allow staff to fully engage in development and delivery activities.

7. Organisational turbulence can play a significant role in inhibiting the development and delivery of an interprofessional education initiative. Given the pace of change within NHS organisations, the viability of practice-based interprofessional education can be at risk. While senior management support is crucial for the survival of an interprofessional education initiative, course planning groups must be aware that financial pressures combined with the need to meet clinical targets, can effectively undermine a practice-based initiative.

8. Course planning groups should pay careful attention (i.e. identity all strengths and weaknesses) if they decide to incorporate an existing model into their own initiative. Similarly, if course planning groups decide to create their own model, careful analysis is required to ensure that the emergence of problems is kept to a minimum. A lack of critical analysis in this part of an initiative can result in a number of challenges for its participants.

9. Course planning groups about to undertake (or those already undertaking) development and delivery activities should draw upon the issues and theories presented in this thesis in their thinking work. Indeed, staff development sessions could be provided that employ work from this thesis. Such sessions would help ensure that course planning groups understand the key issues related to developing

and delivering interprofessional education and are therefore better equipped to deal with the numerous challenges that arise during this type of work.

10.2.2. Research

The following implications for future research into the development and delivery of interprofessional education are offered:

10. This study provided a rare exploration of the factors that influenced the development and delivery of interprofessional education. In doing so, it opened the black boxes associated with these two activities and began to explore their contents. Further exploratory research is required to build upon the findings from this study in order to provide a more comprehensive understanding of the subject area.

11. While this work offers an in-depth account of the development and delivery of an interprofessional education initiative, the generalisability of its findings are limited by its use of a single study setting. To build upon this work, future research should employ multiple case study designs to further explore the development and delivery of interprofessional education, in order to increase the relevance of such research to a broader range of contexts.

12. Enthusiasm, backstage work, negotiation and group development emerged as key factors in the development and delivery of interprofessional education. The closely entwined relationship between development and delivery activities emerged as another key factor. Further research is needed to test the applicability of the study's findings against data gathered from other interprofessional education initiatives.

13. The thesis employed Janis' (1982) theory of groupthink, Goffman's (1963) concept of backstage performance, Strauss' (1978) negotiated order perspective and Tuckman & Jensen's (1977) model of group development to offer new ways thinking about the development and delivery of practice-based interprofessional education. Further work is now required to establish, with more certainty, how effective these perspectives are in illuminating these two activities.

10.2.3. Interprofessional education policy

The following implications for national and international policy-makers are offered:

14. A key factor that inhibited the success of the Training Ward was the need to navigate around the regulations of the different validation bodies for the four professions involved in the project. Despite being generally supportive of incorporating interprofessional education into the respective pre-qualification courses they validate (e.g. College of Occupational Therapists 2000, General Medical Council 2001, Nursing and Midwifery Council 2002), the separateness of these different validation bodies and their regulations can impede the development and delivery of interprofessional education initiatives. These organisations therefore need to consider, collectively, how they might develop a more collaborative approach in their validation policies to ensure they offer more effective support for interprofessional education.

15. While there is an interest from the UK government (Department of Health 2001) and from governments in countries such as Canada (Health Canada 2003) in interprofessional education, they provide little information about how organisations can successfully implement this form of education. Therefore, national and international policy-makers may wish to consider using the study's findings to provide guidance for educational and clinical institutions on how they can overcome the challenges associated with the development and delivery of interprofessional education in order to optimise success in this type of work.

16. Traditionally, research undertaken into interprofessional education has tended to focus on reporting outcomes. In concentrating upon one dimension of interprofessional education the literature has overlooked the *processes* that underpin the production of outcomes. To ensure that future research provides a better focus on the processes associated with interprofessional education, commissioning bodies in this country and abroad should provide research grants for studies that investigate this area in more depth. In doing so, over the next few years, a more substantial knowledge of the nature of development and delivery activities can be produced, which should help ensure the future success of interprofessional education.

Appendices

Appendix 1: Links between the funded evaluation and this PhD study

As discussed in Section 1.1.3, the PhD study was linked to the funded evaluation undertaken by Della Freeth (DF) and myself (SR). To ensure the reader is confident that this PhD study stands in its own right, the activities, roles and contributions that link these two pieces of work need to be explained. Figure 4 therefore provides an insight into the convergent and divergent activities undertaken on both pieces of work.

Year	Funded evaluation	PhD study
1997	Training Ward steering group formed following a visit to the Swedish ward in the previous year (January)	SR registers and begins PhD training (October)
	DF invited to some steering group meetings (June)	
	Steering group secure funding for evaluation post (October)	SR decides to focus PhD on Training Ward, supervised by Richard Barron (RB) and Julienne Meyer (JM) (December)
	SR appointed to Training Ward evaluation post (November)	
1998	DF (principal investigator) and SR jointly plan evaluation and obtain ethical approval (January-March)	SR negotiates separate strand of work focusing on the steering group and undertakes collection of steering group data (January-December)
	DF/SR attend steering group meetings to update members on evaluation (January-December)	
	SR/DF visit the Swedish ward to talk to evaluators, staff and students (October)	
1999	SR collects Training Ward pilot data (February-March)	SR collects and analyses steering group data (January-December)
	SR/DF analyse pilot ward data and produce final project report (March-November)	RB retires in June. Supervision provided solely by JM
	SR attends steering group meetings. DF withdraws, although covers for SR on two occasions (March-December)	SR continues to re-analyse student and facilitator data (March-December)
2000	SR attends steering group meetings (March-June)	SR continues to collect and analyse steering group data (January-April)
	Steering group members disband (June)	SR continues to re-analyse student and facilitator data (January-December)
	DF/SR disseminate evaluation findings (January-December)	
2001	-	SR continues analysis and writing up
2002	-	DF begins as second supervisor (in February) to work with JM
		SR continues analysis and writing up
2003-05	-	SR continues write up / produces thesis

Figure 4: Relationship between the funded evaluation and the PhD study

Appendix 2: Search strategies

Interprofessional education

I modified the search strategy used in my systematic review work on interprofessional education (Zwarenstein et al. 1999, 2001, Freeth et al. 2002) to obtain a broad spread of the interprofessional education literature (e.g. discussion, opinion and policy papers). In doing so, I removed focus on obtaining only 'research' or 'evaluation' papers and added another pre-fix 'trans' to the terms 'profession', 'discipline', 'occupation', 'agency', 'organisation' and 'organization'.

#1	INTER-PROFESSION* or INTERPROFESSION*
#2	INTER-DISCIPLIN* or INTERDISCIPLIN*
#3	INTER-OCCUPATION* or INTEROCCUPATION*
#4	INTER-INSTITUTION* or INTERINSTITUTION*
#5	INTER-AGEN* or INTERAGEN*
#6	INTER-SECTOR* or INTERSECTOR*
#7	INTER-DEPARTMENT* or INTERDEPARTMENT*
#8	INTER-ORGANISATION* or INTERORGANISATION*
#9	INTER-ORGANIZATION* or INTERORGANIZATION*
#10	INTERPROFESSIONAL RELATIONS
#11	COLLABORAT* or TEAM*
#12	#1 or #2 or #3 or #4 or #5 or #6 or #7 or #8 or #9 or #10 or #11
#13	MULTI-PROFESSION* or MULTIPROFESSION*
#14	MULTI-DISCIPLIN* or MULTIDISCIPLIN*
#15	MULTI-INSTITUTION* or MULTIINSTITUTION*
#16	MULTI-OCCUPATION* or MULTIOCCUPATION*
#17	MULTI-AGEN* or MULTIAGEN*
#18	MULTI-SECTOR* or MULTISECTOR*
#19	MULTI-ORGANISATION* or MULTIORGANISATION*
#20	MULTI-ORGANIZATION* or MULTIORGANIZATION*
#21	#13 or #14 or #15 or #16 or #17 or #18 or #19 or #20
#22	TRANS-PROFESSION* or TRANSPROFESSION*
#23	TRANS-DISCIPLIN* or TRANSDISCIPLIN*
#24	TRANS-INSTITUTION* or TRANSINSTITUTION*
#25	TRANS-OCCUPATION* or TRANSOCCUPATION*
#26	TRANS-AGEN* or TRANSAGEN*
#27	TRANS-SECTOR* or TRANSSECTOR*
#28	TRANS-ORGANISATION* or TRANSORGANISATION*
#29	TRANS-ORGANIZATION* or TRANSORGANIZATION*
#30	#22 or #23 or #24 or #25 or #26 or #27 or #28 or #29
#31	EDUCAT* or LEARN* or TEACH* or TRAIN*
#32	#12 and #21 and #30 and #31

Interprofessional practice

Given the limited amount of empirical work exploring interactions within the interprofessional education literature, a search of the literature on interprofessional practice was undertaken. While a similar search strategy was employed, it was modified by removing key search terms of 'education', 'learning', 'teaching' and 'training' and adding the terms of 'practice', 'work' and 'task' to ensure it was focused on obtaining the literature on interprofessional practice.

#1   INTER-PROFESSION* or INTERPROFESSION*
#2   INTER-DISCIPLIN* or INTERDISCIPLIN*
#3   INTER-OCCUPATION* or INTEROCCUPATION*
#4   INTER-INSTITUTION* or INTERINSTITUTION*
#5   INTER-AGEN* or INTERAGEN*
#6   INTER-SECTOR* or INTERSECTOR*
#7   INTER-DEPARTMENT* or INTERDEPARTMENT*
#8   INTER-ORGANISATION* or INTERORGANISATION*
#9   INTER-ORGANIZATION* or INTERORGANIZATION*
#10 INTERPROFESSIONAL RELATIONS
#11 COLLABORAT* or TEAM*
#12 #1 or #2 or #3 or #4 or #5 or #6 or #7 or #8 or #9 or #10 or #11
#13 MULTI-PROFESSION* or MULTIPROFESSION*
#14 MULTI-DISCIPLIN* or MULTIDISCIPLIN*
#15 MULTI-INSTITUTION* or MULTIINSTITUTION*
#16 MULTI-OCCUPATION* or MULTIOCCUPATION*
#17 MULTI-AGEN* or MULTIAGEN*
#18 MULTI-SECTOR* or MULTISECTOR*
#19 MULTI-ORGANISATION* or MULTIORGANISATION*
#20 MULTI-ORGANIZATION* or MULTIORGANIZATION*
#21 #13 or #14 or #15 or #16 or #17 or #18 or #19 or #20
#22 TRANS-PROFESSION* or TRANSPROFESSION*
#23 TRANS-DISCIPLIN* or TRANSDISCIPLIN*
#24 TRANS-INSTITUTION* or TRANSINSTITUTION*
#25 TRANS-OCCUPATION* or TRANSOCCUPATION*
#26 TRANS-AGEN* or TRANSAGEN*
#27 TRANS-SECTOR* or TRANSSECTOR*
#28 TRANS-ORGANISATION* or TRANSORGANISATION*
#29 TRANS-ORGANIZATION* or TRANSORGANIZATION*
#30 #22 or #23 or #24 or #25 or #26 or #27 or #28 or #29
#31 PRACTICE* or WORK* or TASK*
#32 #12 and #21 and #30 and #31

Appendix 3: Facilitator training sessions

Day one[49]
The training began with a presentation on the ward development and details of the Linköping ward. This was followed by a presentation on the principles of PBL and a video presentation of the Maastricht 'Seven Step' PBL approach.

The afternoon centred upon a PBL group exercise in which facilitators were presented with the 'problem' of setting up a Training Ward. This exercise began with the group generating a list of potential problems and then dividing these problems between them in order to find 'solutions'. These were to be fed back in the second day of the training.

Day Two
The morning was taken up with facilitator feedback on their 'solutions' to wider group.
This feedback process continued into the afternoon, by which time the group had agreed all possible 'solutions'. This was followed by a short presentation and discussion around facilitating small groups.

---

[49] Due to pressure of work commitments and the recent rotation of junior doctors, no medical staff could attend this first training session. Therefore, an additional (shorter) session was arranged for them, which condensed the original two-day training into one day.

Appendix 4: Learning objectives for the Pilot Ward

Shared learning outcomes

1. To promote and facilitate team working within a real clinical setting.
2. To identify outcomes of Interprofessional working.
3. To promote and facilitate an holistic approach to health ant social care through collaboration.
4. To clarify roles and responsibilities of individual professionals within the team.
5. To gain an understanding into the knowledge, skills and attitudes expected of individual professionals within the team.
6. To develop individual professional roles within the interprofessional team
7. To communicate effectively with patients, patients' relatives, other health care professionals and people in the community.
8. To develop and maintain respect for the dignity, privacy and rights of patients and patients' relatives.
9. To work in a team and accept principles of collective responsibility.
10. To reflect critically upon my own and others' performances in the team.
11. To develop knowledge and understanding of the natural history of disease and possibilities for rehabilitation.
12. To deepen awareness of ethical and legal issues through team discussion.
13. To apply the principles of professional confidentiality in everyday practice.
14. To demonstrate the principles of evidence-based practice.
15. To discuss the relationship between primary/social care and hospital care as it affects individual patients.
16. To recognise and use opportunities for disease prevention and health promotion.
17. To demonstrate self-direction and manage time effectively in relation to the care being given.
18. To co-ordinate my ward team for a shift.
19. To apply the Trust's Health and Safety procedures and general policies.
20. To experience and analyse and discuss different management styles and their usage.
21. To demonstrate professional behaviour within the hospital ward environment.

Profession-specific learning objectives

Medical students

1. To work, observe, assist and co-operate with nursing, occupational therapy and physiotherapy students in the care of patients.
2. To take part in morning rounds, the reassessment of patients, the handover of patients.
3. To admit and clerk new patients and fill in patient medical records.
4. To order, check and interpret laboratory findings, x-ray reports and drug charts (with the agreement of the radiologist or the doctor in charge).
5. To prescribe medicines for the patients (with the agreement of the doctor in charge).
6. To take part in the handover from one set of students to another.
7. To explain drugs and define management of treatment plans (with the agreement of the doctor in charge).
8. To undertake the pre-operative care of patients.
9. To agree patient records with the doctor in charge.
10. To provide word-processed documents for inclusion in patient notes.
11. To agree discharge plans with the doctor in charge and discharge patients (with the agreement of the doctor in charge).

Nursing students

1. To manage and co-ordinate the care of a group of patients.
2. To ensure safe custody of medicines, ward keys and patient valuables.
3. To develop an understanding of nursing patients with orthopaedic/rheumatological conditions.
4. To prepare a patient for surgery and care for a patient's immediate post-operative care.
5. To safely administer medicines with the nurse supervisor.
6. To admit a patient into the clinical area.
7. To undertake a nursing assessment of a patient.
8. To enable the planning, implementation and evaluation of care.
9. To co-ordinate the discharge of a patient involving nursing care, social services care and follow-up appointments.
10. To develop an expertise in nursing patients with orthopaedic/rheumatological conditions.
11. To report side effects (e.g. surgery, chronic and acute pain).
12. To appreciate the support other members of the team may require.

Occupational therapy students

1. To demonstrate expertise in the assessment of patients' occupational performance and function.
2. To design treatment plans informed by the occupational therapy process.
3. To analyse the patients' problems.
4. To select appropriate occupational therapy intervention.
5. To discuss therapy with the supervising clinician.
6. To identify the precautions that need to be taken following total hip replacement/hemiarthroplasty.
7. To communicate to patients the need for safe techniques in the functional performance of daily living activities.
8. To demonstrate knowledge and understanding of the disease process in inflammatory arthritis particularly the effect on synovial joints.
9. To demonstrate to patients the principles of joint protection in the functional performance of daily living activities.
10. To identify the adaptations and equipment required to make the patients' home environment suitable for their functional needs.
11. To understand the basic principles of stress management.
12. To discuss appropriate relaxation techniques for use with patients with inflammatory arthritis demonstrate basic knowledge of specific seating needs.
13. To reflect on my own role and my knowledge base.

Physiotherapy students

1. To carry out systematic and comprehensive process of enquiry in order to identify the patient's main problems.
2. To set realistic goals and plan treatment taking into account the patient's lifestyle.
3. To offer appropriate advice.
4. To apply a range of treatment modalities effectively and accurately.
5. To assess and identify when to modify and institute the treatment programme and when transfer or discharge the patient is appropriate.
6. To initiate discussion with the other members of the team.
7. To offer a range of treatment and management strategies to the other members of the team.
8. To demonstrate organisational skills and cope with an appropriate workload
9. To reflect on practice.
10. To develop an awareness of oneself as a practitioner.
11. To demonstrate use of analytical, evaluative and reflective skills appropriate to the development of an autonomous practitioner.

Appendix 5: Interview schedules: developing the Training Ward

Interview schedule 1 (1998)

1. What do you know about the Training Ward?

2. How do you think the Training Ward will affect your job?

3. What gains do you see with establishing the Training Ward? (e.g. student, patient, tutor, staff, organisational, professional)

4. What concerns do you have with establishing the Training Ward? (e.g. student, patient, tutor, staff, organisational, professional)

5. What do you feel the students will obtain from their period in the Training Ward? (e.g teamworking, attitudes, skills, understanding roles)

6. What outcomes do you expect to come from the Training Ward? (e.g. educational, patient care)

7. Is there anything else you would like to raise?

Interview schedule 2 (2000)

1. What do you consider the main successes of the steering group's work on the Training Ward?

2. In your opinion, what have been the main challenges inhibiting the group's work on this project?

3. How well do you think the steering group have worked together on the Training Ward project?

4. What do you feel were the areas of difficulty in your work as a steering group member?

5. What is your vision of the future for the Training Ward project?

6. Is there anything else you would like to raise?

Appendix 6: Interview schedules: delivering the Training Ward Pilot

Student interview schedule

1. What were the most useful aspects of the Training Ward experience?

2. What were the least useful aspects of the Training Ward experience?

3. In your opinion what things should change, to improve the Training Ward experience?

4. In your opinion, what things should not changed, because to do so would diminish the Training Ward experience?

5. What would you say to the next group of students before they join the Training Ward?

6. Is there anything else you would like to raise?

Facilitator interview schedule

1. What was the extent of your involvement in the Training Ward?

2. What were the most useful aspects of the Training Ward experience? (e.g. student, patient, tutor, staff, organisation)

3. What were the least useful aspects of the Training Ward experience? (e.g. student, patient, tutor, staff, organisation)

4. In your opinion what things should be changed, to improve the Training Ward experience? (e.g. student, patient, tutor, staff, organisation)

5. In your opinion, what things should not be changed, because to do so would diminish the Training Ward experience? (e.g. student, patient, tutor, staff, organisation)

6. Is there anything else you would like to raise?

Appendix 7: Selected themes from the first stage of the analysis

Below is an extract from the first stage of the data analysis that provides an indication of how data were initially categorised.

Main theme: Developing the ward	
Sub-theme: Collaboration Enthusiasm Enjoyment Subgroup formation Exclusionary practices Talkers and doers Subgroup steam-rolling Feelings of marginalism Communication Leadership issues	**Sub-theme: Problematic progress** Lack of Momentum No targets Missing meetings Supplying students Time and change Heavy workloads Lack of co-ordinated effort Group function Differing agendas Self-interest/promotion
Sub- theme: Institutional Issues School problems Different institutional regulations New directorate management Trust problems Senior management support Organisational constraints Funding issues	**Sub-theme: Informal work** Developing the pilot Meeting with senior managers Professional body representatives Subgroup activities Covert work

Main theme: Delivering the ward	
Sub-theme: Working together Effective teamwork Heavy workloads Preparation Off-ward activities Leadership Getting it right Communication within team Handovers Humour Patient care	**Sub-theme: On the ward** Being there as a team Sharing shifts Two weeks is too short Attendance problems Working together No time to talk Going to the pub Team time Togetherness
Sub-theme: Team duties Its nursing work Limited participation Resistance Mucking in Dirty work	**Sub-theme: selection and assessment** Differences in selection Voluntarism Professional accreditation issues Getting assessed Imbalances

Appendix 8: Selected themes from the second stage of the analysis

Below is an extract from the second stage of the data analysis that provides an indication of how the data categories became more focused in nature.

Main theme: Developing the ward	
Sub-theme: Facilitative Enthusiasm Shared enthusiasm Commitment Senior management enthusiasm	**Sub- theme: External constraints** Missing meetings Heavy workloads Group turnover Management changes Trust reforms
Sub-theme: inhibitory enthusiasm Subgroup enthusiasm Exclusionary work Task orientation Unvoiced Concerns Feedback Informal Leadership	**Sub-theme: backstage work** Overt work Covert work

Main theme: Delivering the ward	
Sub-theme: Collaboration Effectiveness Poor preparation Backstage work Handovers	**Sub-theme: Time and space** Sharing ward space Sharing shifts Team performances Time restrictions Attendance
Sub-theme: Role sharing Participation Resistance	**Sub-theme: equality issues** Selection Accreditation Examination

References

Adair J (1986) *Effective Teamworking*. Pan, London.

Alderson P, Farsides B & Williams C (2002) Examining ethics in practice: health service professionals' evaluations of in-hospital ethics seminars. *Nursing Ethics*; 9:508-521.

Allen D (1996) *The Shape of General Hospital Nursing: the Division of Labour at Work.* Unpublished PhD Thesis, University of Nottingham.

Allen D (1997) The nursing-medical boundary: a negotiated order? *Sociology of Health and Illness*; 19:498-520.

Allen D (2002) Time and Space on the hospital ward: shaping the scope of nursing practice. In: D Allen & D Hughes (eds). *Nursing and the Division of Labour in Healthcare.* Palgrave, Basingstoke.

Allport G (1954) *The Nature of Prejudice.* Addison-Wesley, Reading MA.

Almaraz J (1994) Quality management and the process of change. *Journal of Organisational Change Management*; 7:6-12.

Alvesson M & Skoldberg K (2000) *Reflexive Methodology: New Visas for Qualitative Research.* Sage, London.

Anderson L, Persky N, Whall A, Campbell R, Algase D, Gillis G & Halter J (1994) Interdisciplinary team training in geriatrics: reaching out to small and medium size communities. *The Gerontologist*; 34:833-838.

Annandale E, Clark J & Allen E (1999) Interprofessional working: an ethnographic case study of emergency health care. *Journal of Interprofessional Care*; 13:139-150.

Antoniadis A & Videlock J (1991) In search of teamwork: a transactional approach to team functioning. *The Transdisciplinary Journal*; 1:157-167.

Arlton D (1986) A paying health promotion clinic: combining client services and student learning. *Journal of Allied Health*; 15:3-10.

Argyris C & Schön D (1978) *Organisational Learning.* Addision-Wesley, Reading MA.

Ashbury J (1995) Overview of focus groups. *Qualitative Health Research*; 5:414-420.

Bailey D (2002) Training together – part 2: an exploration of the evaluation of a shared learning programme on dual diagnosis for specialist drugs workers and approved social workers (ASWs). *Social Work Education*; 21:685-699.

Banks S & Junke K (1998) Developing and implementing interprofessional learning in a faculty of health professions. *Journal of Allied Health*; 27:132-36.

Barber G, Borders K, Holland B & Roberts K (1997) Life Span Forum: an interdisciplinary training experience. *Gerontology and Geriatrics Education*; 18:47-59.

Barker J (1964) Team work in the service of the mentally ill. *Nursing Mirror*; 199:285-287.

Barnes D, Carpenter J & Dickinson C (2000a) Interprofessional education for community mental health: attitudes to community care and professional stereotypes. *Social Work Education*; 19:565-583.

Barnes D, Carpenter J & Bailey D (2000b) Partnerships with service users in interprofessional education for community mental health: a case study. *Journal of Interprofessional Care*; 14:189-200.

Barnett R (1994) *The Limits of Competence Knowledge, Higher Education and Society*. Society for Research into Higher Education & Open University Press, Milton Keynes.

Barr H (1994a) NVQs and their implications for interprofessional education. In A Leathard (ed) *Going Interprofessional: Working Together in Health and Welfare*. Routledge, London.

Barr H (1994b) *Perspectives on Shared Learning*. CAIPE, London.

Barr H (1996) Ends and means in interprofessional education: towards a typology. *Education for Health*; 9:341-352.

Barr H (2000) *Interprofessional Education 1997-2000: A Review*. CAIPE, London.

Barr H (2002) *Interprofessional Education: Today, Yesterday and Tomorrow*. Learning and Support Network: Centre for Health Sciences and Practice, London.

Barr H (2005) Evaluating interprofessional education. In: C Carlisle, H Cooper & D Mercer (eds). *Interprofessional Education: an Agenda for Healthcare Professionals*. Quay Books, Salisbury.

Barr H, Freeth D, Hammick M, Koppel I, Reeves S (2000) *Evaluations of Interprofessional Education: A United Kingdom Review for Health and Social Care*. BERA/CAIPE, London.

Barr H, Hammick M, Koppel I & Reeves S (1999a) Evaluating interprofessional education: Two Systematic Reviews for health and social care. *British Educational Research Journal*; 25:533-543.

Barr H, Hammick M, Koppel I & Reeves S (1999b) Systematic Review of the Effectiveness of Interprofessional Education: Towards Transatlantic Collaboration. *Journal of Allied Health*; 28:104-108.

Barrows H & Tamblin R (1980) *Problem Based Learning*. Springer Publications, New York.

Becker H (1963) *Outsiders: Studies in the Sociology of Deviance*. Free Press, New York.

Becker H (1967) Whose side are we on? *Social Problems*; 14:239-48.

Becker H, Geer B, Hughes E & Strauss A (1961) *Boys in White: Student Culture in Medical School*. University of Chicago, Chicago.

Benson J (1977) Organisations: a dialectic view. *Administrative Science Quarterly*; 22:1-21.

Biggs J (1993) From theory to practice: a cognitive systems approach. *Higher Education Research and Development*; 12:73-85.

Birmingham C (2002) *Conflict Resolution in Decision-making Teams: a Longitudinal Study*. Unpublished PhD Thesis, University of Oklahoma.

Birnbaum M, Robinson N, Kuska B, Stone H, Fryback D & Rose J (1994) Effect of advanced cardiac life-support training in rural, community hospitals. *Critical Care Medicine*; 22:741-749.

Blaikie N (1993) *Approaches to Social Enquiry.* Polity Press, Cambridge.

Bloor M (1997) Techniques of validation in qualitative research: a critical commentary. In: G Miller & R Dingwall (eds). *Context and Method in Qualitative Research.* Sage, London.

Blumer H (1969) *Symbolic Interactionism: Perspective and Method.* University of California Press, Santa Monica CA.

Blumer H (2001) The ethics of social research. In Gilbert N (ed) *Researching Social Life* (2nd ed). Sage, London.

Bond M (1997) A learning team in the making. *Journal of Interprofessional Care*; 11:89-98.

Bond M (1999) Placing poverty on the agenda of a primary health care team: an evaluation of an action research project. *Health and Social Care in the Community*; 7:9-16.

Booth J & Hewison A (2002) Role overlap between occupational therapy and physiotherapy during in-patient stroke rehabilitation: an exploratory study. *Journal of Interprofessional Care*; 16:31-40.

Borrill C, Carletta J, Carter A, Dawson J, Garrod S, Rees A, Richards A, Shapiro D & West M (2000) *The Effectiveness of Health Care Teams in the National Health Service.* Aston University, Birmingham.

Boyer L, Lee D & Kirchner C (1977) A student-run course in interprofessional relations. *Journal of Medical Education*; 52:183-189.

Brandon R & Knapp M (1999) Interprofessional education and training. *American Behavioural Scientist*; 42:876-891.

Bridges J (2004) *Workforce Matters: Exploring a New Flexible Role in Health Care.* Unpublished PhD Thesis. City University, London.

Brown R, Condor S, Mathews A, Wade G & Williams J (1986) Explaining intergroup differentiation in an industrial organization. *Journal of Occupational Psychology;* 59:273-286.

Brown B, Crawford P & Darongkamas J (2000) Blurred roles and permeable boundaries: the experience of multidisciplinary working in community mental health. *Health and Social Care in the Community*; 8:425-435.

Brown V & Adkins B (1989) A comprehensive training program for multidisciplinary treatment plans, *Journal of Nursing Staff Development*; 5:25-29.

Buchanan D & Huczynski A (1997) *Organisational Behaviour.* (3rd ed). Prentice-Hall, London.

Busch L (1982) History, negotiation and structure in agricultural research. *Urban Life*; 11:368-384.

Butler-Sloss E (1988) *The Report of the Inquiry into Child Abuse in Cleveland.* HMSO, London.

Cable S (2000) Clinical Experience: *Preparation of Medical and Nursing Students for Collaborative Practice.* Unpublished PhD Thesis, University of Dundee.

Cable S (2002) Why the current interest? In: S Glen & T Leiba (eds). *Multiprofessional Learning for Nurses: Breaking the Boundaries.* Palgrave, Basingstoke.

Carlisle C, Cooper H & Watkins C (2004) "Do none of you talk to each other?": the challenges facing the implementation of interprofessional education. *Medical Teacher,* 26:545-552.

Carpenter C, Ericksen J, Purves B & Hill D (2004) Evaluation of the perceived impact of an interdisciplinary healthcare ethics course on clinical practice. *Learning in Health and Social Care;* 4:223-236.

Carpenter J (1995a) interprofessional education for medical and nursing students: Evaluation of a programme. *Medical Education;* 29:265-272.

Carpenter J (1995b) Doctors and nurses: Stereotype and stereotype change in interprofessional education. *Journal of Interprofessional Care;* 9:151-62.

Carpenter J (1995c) Implementing community care. In: K Soothill, L Mackay & C Webb (eds). *Interprofessional Relations in Health Care.* Edward Arnold, London.

Carpenter J & Hewstone M (1996) Shared learning for doctors and social workers. *British Journal of Social Work;* 26:239-57.

Carpenter J, Barnes D & Dickinson C (2003a) *Making a Modern Mental Health Care Force: Evaluation of the Birmingham University Interprofessional Training Programme in Community Mental Health 1998-2002.* Internal Research Report. University of Durham, Durham.

Carpenter J, Schneider J, Brandon T & Wooff D (2003b) Working in multidisciplinary community mental health teams: the impact on social workers and health professionals of integrated mental health care. *British Journal of Social Work;* 33:1081-1103.

Casto M (1994a) Education for interprofessional practice. In: M Casto & M Julia (eds). *Interprofessional Care and Collaborative Practice.* Brooks/Cole, Belmont.

Casto M (1994b) Interprofessional work in the USA. In A Leathard (ed) *Going Interprofessional: Working Together in Health and Welfare.* Routledge, London.

Chapman T, Hugman R, Williams A (1995) Effectiveness of interprofessional relationships: a case illustration of joint working. In: K Soothill, L Mackay & C Webb (eds). *Interprofessional Relations in Health Care.* Edward Arnold, London.

Chesney B & Chesney A (1981) Student reactions to a community-based experience for health professions education. *Journal of Allied Health;* 10:120-125.

Cilliers P (1998) *Complexity and Postmodernism.* Routledge, London.

Clark P (2004) Institutionalizing interdisciplinary health professions programs in higher education: the implications of one story and two laws. *Journal of Interprofessional Care;* 18:251-261.

Clay M, Lilley S, Borre K & Harris J (1999) Applying adult education principles to the design of a preceptor development program. *Journal of Interprofessional Care;* 13:405-415.

Cleghorn G & Baker G (2000) What faculty need to learn about improvement and how to teach it to others. *Journal of Interprofessional Care;* 14:147-59.

College of Occupational Therapists (2000) *Code of Ethics and Professional Conduct for Occupational Therapists*. College of Occupational Therapists, London.

Collier I (1981) Educational co-operation among nursing, medicine and pharmacy: a success story. *Journal of Nursing Education*; 20:23-26.

Collins R (1980) Erving Goffman and the development of social theory. In J Ditton (ed) *The View from Goffman*. Macmillan, London.

Committee of Vice Chancellors and Principals (1997) *Survey of Interprofessional Education and Training*. Health Professionals Committee. CVCP, London.

Connolly P (1995) Transdisciplinary collaboration of academia and practice in the area of serious mental illness. *Australian and New Zealand Journal of Mental Health Nursing*; 4:168-180.

Cooper H (2005) Chronic illness: empowering patients for self-care in diabetes. In: C Carlisle, H Cooper & D Mercer (eds). *Interprofessional Education: an Agenda for Healthcare Professionals*. Quay Books, Salisbury.

Cooper H, Carlisle C, Gibbs T & Watkins C (2001) developing an evidence base for interdisciplinary learning: a systematic review. *Journal of Advanced Nursing*; 35:228-237.

Cooper H, Braye S, Geyer R (2004) Complexity and interprofessional education. *Learning in Health and Social Care*; 3:179-189.

Cooper G (2001) Conceptualising social life. In N Gilbert (ed) *Researching Social Life* (2nd ed). Sage, London.

Cornish P, Church E, Callanan T, Bethune C, Robbins C & Miller R (2003) Rural interdisciplinary mental health team building via satellite: a demonstration project. *Telemedicine Journal & E-Health*; 9:63-71.

Couchman P & Fulop L (2004) Managing risk in cross-sector R&D collaborations: lessons from an international case study. *Prometheus*; 22:151-167.

Cox S, Wilcock P & Young J (1999) Improving the repeat prescribing process in a busy general practice. A study using continuous quality improvement methodology. *Quality in Health Care*; 8:119-125.

Cozijnsen A, Vrakking W & van Ijzerloo M (2000) Success and failure of 50 innovation project in Dutch companies. *European Journal of Innovation Management*; 3:150-159.

Crawford M, Turnbull G & Wessely S (1998) Deliberate self-harm assessment by accident and emergency staff - an intervention study. *Journal of Accident and Emergency Medicine*; 15:18-22.

Crotty M (1998) *The Foundations of Social Research*. Sage, London.

Crutcher R, Then K, Edwards A, Taylor K & Norton P (2004) Multiprofessional education in diabetes. *Medical Teacher*; 26:435-443.

Davies H, Nutley S & Smith P (2000) *What works? Evidence-based Policy and Practice in Public Services*. Policy Press, Bristol.

Day R & Day J (1977) A review of the current state of negotiated order theory: an appreciation and critique. *The Sociological Quarterly*; 19:499-501.

Denzin N (1970) *The Research Act in Sociology*. Butterworths, London.

Denzin N (1978) *The Research Act: A Theoretical Introduction to Sociological Methods.* McGraw-Hill, New York.

Denzin N (1989) *Interpretative Interactionism.* Sage, London.

Department of Health (1988) *Working Together – A Guide to Inter-agency Cooperation for the Protection of Children from Abuse.* HMSO, London.

Department of Health (1989) *Caring for People: Community Care in the Next Decade and Beyond.* HMSO, London.

Department of Health (1994) *The Report of the Inquiry into the Care and Treatment of Christopher Clunis.* HMSO, London.

Department of Health (1996) *The National Health Service: A Service with Ambitions.* HMSO, London.

Department of Health (1997) *The New NHS. Modern. Dependable.* DoH, London.

Department Of Health (1998) *A First Class Service. Quality in the NHS.* DoH, London.

Department of Health (2000) *A Health Service of all the Talents: Developing the NHS Workforce.* DoH, London.

Department of Health (2001) *Working Together – Learning Together: A Framework for Lifelong learning for the NHS.* DoH, London.

Department of Health (2002) *Learning from Bristol: The DH Response to the Report of the Public Inquiry into Children's Health Surgery at the Bristol Royal Infirmary 1984-1995.* DoH, London.

Department of Health and Social Security (1974) *The Joseph Report.* HMSO, London.

DePoy E, Wood C & Miller M (1997) Educating allied health professionals: an interdisciplinary effort. *Journal of Allied Health*; 26:127-32.

Dienst E & Byl N (1981) Evaluation of an educational program in health care teams. *Journal of Community Health*; 6:282-298.

Dingwall R (1980a) Problems of teamwork in primary care. In: S Lonsdale, A Webb & T Briggs (eds). *Teamwork in the Personal Social Services and Health Care.* Croom Helm, London.

Dingwall R (1980b) Ethics and Ethnography, *Sociological Review*, 28:4:871-91.

Dombeck M (1997) Professional personhood: training, territoriality and tolerance. *Journal of Interprofessional Care*; 11: 9-21.

Donovan T, Mercer D & Sutton R (2005) Communication skills training in cancer care using actors as simulated patients. In: C Carlisle, H Cooper & D Mercer (eds). *Interprofessional Education: an Agenda for Healthcare Professionals.* Quay Books, Salisbury.

Douglas T (1983) *Groups: Understanding People Gathered Together.* Tavistock, London.

Douglas T (1996) *Survival in Groups: the Basics of Group Membership.* Open University Press, Milton Keynes.

Douglas T (2000) *Basic Groupwork.* Routledge, London.

Doyle M, Earnshaw P, & Galloway A (2003) Developing, delivering and evaluating interprofessional clinical risk training in mental health services. *Psychiatric Bulletin*; 27:73-76.

Drinka T & Ray R (1987) An investigation of power in an interdisciplinary health care team. *Gerontology and Geriatrics Education*, 6:43-53.

Drinka T & Clark P (2000) *Health Care Teamwork: Interdisciplinary Practice and Teaching*. Auburn House, Westport.

Eales-White R (2004) Change management: understanding and harnessing creative diversity. *Industrial and Commercial Training*; 36:171-174.

Edinberg M, Dodson S & Veach T (1978) A preliminary study of student learning in interdisciplinary health teams. *Journal of Medical Education*; 53:667-671.

Edward C & Preece P (1999) Shared teaching in health care ethics: a report on the beginning of an idea. *Nursing Ethics*; 6:299-307

Ellemers N, Spears, R & Doose J (1999) *Social Identity*. Blackwell, Oxford.

Elliott R, Woodward, M & Oborne C (2002) Antithrombotic prescribing in atrial fibrillation: application of a prescribing indicator and multidisciplinary feedback to improve prescribing. *Age and Ageing*; 31:391-396.

Elston M (1991) The politics of professional power: medicine in a changing health service. In: J Gage, M Calnan & M Bury (eds). *The Sociology of the Health Service*. Routledge, London.

Elywin G, Rapport F & Kinnersley P (1998) Primary health care teams re-engineered. *Journal of Interprofessional Care*; 12:189-98.

Emerson R (1981) Observational fieldwork. *Annual Review of Sociology*; 7:351-378.

Eraut M (1994) *Developing Professional Knowledge and Competence*. Falmer Press, Brighton.

Evers H (1981) Multidisciplinary teams in geriatric wards: myth or reality? *Journal of Advanced Nursing*; 6:205-214.

Falconer J, Roth E, Sutin J, Strasser D & Chang R (1993) The critical path method in stroke rehabilitation: lessons from an experiment in cost containment and outcome improvement. *Quarterly Review Bulletin*; 19:8-16.

Fallsberg M & Wijma K (1999) Student attitudes towards the goals of an interprofessional Training Ward. *Medical Teacher*, 6:576-581.

Fallsberg M & Hammar M (2000) Strategies and focus at an integrated, interprofessional Training Ward, *Journal of Interprofessional Care*; 14:337-350.

Farrell M (2005) Enabling interprofessional education: the potential of e-learning. In: C Carlisle, H Cooper & D Mercer (eds). *Interprofessional Education: an Agenda for Healthcare Professionals*. Quay Books, Salisbury.

Farrell M, Heinemann G & Schmitt M (1986) Informal roles, rituals and style of humor in interdisciplinary teams: their relation to stages of team development. *International Journal of Small Group Research*; 2:143-162.

Farrell M, Schmitt M & Heinemann G (2001) Informal roles and the stages of team development. *Journal of Interprofessional Care*; 15:281-295.

Fay B (1974) *Social Theory and Political Practice*. Allen & Unwin, London.

Feiger S & Schmitt M (1979) Collegiality in interdisciplinary health teams: its measurements and its effects. *Social Science and Medicine*; 13:217-229

Fetterman D (1998) *Ethnography: Step by Step* (2nd ed). Sage, London

Field R & West M (1994) Teamwork in primary health care: perspectives from practices. *Journal of Interprofessional Care*; 9:123-130.

Fielding N & Fielding J (1986) *Linking Data*. Sage, London.

Finch J (2000) Interprofessional education and teamworking: a view from the education providers. *British Medical Journal*; 321:1138-1140.

Finley L (2002) Negotiating the swamp: the opportunity and challenge of reflexivity in research practice. *Qualitative Research*; 2:209-230.

Finset A, Krogstad J, Hansen H, Berstad J, Haarberg D, Kristansen G, Saether K & Wang M (1995) Team development and memory training in traumatic brain injury rehabilitation: two birds with one stone. *Brain Injury*; 9:495-507.

Firth-Cozens J (1998) Celebrating teamwork. *Quality in Health Care*; 7(Suppl):S3-S7.

Firth-Cozens J & Mowbray D (2001) Leadership and the quality of care. *Quality in Health Care*; 10(Suppl II):ii3-ii7.

Flick U (2002) *An Introduction to Qualitative Research* (2nd ed). Sage, London.

Forbes E & Fitzsimons V (1993) Education: the key for holistic interdisciplinary collaboration. *Holistic Nurse Practice*; 7:1-10.

Forman D & Nyatanga L (1999) The evolution of shared learning: some political and professional imperatives. *Medical Teacher*; 21:489-496.

Foucault M (1972) *The Archaeology of Knowledge*. Tavistock, London.

Foucault M (1979) *Discipline and Punish: the Birth of the Prison*. Penguin, Harmondsworth.

Freeth D (2001) Sustaining interprofessional collaboration. *Journal of Interprofessional Care*; 15:37-46.

Freeth D, Hammick M, Koppel I, Reeves S, Barr H (2002) *A Critical Review of Evaluations of Interprofessional Education*. Learning and Support Network: Centre for Health Sciences and Practice. London.

Freeth D, Meyer J, Reeves S & Spilsbury K (1998) *Interprofessional Education and Training in Wales: Stages 2 & 3 of the CAIPE Consultation*. Internal Research Report. City University, London.

Freeth D, Meyer J, Reeves S & Spilsbury K (1999) Linking interprofessional education to user benefit: of drops in the ocean and stalactites. *Advancing Clinical Nursing*; 3:127-135.

Freeth D & Nicol M (1998) Learning clinical skills: an interprofessional approach. *Nurse Education Today* 18, 455-61.

Freeth D & Reeves S (1999) *Interprofessional Training Ward Pilot Phase: Evaluation Project Report*. Internal Research Report. City University, London.

Freeth D & Reeves S (2004) Learning to work together: using presage, process, product (3P) model to highlight decisions and possibilities. *Journal of Interprofessional Care*; 18:43-56.

Freeth D, Reeves S, Goreham C, Parker P, Haynes S, Pearson S (2001) Real life clinical learning on an interprofessional Training Ward. *Nurse Education Today*; 21:366-72.

Freidson E (1970) *Profession of Medicine: A Study of the Sociology of Applied Knowledge*. Harper and Row, New York.

Fry H, Ketteridge S & Marshall S (1999) *A Handbook for Teaching and Learning in Higher Education: Enhancing Academic Practice*. Kogan Page, London.

Funnell P (1995) Exploring the value of interprofessional shared learning. In: K Soothill, L Mackay & C Webb (eds). *Interprofessional Relations in Health Care*. Edward Arnold, London.

Gair G & Hartery T (2001) Medical dominance in multidisciplinary teamwork: a case study of discharge decision-making in a geriatric assessment unit. *Journal of Nursing Management*; 9:3-11.

Gamarnikow E (1978) Sexual division of labour: the case of nursing. In: A Kuhn & A Wolpe (eds). *Feminism and Materialism*. Routledge & Kegan Paul, London.

Geertz C (1988) *Works and Lives: the Anthropologist as Author*. Stanford University Press, Stanford.

General Medical Council (2001) *Good Medical Practice*. General Medical Council, London.

Gentry M, Iceton J & Milne D (2001) Managing challenging behaviour in the community: methods and results of interactive staff training. *Health & Social Care in the Community*; 9:143-150.

Giddens A (1984) The Constitution of Society: Outline of the Theory of Structuration. Polity Press, Cambridge.

Giddens A (1993) *Sociology*. Polity Press, Cambridge.

Gibbon B (1999) An investigation of interprofessional collaboration in stoke rehabilitation team conferences. *Journal of Clinical Nursing*; 8:246-252.

Gilbert J, Camp R, Cole C, Bruce C, Fielding D & Stanton S (2000) Preparing students for interprofessional teamwork in health care. *Journal of Interprofessional Care*; 14:223-235.

Gill J & Ling J (1995) Interprofessional shared learning: a curriculum for collaboration. In: K Soothill, L Mackay & C Webb (eds). *Interprofessional Relations in Health Care*. Edward Arnold, London.

Glanz K, Brekke M, Harper D, Bache-Wiig M & Hunninghake D (1992) Evaluation of implementation of a cholesterol management program in physicians' offices *Health Education Research*; 7:151-64.

Glen S & Reeves S (2003) Developing interprofessional education in the pre-qualification curricula: mission impossible? *Nurse Education in Practice*; 4:45-52.

Glennie S & Cosier J (1994) Collaborative inquiry: developing multidisciplinary learning and action. *Journal of Interprofessional Care*; 8:255-263.

Goble R (1994) Multiprofessional education in Europe: an overview. In Leathard A (ed) Going Interprofessional: Working Together for Health and Welfare. Routledge, London.

Goffman E (1963) *The Presentation of Self in Everyday Life.* Penguin, London.

Gosling S (2005) The education and practice agenda for interprofessional teaching and learning. In: C Carlisle, H Cooper & D Mercer (eds). *Interprofessional Education: an Agenda for Healthcare Professionals.* Quay Books, Salisbury.

Gould K, Eickhoff-Shemek J, Stacy R & Mecklenburg R (1998) The impact of National Cancer Institute training on clinical tobacco use cessation services by oral health teams. *Journal of the American Dental Association*; 129:1442-1449.

Graham J & Wealthall S (1999) Interdisciplinary education for the health professions: taking the risk for community gain. *Focus on Health Professional Education;* 1:49-69.

Green R. Cavell G. & Jackson S. (1996) Interprofessional clinical education of medical and pharmacy students. *Medical Education*; 30:129-133.

Greenhalgh T, Robert G, Bate P, Kyriakidou O, Macfarlane F & Peacock R (2004) *Diffusion, Dissemination and Sustainability of Innovations in Health Service Delivery and Organisations: a Systematic Review.* University College London, London.

Gregson B, Cartlidge A & Bond J (1991) *Interprofessional collaboration in primary health care organisations.* Royal College of General Practitioners, London.

Guest C, Smith L, Bradshaw M & Hardcastle W (2002) Facilitating interprofessional learning for medical and nursing students in clinical practice. *Learning in Health and Social Care;* 1:132-138.

Hall P & Spencer-Hall D (1982) The social conditions of the negotiated order. *Urban Life*; 11:328-349.

Hall P & Weaver L (2001) Interdisciplinary education and teamwork: a long and winding road. *Medical Education*; 35:867-875.

Hammersley M (1985) Ethnography: what it is and what it offers. In: S Hegarty & P Evans (eds). *Research and Evaluation Methods in Special Education.* Nefar-Nelson, Philadelphia.

Hammersley M (1990) *Reading Ethnographic Research: a Critical Guide.* Longman, London.

Hammersley M (1992) *What's Wrong with Ethnography? Methodological Explorations.* Routledge, London.

Hammersley M & Atkinson P (1995) *Ethnography: Principles in Practice* (2nd ed). Routledge, London.

Hammick M (1998) Interprofessional education: concept, theory and application. *Journal of Interprofessional Care*, 12:323-32.

Hammick M, Barr H, Freeth D, Koppel I & Reeves (2002) Systematic reviews of evaluations of interprofessional education: results and work in progress. *Journal of Interprofessional Care*; 16:80-84

Harden R (1998) AMEE Guide No. 12: Multiprofessional education: Part 1 – effective multiprofessional education: a three-dimensional perspective. *Medical Teacher*, 20:402-408.

Harmon R, Sheehy L & Davis D (1998) The utility of external performance measurement tools in program evaluation. *Rehabilitation Nursing*; 23:8-11.

Harris D, Henry R, Bland C, Starnaman S & Voytek K (2003) Lessons learned from implementing multidisciplinary health professions educational models in community settings. *Journal of Interprofessional Care*; 17:7-20.

Hart P, Sterns E, Sundelius B & Hermann C (1996) Beyond Groupthink: political group dynamics and foreign policy-making. *American Political Science Review*; 93:766 -767.

Harvey D & Reed M (1997) Social science as the study of complex systems. In: L Kiel & E Elliott (eds). *Chaos Theory and the Social Sciences: Foundations and Applications.* University of Michigan Press, Michigan.

Hasler J & Klinger M (1976) Common ground in general practice and health-visitor training – an experimental course. *Journal of the Royal College of General Practitioners*; 26:266-276.

Haug M (1993) De-professionalisation: an alternative hypothesis for the future. *Sociological Review Monograph*; 20:195-211.

Hayward K, Powell L & McRoberts J (1996) Changes in student perceptions of interdisciplinary practice in the rural setting. *Journal of Allied Health*; 25:315-27.

Headrick L, Wilcock P, Batalden P (1998) Interprofessional working and continuing medical education. *British Medical Journal*; 316:771-74.

Health Canada (2003) *First Ministers' Accord on Health Care Renewal.* Health Canada, Toronto.

Heckman M, Ajdari S, Esquivel M, Chernof B, Tamm N, Landowski L & Guterman J (1998) Quality improvement principles in practice: the reduction of umbilical cord blood errors in the labor and delivery suite. *Journal of Nursing Care Quality*; 12:47-54.

Hemman E, McClendon B & Lightfoot S (1995) Networking for educational resources in a rural community. *Journal of Continuing Education in Nursing*; 26:170-173.

Henneman E, Lee J & Cohen J (1995) Collaboration: a concept analysis. *Journal of Advanced Nursing*; 21:103-109.

Hertz R (1997) *Reflexivity and Voice.* Sage, London

Hewstone M & Brown R (1986) Contact is not enough: an intergroup perspective on the "contact hypothesis". In: M Hewstone & R Brown (eds). *Contact and Conflict in Intergroup Encounters.* Blackwell, Oxford.

Hickey M, Kleefield S, Pearson S, Hassan S, Harding M, Haughie P, Lee T & Brennan T (1996) Payer-Hospital collaboration to improve patient satisfaction with hospital discharge. *Joint Commission Journal on Quality Improvement*; 22:336-344.

Hilton R, Morris D & Wright A (1995) Learning to work in the heath care team. *Journal of Interprofessional Care*; 9:167-74.

Hind M, Norman I, Cooper S, Gill E, Hilton R, Judd P & Newby S (2003) Interprofessional perceptions of health care students. *Journal of Interprofessional Care*; 17:21-34.

Hodges B (2003) OSCE! Variations on a theme by Harden. *Medical Education*; 37:1134-1140.

Holman C & Jackson S (2001) A team education project: an evaluation of a collaborative education and practice development in a continuing care unit for older people. *Nurse Education Today*; 21:97-103.

Horder J (1996) The Centre for the Advancement of Interprofessional Education. *Education for Health*; 9:397-400.

Hughes D (1988) When nurse knows best: some aspects of nurse/doctor interaction in a casualty department. *Sociology of Health and Illness*; 16:184-202.

Hughes L & Lucas J (1997) An evaluation of problem based learning in the multiprofessional education curriculum for the health professions. *Journal of Interprofessional Care*; 11:77-88.

Hugman R (1991) *Power in the Caring Professions*. Macmillan, London.

Humphris D & Hean S (2004) Educating the future workforce: building the evidence about interprofessional education. *Journal of Health Services Research and Policy*; 9:(Suppl)S24-S27.

Hunter D (1994) From Tribalism to corporatism: the managerial challenge to medical dominance. In: J Gabe, D Kelleher & G Williams (eds). *Challenging Medicine*. Routledge, London.

Hunter M & Love C (1996) Total quality management and the reduction of inpatient violence and cost in a forensic psychiatric hospital. *Psychiatric Services*; 47:751-754.

Hyer K, Fairchild S, Abraham I, Mezey M & Fulmer T (2000) Measuring attitudes related to interdisciplinary training: revisiting the Heinemann, Schmitt and Farrell 'attitudes toward health care teams' scale. *Journal of Interprofessional Care*; 14:249-258.

Hyland L & Morse J (1995) Orchestrating comfort: the role of funeral directors. *Death Studies*; 19:453-474.

Illeris K (2003) Workplace learning and learning theory. *The Journal of Workplace Learning*; 15:167-178.

Itano J, Williams J, Deaton, M & Oishi N (1991) Impact of a student interdisciplinary oncology team project, *Journal of Cancer Education*, 6:219-226.

James S & Anderson A (1999) Interdisciplinary health care as the link between nursing homes and educational institutions. *Geriatric Nursing*; 20:214-216.

Janicik G & Bartel C (2003) Talking about time: effects of temporal planning and time awareness norms on group co-ordination and performance. *Group Dynamics*; 7:122-134.

Janis I (1982) *Groupthink: A Study of Foreign Policy Decisions and Fiascos* (2nd ed). Houghton Mifflin, Boston, MA.

Jarvis P (1995) *Adult and Continuing Education: Theory and Practice*. Routledge/Falmer, London.

Jaques D (1998) *Learning in Groups* (2nd ed). Kogan Page, London.

Johnson R (2003) Exploring students' views of interprofessional education. *International Journal of Therapy and Rehabilitation*; 10:314-320.

Jones R (1986) *Working Together, Learning Together*. Royal College of General Practitioners, London.

Jones M & Salmon D (2001) The practitioner as policy analyst: a study of student reflections of an interprofessional course in higher education. *Journal of Interprofessional Care*; 15:67-77.

Joseph M (1990) *Sociology for Everyone* (2nd ed). Polity, Cambridge.

Kaner E, Steven A, Cassidy P & Vardy C (2003) Implementation of a model for service delivery and organisation in mental healthcare: a qualitative exploration of service provider views. *Health and Social Care in the Community*; 11:519-527.

Kaplan B & Shaw N (2002) People, organisation and social issues: evaluation as an exemplar. In: R Haux & C Kulikowski (eds). *Yearbook of Medical Informatics*. Schattauer, New York.

Kelly J & McGrath J (1985) Effects of time limits and task types on task performance and interaction. *Journal of Personality & Social Psychology*; 49:395-407.

Kelman H (1977) Privacy and research with human beings. *Journal of Social Issues*; 33:169-195.

Kennard J (2002) Illuminating the relationship between shared learning and the workplace. *Medical Teacher*; 24:379-384.

Kennedy I (2001) *The Inquiry into the Management of Care of Children Receiving Complex Heart Surgery at the Bristol Royal Infirmary*. DoH, London.

Ker J, Mole L & Bradley P (2003) Early introduction to interprofessional learning: a stimulated ward environment. *Medical Education*; 37:248-255.

Kindig D (1975) Interdisciplinary education for primary health care team delivery. *Journal of Medical Education*; 50:97-110.

Knowles M (1975) *The Adult Learner: a Neglected Species*. Gulf, Houston.

Kolb D (1984) *Experiential Learning: Experiences as the Source of Learning and Development*. Prentice Hall, New Jersey.

Koppel I, Barr H, Reeves S, Freeth D & Hammick M (2001) Establishing a systematic approach to evaluating the effectiveness of interprofessional education. *Issues in Interdisciplinary Care*: 3:41-49.

Koppel I (2003) *Autonomy Eroded? Changing Discourses in the Education of Health and Community Care Professionals*. Unpublished PhD Thesis. University of London.

Kraus W (1980) *Collaboration in Organisations: Alternatives to Hierarchy*. Human Sciences Press, New York.

Krogstad U, Hofoss D & Hjortdahl P (2002) Continuity of hospital care: beyond the question of personal contact. *British Medical Journal*; 324:36-38.

Krueger R (1994) *Focus groups: A Practical Guide for Applied Research* (2nd ed). Sage, London.

Lacey C (1976) Problems of sociological fieldwork: a review of the methodology of "Hightown Grammar". In M Shipman (ed) *The Organisation and Impact of Social Research*. Routledge & Kegan Paul, London.

Lacey P (1996) Improving practice through reflective enquiry: confessions of a first-time action researcher. *Educational Action Research*; 4:349-361.

Lacey P (1998) Interdisciplinary training for staff working with people with profound and multiple learning disabilities. *Journal of Interprofessional Care*; 12:43-52.

Lajara B, Lillo F & Sempere V (2003) Human resources management: a success and factor in strategic alliances. *Employee Relations*; 25:61-80.

Laming H (2003) *The Victoria Climbié Inquiry.* Department of Health and Home Office. London.

Larson C & LaFasto F (1989) *Teamwork: What Must go Right, What can go Wrong.* Sage: Newbury Park, CA.

Larson E (1999) The impact of physician-nurse interaction on patient care. *Holistic Nursing Practice*; 13:38-46,

Lary M, Lavigne S, Muma S, Jones S & Hoeft H (1997) Breaking down barriers: multidisciplinary education model. *Journal of Allied Health*; 26:63-69.

LaSala K, Hopper S, Rissmeyer D & Shipe D (1997), Rural health care & interdisciplinary education, *Nursing and Health Care Perspectives*; 18:292-298.

Lave J & Wenger E (1991) *Situated Learning: Legitimate Peripheral Participation.* University Press Cambridge, Cambridge.

Lia-Hoagberg B, Nelson P & Chase R (1997) An interdisciplinary health team training program for school staff in Minnesota. *Journal of School Health*; 67:94-97.

Lies V & Sunderland K (2001) *Organisational Change. A Review for Health Care Managers, Professionals and Researchers.* London School of Hygiene and Tropical Medicine, London.

Lincoln Y & Guba E (1985) *Naturalistic Enquiry.* Sage, Beverly Hills, CA.

Litaker D, Mion L, Planavsky L, Kippes C, Mehta N & Frolkis J (2003) Physician-nurse practitioner teams in chronic disease management: the impact on costs, clinical effectiveness and patients' perception of care. *Journal of Interprofessional Care*; 17:223-238.

Leathard A (1994) Interprofessional developments in Britain. In A Leathard (ed) *Going Interprofessional: Working Together for Health and Welfare.* Routledge, London.

Leathard A (2003) Introduction. In A Leathard (ed) *Interprofessional Collaboration: From Policy to Practice in Health and Social Care.* Brunner-Routledge, London.

Lee D & Newby H (1984) *The Problem of Sociology.* Hutchinson, London.

Leiba T (1993) Current developments in interprofessional education. *British Journal of Nursing*; 2:631-633.

Lempp H, Maclellan M, Kenn S & Nesbitt A (2003) An example of interprofessional teaching in the community for final-year medical students: challenges and rewards. *Education for Primary Care*; 14:317-328.

Leucht R, Madson M, Taugher M & Petterson J (1990) Assessing perceptions: design and validation of an interdisciplinary education perception scale. *Journal of Allied Health*; 19:181-191.

Long S (1996) Primary health care team workshop: team members' perspectives. *Journal of Advanced Nursing*; 23:935-41.

Lorenzi N & Riley R (2003) Organisational issues – change. *International Journal of Medical Informatics*; 69:197-203

Lough M, Schmidt K & Swain, G (1996) An interdisciplinary educational model for professions students in a family practice center. *Nurse Educator*, 21(1):27-31.

Loxley A. (1997) *Collaboration in Health and Welfare: Working with Difference*. Jessica Kingsley, London.

MacDougall M & Elahi V (1974) A multidisciplinary learning experience. *Journal of Medical Education*; 49:752-755.

Mackay S (2004) The role perception questionnaire (RPQ): a tool for assessing undergraduate students' perceptions of the role of other professions. *Journal of Interprofessional Care*; 18:289-302.

Mandy A, Milton C & Mandy P (2004) Professional stereotyping and interprofessional education. *Learning in Health & Social Care*; 3:154-170

Mann K, Viscount P, Cogdon A, Davidson K, Langille D & Maccara M (1996) Multidisciplinary learning in continuing professional education: the Heart Health Nova Scotia experience. *Journal of Continuing Education in the Health Professions*; 16:50-60.

Marris P (1986) *Loss and Change*. Routledge, London.

Mathias P & Thompson T (1997) Preparation for interprofessional work: trends in education, training and the structure of qualification in the United Kingdom. In: J Øvretveit, P Mathias & T Thompson (eds). *Interprofessional Working for Health and Social Care*. Macmillan, Basingstoke.

Mattessich P, Murray-Close M & Monsey B (2001) *Collaboration: What Makes it Work?* (2nd ed). Saint Paul, Minnesota.

May T (1993) *Social Research: Issues, Methods and Process*. Open University Press, Milton Keynes.

McCarey M & Mires G (2002) Interprofessional teaching on normal labour for midwifery and medical students. In: S Glen & T Leiba (eds). *Multiprofessional Learning for Nurses: Breaking the Boundaries*. Palgrave, Basingstoke.

McCauley C (1998) Group dynamics in Janis's theory of groupthink: backward and forward. *Organizational Behavior and Human Decision Processes*; 73:142-162.

McCormack B & Wright J (1999) Achieving dignified care for older people through practice development: a systematic approach. *NT Research*; 4:340-352.

McGrath J (1990) Time matters in groups. In: J Galegher, R Kraut & C Egido (eds). *Intellectual Teamwork*. Lawrence Erlbaum, New Jersey.

McGrath M (1991) *Multidisciplinary Teamwork*, Avebury, Aldershot.

McKeown M, Blundell P, Lord J & Haigh C (2005) Organic training and development: working with mental health teams directly in the workplace. In: C Carlisle, H Cooper & D Mercer (eds). *Interprofessional Education: an Agenda for Healthcare Professionals*. Quay Books, Salisbury.

McNulty T & Ferlie E (2002) *Reengineering Health Care: the Complexities of Organisational Transformation*. Open University Press, Oxford.

Meerabeau L & Page S (1999) I'm sorry if I panicked you: nurses' accounts of teamwork in cardiopulmonary resuscitation. *Journal of Interprofessional Care*; 13:29-40.

Melia K (1987) *Learning and Working: The Occupational Socialisation of Nurses.* Tavistock, London.

Meyer J (2001) *Lay Participation in Care in a Hospital Setting: An Action Research Study.* Nursing Praxis International, Portsmouth.

Miller C, Freeman M & Ross N (2001) *Interprofessional Practice in Health and Social Care.* Arnold, London.

Mires G, Williams F, Harden R, Howie P, McCarey M & Robertson A (1999) Multiprofessional education in undergraduate curricula can work. *Medical Teacher*; 21:281-285.

Mitchell J (1977) The logic and methods of sociological enquiry. In P Worsley (ed). *Introducing Sociology.* Penguin, Harmonsworth.

Mitchell J (1983) Case and situation analysis. *Sociological Review*; 31:187-211.

Molyneux, J. (2001) Interprofessional teamworking: what makes teams work well. *Journal of Interprofessional Care*; 15:29-36.

Morison S, Boohan M, Jenkins J & Moutray M (2003) facilitating undergraduate interprofessional learning in healthcare: comparing classroom and clinical learning for nursing and medical students. *Learning in Health and Social Care*; 2:92-104.

Mullen B, Anthony T, Salas E & Driskell J (1994) Group cohesiveness and quality of decision making: an integration of tests of the groupthink hypothesis. *Small Group Research*; 25:189-204.

Nash A & Hoy A (1993) Terminal care in the community – an evaluation of residential workshops for general practitioner/district nurse teams. *Palliative Medicine*; 7:5-17.

Newton P, Long S, Joesberg H, Matthews D & Usherwood (1998) *Competencies in Primary Health Care Teams.* DfEE/NHS(E), London.

Norman G (1999) The adult learner: a mythical species. *Academic Medicine*; 74:886-889

Norman I & Peck E (1999) Working together in adult community mental health services: an interprofessional dialogue. *Journal of Mental Health*; 8:217-230.

Nursing and Midwifery Council (2002) *Code of Professional Conduct.* Nursing and Midwifery Council, London.

O'Boyle M, Paniagua F, Wassef A & Holzer C (1995), Training health professionals in the recognition and treatment of depression, *Psychiatric Services*; 46:616-618.

O'Neil E & Pew Health Professions Commission (1993) *Recreating Health Professional Practice for a New Century.* Pew Health, San Francisco.

Onyett S (2003) *Teamworking in Mental Health.* Palgrave, Basingstoke.

Opie A (1997) Thinking teams thinking clients: issues of discourse and representation in the work of health care teams. *Sociology of Health and Illness*; 19:259-280.

Øvretveit J (1990) Making the team work. *Professional Nurse*; March: 284-288.

Øvretveit J (1993) *Co-ordinating Community Care: Multidisciplinary Teams and Care Management.* Open University Press, Milton Keynes.

Øvretveit J (1997a) Leadership in multiprofessional teams. *Health and Social Care in the Community*; 5:276-283.

Øvretveit J (1997b) Planning and managing teams. *Health and Social Care in the Community*; 5:269-276.

Parikh A, McReelis K & Hodges B (2001) Student feedback in problem based learning: a survey of 103 final year students across five Ontario medical schools. *Medical Education*; 35:632-636.

Parker H (2001) The role of occupational therapists in community mental health teams: generic or specialist? *British Journal of Occupational Therapy*; 64:609-611.

Parsell G & Bligh J (1998) Educational principles underpinning successful shared learning. *Medical Teacher*, 20:522-29.

Parsell G & Bligh J (1999) The development of a questionnaire to assess the readiness of health care students for interprofessional learning (RIPLS). *Medical Education*; 33:95-100.

Parsell G. Spalding R. & Bligh J. (1998) Shared Goals, shared learning: evaluation of a multiprofessional course for undergraduate students. *Medical Education*; 32:304-11.

Perkins J & Tryssenaar J (1994) Making interdisciplinary education effective for rehabilitation students. *Journal of Allied Health*; 23:133-141.

Pethybridge J (2004) How team working influences discharge planning from hospital: a study of four multi-disciplinary teams in an acute hospital in England. *Journal of Interprofessional Care*; 18:29-41.

Pilon C, Leathley M, London R, McLean S, Phang P, Priestley R, Rosenberg F, Singer J, Anis A & Dodek P (1997) Practice guideline for arterial blood gas measurement in the intensive care unit decreases numbers and increases appropriateness of tests. *Critical Care Medicine*; 25:1308-1313.

Pirrie A, Wilson V, Harden R & Elsegood J (1998) AMEE Guide No. 12: Multiprofessional education part 2 – promoting cohesive practice in health care. *Medical Teacher*, 20:409-416.

Pirrie A (1999) Rocky mountains and tired Indians: on territories and tribes. Reflections on multidisciplinary education in the health professions. *British Education Research Journal*; 25:113-126.

Pittilo M & Ross F (1998) Policies for interprofessional education: current trends in the UK. *Education for Health*; 11:285-295.

Ponzer S, Hylin U, Kusoffsky A, Lonka K, Mattiasson A-C & Nordström G (2004) Interprofessional training in the context of clinical practice: goals and students' perceptions on clinical education wards. *Medical Education*; 38:727-736.

Poole M (1981) Decision development in small groups: a comparison of two models. *Communication Monographs*; 48:1-24.

Poole M & Roth J (1989) Decision development in small groups: a typology of group decision paths. *Human Communication Research*; 15:323-356.

Pope C & Mays N (1996) Opening the black box: an encounter in the corridors of health service research. In: N Mays & C Pope (eds). *Qualitative Research in Health Care*. British Medical Association, London.

Porter S (1995) *Nursing's Relationship with Medicine*. Avebury, Aldershot.

Porter S (1996) Contra-Foucault: soldiers, nurses and power. *Sociology*; 30:59-78.

Porter S (1999) Working with doctors. In: G Wilkinson & M Miers (eds). *Power and Nursing Practice*. Macmillan, Basingstoke.

Poulton B & West M (1999) The determinants of effectiveness in primary health care teams. *Journal of Interprofessional Care*; 13:7-18.

Prideaux D (2000) On theory in medical education. *Medical Education*; 34:888-889.

Pritchard P (1995) Learning to work effectively in teams. In: P Owens, J Carrier & J Horder (eds). *Interprofessional Issues in Community and Primary Health Care*. Macmillan, Basingstoke.

Pryce A & Reeves S (1997) *An Evaluation of the Effectiveness of Multidisciplinary Education for Medical, Dental and Nursing students: a Case Study*. Internal Research Report. City University, London.

Pryce A, Mann S, Stokes J & Reeves S (2000) *Report on the Scoping Study for a Programme of Interprofessional Education on Chlamydia*. Internal Research Report. City University, London.

Punch, M (1994) *The Politics and Ethics of Fieldwork*. In: N Denzin & Y Lincoln (eds). *Handbook of Qualitative Research*. Sage, Thousand Oaks, CA.

Rafferty A, Ball J & Aiken H (2001) Are teamwork and professional autonomy compatible, and do they result in improved hospital care? *Quality in Health Care*; 10(Suppl):S32-S37.

Raven B (1998) Groupthink, Bay of Pigs and Watergate reconsidered. *Organisational Behavior and Human Decision Processes*; 73:352-361.

Reeves S (2000) Community-based interprofessional education for medical, nursing and dental students. *Health and Social Care in the Community*; 8:269-276.

Reeves S (2001) A review of the effects of interprofessional education on staff involved in the care of adults with mental health problems. *Journal of Psychiatric and Mental Health Nursing*; 8:533-542.

Reeves S (2002) Interprofessional *Workshops for Community Mental Health Teams*. Internal Research Report. City University, London.

Reeves S (2004) Work-based interprofessional education for community mental health teams. In: S Glen & T Leiba (eds). *Interprofessional Post-qualifying Education for Nurses*. Palgove, Basingstoke.

Reeves S & Freeth D (2002) The London Training Ward: an innovative interprofessional learning initiative. *Journal of Interprofessional Care*; 16:41-52.

Reeves S, Freeth D, McCrorie P & Perry D (2002a) 'It teaches you what to expect in real life' interprofessional learning on a Training Ward for medical, nursing, occupational therapy and physiotherapy students. *Medical Education*; 36:337-344.

Reeves S, Freeth D, Nicol M & Wood D (2000) A joint learning venture between new nurses and junior doctors. *Nursing Times*; 96(38):39-40.

Reeves S, Koppel I, Barr H, Freeth D & Hammick M (2002b) Twelve tips for undertaking a systematic review. *Medical Teacher*; 24:358-363.

Reeves S & Parker P (2003) Interprofessional learning in practice. In: S Glen & P Parker (eds). *Supporting Learning in Nursing Practice: A Guide for Practitioners*. Palgrave, Hampshire.

Reeves S & Pryce A (1998) Emerging Themes: an exploratory research project of a multidisciplinary education module for medical, dental and nursing students. *Nurse Education Today*; 18:534-541.

Reeves S & Summerfield Mann L (2003) Key issues in developing and delivering interprofessional education. *International Journal of Therapy and Rehabilitation*; 10:310-313.

Regan de Bere S (2003) Evaluating the implications of complex interprofessional education for improvement in collaborative practice: a multidimensional model. *British Educational Research Journal*; 29:105-124.

Richards G & Horder W (1999) Mental health training: the process of collaboration. *Social Work Education*; 18:449-458.

Richardson B & Cooper N (2003) Developing a virtual interdisciplinary research community in higher education. *Journal of Interprofessional Care*; 17:173-182

Richardson L (1991) Postmodern social theory: representational realities. *Sociological Theory*; 9:173-179.

Rickards T & Moger S (2000) Creative leadership processes in project team development: an alternative to Tuckman's stage model. *British Journal of Management*; 11:273-283.

Roberts C, Howe A, Winterburn S & Fox N (2000) Not as easy as it sounds: a qualitative study of a shared learning project between medical and nursing undergraduate students. *Medical Teacher*; 22:386-387.

Robson, C (1993) *Real World Research*, Blackwell, London.

Rock P (2001) Symbolic interactionism and ethnography. In: P Atkinson, A Coffey, S Delamont, J Lofland & L Lofland (eds). *Handbook of Ethnography*. Sage, London.

Rogers G (1969) *Freedom to Learn*. Merrill, Columbus, MA.

Rorty R (2000) *Philosophy and Social Hope*. Penguin, Harmondsworth.

Rosander M, Stiwne D & Granström K (1998) "Biopolar groupthink": assessing groupthink tendencies in authentic work groups. *Scandinavian Journal of Psychology*; 39:81-92.

Ross F & Harris R (2005) Can interprofessional education make a difference in the care of people with chronic disease? *Chronic Illness*; 1:81-86.

Ross F, Rink E & Furne A (2000) Integration or pragmatic coalition? An evaluation of nursing teams in primary care. *Journal of Interprofessional Care*; 14:259-267.

Ross F, O'Tuathail C & Stubberfield D (2005) Towards multidisciplinary assessment of older people: exploring the change process. *Journal of Clinical Nursing*; 14:518-529.

Ross F & Southgate L (2000) Learning together in medical and nursing training: aspirations and activity. *Medical Education*; 34:739-743.

Rutter D & Hagart J (1990), Alcohol training in south-east England: a survey and evaluation, *Alcohol & Alcoholism*; 25:699-709.

Sandén I & Wahlström O (1996) *Training Ward 30*. University of Linköping, Linköping.

Satin D (1987) The difficulties of interdisciplinary education: lessons from three failures and a success. *Educational Gerontology*; 13:53-69.

Savage C & MacDowell M (2000) Evaluating electronic information strategies in a master of science in nursing and master in health services administration interdisciplinary learning experience. *Journal of Nursing Education*; 39:94-96.

Schafer M & Crichlow S (2002) The process-outcome connection in foreign policy decision-making: a quantitative study building on Groupthink. *International Studies Quarterly*; 46:45-68.

Schlomann P (1996) Ethical decision making in a neonatal intensive care unit: the nurse's role. *Neonatal Intensive Care*; 9:44-53.

Schmitt M (2001) Collaboration improves the quality of care: methodological challenges and evidence from US health care research. *Journal of Interprofessional Care*; 15:47-66.

Schön D (1983) *The Reflective Practitioner*. Temple Smith, London.

Schwandt T (1994) Three epistemological stances for qualitative inquiry: interpretivism, Hermeneutics and social constructivism. In: N Denzin & Y Lincoln (eds). *Handbook for Qualitative Research*. Sage, Thousand Oaks, CA.

Scott S, Harrison A, Baker T & Wills J (2005) Interdisciplinary community partnership for health professional students. *Journal of Allied Health*; 34:31-35.

Seale C (1999) *The Quality of Qualitative Research*. Sage, London.

Seel I (1994) Total quality at Thomas Cork. *Managing Service Quality*; 4:21-25.

Sengupta S, Dobbins S & Roberts J (2003) Multi-agency training for quality: reflections and recommendations. *Journal of Interprofessional Care*; 17:58-68.

Shaw I (1994) *Evaluating Interprofessional Education*. Avebury, Aldershot.

Shaw M (1970) *Communication Processes*. Penguin, London.

Skjørshammer M (2001) Co-operation and conflict in a hospital: interprofessional differences in perception and management of conflicts. *Journal of Interprofessional Care*; 15:7-18

Skovholt C, Lia-Hoagberg B, Mullett S, Siiteri R, Vanman R, McKay C & Oberg C (1994) The Minnesota Prenatal Care Coordination Project: successes and obstacles, *Public Health Reports*; 109:774-781.

Silverman, D (1993) *Interpreting Qualitative Data*, Sage: London.

Sims D (2002) Joint training for integrated care. In: S Glen & T Leiba (eds). *Multiprofessional Learning for Nurses: Breaking the Boundaries*. Palgrave, Basingstoke.

Sinclair S (1997) *Making Doctors: An Institutional Apprenticeship*. Berg, Oxford.

Smith M (2003) Changing an organisation's culture: correlates of success and failure. *Leadership and Organization Development Journal*; 24:249-261.

Spratley J (1990) *Disease Prevention and Health Promotion in Primary Health Care: Team Workshops Organised by the Health Education Authority*. Health Education Authority, London.

Stanford R & Yelloly M with Loughlin B, Rolph K, Talbot M & Trowell J (1994) *Shared Learning in Child Protection*. ENB, London.

Stark R, Yeo G, Fordyce M, Grudzen M, Hopkins J, McGann L & Shepard D (1984) An interdisciplinary teaching program in geriatrics for physician's assistants. *Journal of Allied Health*; 13:280-287.

Stone J, Haas B, Harmer-Beem M & Baker D (2004) Utilization of research methodology in designing and developing an interdisciplinary course in ethics. *Journal of Interprofessional Care*; 18:57-62.

Strasser R (1995) Innovative interactive multidisciplinary workshops. *Australian Journal of Rural Health*; 3:56-61.

Strauss A, Schatzman D, Ehrlich R, Bucher M & Sabshin C (1963) The Hospital and its Negotiated Order. In E Freidson (ed). *The Hospital in Modern Society*. The Free Press, New York.

Strauss A (1978) *Negotiations: Varieties, Contexts, Processes and Social Order*. Jossey-Bass, San Francisco.

Strong P (1977) *The Ceremonial Order of the Clinic*. Routledge, London.

Svensson R (1996) The interplay between doctors and nurses – a negotiated order perspective. *Sociology of Health and Illness*; 18:379-398.

Swanson E, Taylor C, Valentine A, & McCarthy A (1998) The integrated health professions education program seminar, *Nurse Educator*; 23:18-21.

Szasz G (1969) Interprofessional education in the health sciences. *Millbank Memorial Fund Quarterly*; 47:449-475.

Tanner J & Timmons S (2000) Backstage in the theatre. *Journal of Advanced Nursing*; 32:975-980.

Tepper M (1997) Providing comprehensive sexual health care in spinal cord injury: implementation and evaluation of a new curriculum for health professionals. *Sexuality & Disability*; 15:131-165.

Thomas M (1995) Learning to be a better team player: initiatives in continuing education in primary care. In: K Soothill, L Mackay & C Webb (eds). *Interprofessional Relations in Health Care*. Edward Arnold, London.

Tope R (1996) *Integrated Interdisciplinary Learning Between Health and Social Care Professions: A Feasibility Study*. Avebury, Aldershot.

Townes C, Petit B & Young B (1995) Implementing total quality management in an academic surgery setting: lessons learned. *Swiss Surgery*; 1:15-23.

Tuckman B (1965) Developmental sequence in small groups. *Psychological Bulletin*; 63:384-399.

Tuckman B & Jenson M (1977) Stages of small group development re-visited. *Group and Organisational Studies*; 2:419-427.

Tunstall-Pedoe S, Rink E & Hilton S (2003) Student attitudes to undergraduate interprofessional education. *Journal of Interprofessional Care*; 17:161-172.

Turner J (1999) Some current issue in research on social identity and self-categorisation theories. In: N Ellemers, R Spears & B Doosje (eds). *Social Identity*. Blackwell, Oxford.

Tye C & Ross F (2000) Blurring boundaries: professional perspectives of the emergency nurse practitioner role in a major accident and emergency department. *Journal of Advanced Nursing*; 31:1089-1096.

UK Centre for the Advancement of Interprofessional Education (CAIPE) (1996) *The Principles of Interprofessional Education*. CAIPE, London.

UK Centre for the Advancement of Interprofessional Education (CAIPE) (1997) *Interprofessional Education – A Definition*. CAIPE, London.

Van der Horst M. Turpie I & Nelson W (1995) St Joseph's Community Centre model of community-based interdisciplinary health care team education. *Health and Social Care in the Community*; 3:33-42.

Vygotsky L (1978) *Mind in Society: The Development of Higher Psychological Processes*. Harvard University Press, Cambridge MA.

Wahlström O, Sandén I & Hammar M (1996) The student ward at the University Hospital, Faculty of Health Sciences, Linköping, Sweden. *European Nurse*; 1:262-268.

Wahlström O, Sandén I & Hammar M (1997) Multidisciplinary training within the undergraduate medical curriculum. *Medical Education*; 31:425-29.

Wahlström O & Sandén I (1998) Multiprofessional Training Ward at Linköping University: early experience. *Education for Health*; 11:225-31.

Wakefield A, Cooke S & Boggis C (2003) Learning together: use of simulated patients with nursing and medical students for breaking bad news. *International Journal of Palliative Nursing*; 9:32-38.

Walby S, Greenwell J, Mackay L & Soothill K (1994) *Medicine and Nursing: Professions in a Changing Health Service*. Sage, London.

Wallerstein N (1999) Power between evaluator and community: research relationships within New Mexico's heathier communities. *Social Science and Medicine*; 49:39-54.

Watts F & Bennett D (1983) *Theory and Practice of Psychiatric Rehabilitation*. Wiley, Chichester.

West M (1996) *Handbook of Work Group Psychology*. Wiley, Chichester.

West M & Markiowicz L (2004) *Building Team-based Working: A Practical Guide to Organisational Transformation*. British Psychology Society/Blackwell, London.

West M & Slater J (1996) *Teamworking in Primary Health Care: A Review of its Effectiveness*. Health Education Authority, London.

Whyte W (1981) *Street Corner Society: The Social Structure of an Italian Slum* (3rd Ed). University of Chicago, Chicago.

Wickes D (1998) *Nurses and Doctors at Work: Rethinking Professional Boundaries*. Open University Press, Milton Keynes.

Wilcock P, Campion-Smith C & Head M (2002) The Dorset Seedcorn Project: interprofessional learning and continuous quality improvement in primary care. *British Journal of General Practice*; 52(Suppl):S39-S44.

Wildridge V, Childs S, Cawthra L & Madge B (2004) How to create successful partnerships – a review of the literature. *Health Information and Libraries Journal*; 21:3-19.

Willkinson G & Miers M (1999) Power and professions. In: G Wilkinson & M Miers (eds). *Power and Nursing Practice*. Macmillan, Basingstoke.

Wilkinson G, Parcell M & Macdonald A (2000) Cerebrovascular accident clinical pathway, *Journal of Quality in Clinical Practice*; 20:109-112.

Williams G & Laungani P (1999) Analysis of teamwork in an NHS community trust: an empirical study. *Journal of Interprofessional Care*; 13:19-28.

Willis K, Cameron P & Igoe P (1997) Building community networks: a road trauma education and training program for rural areas. *Australian Journal of Rural Health*; 5:6-10.

Witz A (1992) *Professions and Patriarchy*. Routledge, London.

World Health Organisation (1976) *Continuing Education of Health Personnel*. WHO Regional Office for Europe, Copenhagen.

World Health Organisation (1988) *Learning together to Work Together*. WHO, Geneva.

Wright Mills, C (1967) *The Sociological Imagination*, Oxford University Press, Oxford.

Yarborough M, Jones T, Cye T, Phillips S & Stelzner D (2000) Interprofessional education in ethics at an academic sciences center. *Academic Medicine*; 75:793-800.

Young M, Gooder V, Oltermann M, Bohman C, French T & James B (1998) The impact of a multidisciplinary approach on caring for ventilator-dependent patients, *International Journal for Quality in Health Care*; 10:15-26.

Zungolo E (1994) Interdisciplinary education in primary care: the challenge. *Nursing and Health Care*; 15:288-292.

Zwarenstein M, Atkins J, Barr H, Bell L, Koppel I, Hammick M & Reeves S (1997) Systematic Review of outcomes from Interprofessional Education. *CAIPE Bulletin*; 14:7-8.

Zwarenstein M, Atkins J, Barr H, Hammick M, Koppel I & Reeves S (1999) Interprofessional Education and Systematic review: a new initiative in evaluation, *Journal of interprofessional Care*; 13:417-424.

Zwarenstein M, Bryant W & Reeves S (2003) In-service interprofessional education improves inpatient care and patient satisfaction. *Journal of Interprofessional Care*; 17:427-428.

Zwarenstein M & Reeves S (2002) Working together but apart: barriers and routes to nurse-physician collaboration. *The Joint Commission Journal on Quality Improvement*; 28:242-247.

Zwarenstein M, Reeves S, Barr H, Hammick M, Koppel I & Atkins J (2001) *Interprofessional Education: Effects on Professional Practice and Health Care Outcomes*. (Cochrane Review). The Cochrane Library, Issue 3, (Oxford, Update Software).

9 783836 481106